SAY YOU WANT A REVOLUTION

WE NOW FIND OURSELVES TRANSPORTED INTO A DECEPTIVE AND DEADLY 90'S CULTURE

ERIC JOHNSON

Printed in the United States of America
International Standard Book Number: 1-883928-03-6
Library of Congress Catalog Card Number: 93-086238

Published by:
Longwood Communications
397 Kingslake Drive
DeBary, FL 32713
(904) 774-1991

To contact author:
Eric Johnson
P.O. Box 17574
Shreveport, LA 71138

Contents

Symptomatic Signs

Conclusion

Acknowledgements

The following people were very encouraging and supportive as I worked to complete this book. I wiould like to express my heart-felt gratitude and appreciation to them: Bill and Ann Gordon – Skip and janelle McCright – John and Jeri Mazur – Joe and Tag Young – Charles L. and Bea Huffman – Thad and Kay Pinnix, Hal Brennan – Dr. Denny Gamble – R. A. Mackey Sr., Don Alexander – Bill Keith – Dr. Billy McCormick – Tam Burford – Harvey and Connie Johnson – Sharon Seward – Donna Bass – Stacy Luttrell – Judy Banks – Neatrice Buehler – Lillian Keeling – Joe and Sharon Partain – Marilyn Jansen – Sandy Burford – Sherry Chambers – Dr. Joe B. Hayes – Jeremy Rimmer – Selena Spicer – Rex Balnkenship – Linden Bethune.

Special thanks t Helen Billingsley who worked hundreds of hours from my handwritten notes to compile the original manuscript.

Also, my deep appreciation to my wife Debbie and our teenagers, Chad and Wendy.

Preface

Say You Want A Revolution is a confrontational book. It is not a simplistic analysis of, or a panacea for, the ills of our nation and the church. It is intended to challenge readers with the seriousness of the present crisis among youth, to reveal the generational impact made by the baby-boomer parents of these youth and the effect of popular culture on their generation, and to provoke thought, questioning, self-examination, prayer and action in this critical hour we face in America.

This book is about two generations — one well into adulthood and the other still approaching it. It is about America and her children, about *our* past and present and *their* future. And what remains for us will be determined largely by what becomes of today's youth. This rising generation may be the most pivotal group in the history of the church in America, perhaps even of America itself.

The evangelical Christian community has a tendency to look for quick, painless and neatly packaged solutions to the complex social and spiritual problems confronting America.

The Christian community has taken a superficial, convenient and man-centered approach to critical spiritual issues. The result is a spiritual crisis confronting America, which has put this generation at risk more than all the other societal forces combined. The current spiritual crisis has created a potential for a spiritual revolution or a revolution of destruction.

This book focuses on the major motivations of a generation, the radical cultural climate of the '90s and unprecedented forces now converging on this generation. Understanding what determines or motivates the actions, beliefs and life-styles of individuals or generations is a critical key to resolving their problems. Deadly generational cycles currently in motion can be broken only through a spiritual awakening, a supernatural move of God — a true commitment to Jesus Christ as individuals and as a nation. This book is not meant to comfort but to break down the barriers of spiritual apathy, that we may understand and recognize the present and future dangers we face.

Introduction

Generation X

"X" has become the metaphor for an entire generation that is lost, says *USA Today,* a generation without identity, without a cause, or a promising future, virtually ignored by society, especially in comparison to the baby boomers. This "thirteenth generation" has grown up in the shadow of the boomers — as though wonder has been followed by disappointment. Its members feel anonymous, alienated, disillusioned, and cynical about everything and everyone.

Authors William Strauss and Neil Howe define the thirteenth generation as those youth born from 1961 to 1981. They are also referred to as baby busters, born from 1965 to 1983. This is the thirteenth generation to know the American nation and flag. The number thirteen is also an omen, a gauntlet, a challenge — an obstacle to be overcome.[1]

Far more than other generations, the post-boomer Generation X feels that the real world is gearing up to punish them. Annual polls of high school seniors show that those born just after 1960 came of age much more fearful of national catastrophe than those born just before. These mid-'60s babies were the kids whose low test scores and high rates of crime, violence, suicide, divorce, drug abuse and teen pregnancy marked postwar extremes. The indicators have not improved for young people born in the late '60s and '70s.

Like its music, Generation X can appear shocking on the outside, unknowable on the inside, like MTV's Beavis and Butthead. Elders find it hard to suppress feelings of disappointment about how Generation Xers are turning out — dismissing them as a lost, ruined, even wasted generation. In an unrelenting, mostly unanswered barrage of what could be termed youth-bashing, the older generation has judged them to be the "dumb and numb" generation, academically inferior to boomers and extremely unemotional.

More than any previous generation, Generation Xers feel estranged from God, separated from each other, lacking significant relationships, void of roots or a societal connection. There is no real sense of where reality leaves off and the media's influence takes over, reshaping and redefining their perceptions.

The television, or electronic guardian, has imparted both wisdom and entertainment to two generations. Members of Generation X crave entertainment, as do their baby-boomer parents; their attention spans are as short as one click of the remote. MTV — with its flashy, provocative images promising instant, continual gratification — further fuels disillusionment and jadedness. Family relationships that were traditionally secure are no longer there for them. They feel betrayed by their parents because of epidemic boomer divorce rates; they've been ripped off and are suspicious of all relationships.

Generation X youth are very pessimistic about their future. They are ever-conscious of the harsh economic realities they face and disheartened by the perception that they will probably never rise to the level of financial independence and security achieved by their parents and grandparents. As one young person put it, "Getting a bachelor's degree isn't enough anymore. Even getting a master's doesn't guarantee you a job." Two thirds of Generation Xers describe the purpose of life as self-gratification and personal fulfillment.

Generation X young people are suffering from what economists describe as a remarkable generational economic disease — a "depression of youth."[2] Money isn't everything, but these youth find themselves both unprepared for and uninvited to most other avenues of social advancement and approval. Money means survival, and for a generation whose earliest life experiences have taught them not to trust anyone, survival must come first.

Generation X youth live in a "world of destructive life-styles, disintegrating homes, self-absorbed parents, violent schools, gangs, confused leadership, unprecedented sexual activity and the ominous emergence of AIDS — a culture shifting from G to R rating."[3] The new enlightened morality is really a moral vacuum where confusion, disillusion and uncertainty reign.

At every phase of life, these youth have encountered a world with more punishing consequences than anything the two generations before them ever experienced. Generation X knows where the youth euphoria of the late '60s actually led. As college student Kim Blum puts it, "The sexual revolution is over, and everybody lost." The Bon Jovi song, "You Give Love a Bad Name," became an instant hit among the teens of the 1980s, reflecting the emotional devastation and relationship confusion left for the current generation. Their music doesn't just talk about sex, it expects its listeners to participate. It's just like MTV says, "Teens today don't just watch it, they live it."

Today's youth are characterized as being an emotionally detached generation. They experience the world only as a source of pleasure and pain. Baby-boomer culture is quick to criticize or punish them but slow to find out what's really going on in their lives. A major characteristic of today's young people is their desire to avoid risk, commitment, reality and rapid change. They feel paralyzed by the social problems they see as their inheritance.

The societal landscape for this generation is deadly — created by the lost family, MTV-produced realities, media-based morality, levels of erotic sex and brutal violence which constitute a cultural revolution that has produced a generational wasteland.

I have described the cultural atmosphere — generational mindset and defined the basic motivating needs and fears — that determine our choices, beliefs and life-styles. Understanding the mind-set of this generation — how they think and what motivates them, is critical in effectively reaching them with the gospel.

Jesus always zeroed in on what motivated people's actions (why we behave a certain way) rather than just focusing on their actions, in order to meet their real needs and confront their problems. If you understand the basic human motivations of an individual or a generation, you're able to focus on the root causes of the problem, rather than the symptoms. I have identified the six (6) crucial needs and fears that determine our motivations and actions, which is the key to resolving conflict and problems.

Introduction

There is a battle for the hearts and minds of teenagers today. I am more convinced of it than I've ever been before, that if we lose the battle for the minds of our young people, the entire understanding of the Judeo-Christian ethic, which was so predominant from the foundation of this country to the present day, can be lost in one generation.

Dr. James Dobson
Focus on the Family

America is in danger of a cultural breakdown, if we do not return to the Christian foundations of our society.

Dr. Billy Graham

There's something happening here.
What it is ain't exactly clear.
Stop, hey, what's that sound?
Everybody look what's going down.
You better stop, now, what's that sound?
Everybody look what's going down.

"For What It's Worth"
Stephen Stills
Buffalo Springfield

There is no precedent for what has happened over the last thirty years and what is happening now in American Society. In no other time or any other place have all these forces and factors been present at one time. American popular culture is experiencing a social, moral and technological revolution.

It was the best of times, it was the worst of times; it was the age of wisdom, it was the age of foolishness; it was the age of belief, it was the age of unbelief; it was the season of light, it was the season of darkness; it was the spring of hope, it was the winter of despair; we had everything before us, we had nothing before us; we were all going direct to heaven, we were all going direct the other way.

—Charles Dickens
A Tale of Two Cities

1

Generational Cycles: The 60s Effect

> There is a generation that is pure in its own eyes, yet is not washed from its filthiness. There is a generation — oh, how lofty are their eyes! And their eyelids are lifted up (Prov. 30:12-13 NKJ).

The Youth Vacuum

David Elkind, in his classic analysis of the new role of teenagers in our society says, "There is no place for teenagers in American society today, not in our homes, not in our schools and not in society. This was not always the case; barely fifteen years ago, teenagers had a clearly defined position in the social structure."[1]

Society today has created a youth vacuum. Where we no longer recognize adolescence as a special stage in life, the transition (rite of passage) from teen to adult has been aborted. Youth have been denied this time of emotional preparation and protection and have had a premature adulthood thrust upon them. Teenagers now are confronted with adult-sized pressures, without clear identity or adequate time to prepare for them emotionally. On the surface, youth today appear extremely cool, sophisticated and physically mature; in reality, they are emotionally immature; many of them are spiritually, psychologically and emotionally crippled.

A Teenage Wasteland

What is happening in American popular culture, and how is it affecting today's generation of youth? There are certainly thousands of talented, intelligent, successful and dynamic teens all across the country. But, why are so many young people today going over the edge?

The journey from childhood to adulthood has become a perilous one as waves of radical and deadly changes are sweeping across the treacherous youth landscape. Unprecedented pressures, problems and dangers have created a vast teenage wasteland. The world of today's teens and their role in that world have undergone extreme change. There are factors and forces present and on the horizon that make this generation unparalleled to past generations. In their book, High School Ministry, authors and youth specialists Yaconelli and Burns describe the perils created by our society for today's youth:

> Adolescence is a phenomenon unique to Western culture. Adolescence exists in our society because there are certain structures or underpinnings designed to support it. In past generations, those underpinnings protected the adolescent from forces in society that could harm or permanently retard his development. But now something is happening to those safeguards of adolescence, and the world of the adolescent has begun to collapse under the weight of change. The security structures are crumbling — and our young people are becoming increasingly exposed to the harsh and often destructive forces of a brave new environment.[2]

A Generation at Risk

Let's examine some of these dangerous trends putting a generation at risk. More than 1.4 million teens are runaways and throwaways each year in America. To survive, they get involved in prostitution, pornography, drug abuse, sex rings, perversion and robbery. Nearly twenty million children-teens live in poverty in America. The explosion of youth gangs, kids packing guns, random vicious violence and revenge has multiplied the chances of teens being victims of assault, rape or murder.

The homicide and suicide rate have both increased 300 percent since 1960. Today's teens are more prone to kill each other and kill themselves than any previous generation in history. The divorce rate has increased 250 percent since 1970. Between 1970 and 1992, over twenty-four million couples divorced. Epidemic child abuse and neglect in the family settings have had a devastating effect.

Alcohol is the drug of choice for this generation, as 70 percent of teens, age thirteen to eighteen, drink on an occasional and regular basis. Four million teens are alcoholics, and another three million are considered problem drinkers. Alcohol-related accidents kill five thousand teens yearly. More teens are sexually active today at earlier ages than any previous generation. Twenty percent now lose their virginity before age thirteen. Three to five million twelve- to fourteen-year-olds are already having sex.

The rise of a satanic youth subculture involved in bizarre, ghoulish occult activities, such as blood rituals, murder and suicide, is another dark phenomenon, another destructive trend.

In a recent ABC News Special Report entitled "Making the Grade — A Report Card on America's Youth" disturbing results were presented:

Subject: Functional Literacy — Grade (F) - Sixty percent of seventeen-year-olds are severely limited in their employment opportunities because of inadequate reading, writing and math skills. Seven out of ten high-schoolers cannot write an effective letter seeking employment or information. Three out of five cannot read a map or total their lunch bill.

Subject: Obeying the Law — Grade (D) - The most violent person in our society is the adolescent male; add drug use and more advanced automatic weapons to the mix and you have a deadly combination. Over two million persons under the age of eighteen are arrested yearly for offenses ranging from disorderly conduct to murder. The murder rate for youth rose 25 percent compared to 4 percent for the rest of the population and has doubled among teens during the last ten years. There is more than one arrest for every ten juveniles age fourteen to seventeen in the United States. Homicide rates increased 50 percent.

Subject: School Completion — Grade (F) - One in four of our nation's youth will not graduate from high school. Over one million teens drop out of school each year. The dropout rate has increased

500 percent since 1960. In most inner cities, the dropout rate is twice the national average with one out of two dropping out. We have millions of teens totally unprepared for a high-tech culture.

Subject: Abstinence from Substance Abuse — Grade (D) - Seventy percent of all teens use alcohol on a regular basis. The United States has the highest rate of teen alcohol and drug use of any industrialized nation in the world. The drug problem in America is ten times that of Japan.

Subject: Postponement of Motherhood — Grade (F) - U.S. teenagers have the highest pregnancy rates in the developed world. Each year in America, more than one million teenage girls get pregnant out of wedlock; that is, one in ten girls fifteen to nineteen years old. Four in ten females become pregnant before age twenty. There is a one-in-three chance that a teen mother will have a second child while still in her teens, and every day forty teenage girls give birth to their third child. Illegitimate births have increased 600 percent since 1960.

Subject: Health and Emotional Well-Being — Grade (F) - Divorce, teen pregnancies, throwaways, missing fathers and runaways have created a poverty crisis among children and youth today. The new poverty in America is compromising children and teens' health and seriously jeopardizing their futures. Recent national statistics indicate as many as 18 million (one in nearly every five) children in the United States are currently living in poverty.

Reflections of Society

The youth culture is a reflection of the needs and problems of the entire society. Nearly every facet of America's culture is mirrored in our youth. If we are to understand where we are as a nation, we must understand where our youth are. We talk about the generation gap, and there's always been and probably to some degree always will be a communication barrier between parents and teens. The irony is that current research indicates how teens actually reflect their parents' values, attitudes and life-styles. If the youth reflect what the adult world believes and how we live, that says volumes about the role of parents in America and our present social situation. Many of the problems that exist today among teens are an extension of an adult world that has greatly disappointed them.

Generational Cycles

A generational cycle can be defined as the positive or negative emotional, psychological and spiritual impact of one generation upon another. The Bible states that the sins of the fathers will be visited on the third and fourth generations. That is a haunting verse of Scripture when you think about the connection between generations and the perpetual ripple effect caused by preceding and following generations. Each generation has distinctive characteristics that identify and separate it from others.

William Strauss and Neil House, in their book, Generations, define peer personality as a generational identity recognized and determined by common age location, common beliefs and behavior, and perceived membership in a common generation.

> A generation has collective attitudes about family life, sex roles, institutions, politics, religion, life-style and the future. It can be safe or reckless, calm or aggressive, self-absorbed or outer-driven, generous or selfish, spiritual or secular, interested in culture or in politics. Between any two generations, as between any two people, such personalities can mesh, clash, be attracted or repelled by one another.[3]
>
> To fully comprehend the current generation of teens, we need to understand the generation before them. Danish theologian and philosopher Søren Kierkegaard noted "that life may be lived forward but can only be understood backwards."[4]

The 60s Effect

"At the same time that more people were entering adolescence than ever before, the period of adolescence itself was longer than ever before. This was something new in history."[5] This was the emergence of the baby-boomer teens, seventy-five million strong, those born between 1946 and 1964, entering their teen years with all attention focused on them. These teens were the privileged, the elite, a special generation. They were the Woodstock Nation, a vast sea of teenagers ready to conquer the world! They were raised on the philosophies of Dr. Spock, whose book, Spock's Baby and Child Care, sold thirty million copies. They grew up with Howdy Doody, Mickey Mouse, Leave It to Beaver and The Adventures of Ozzie and Harriet. The sheer number of baby boomers gave youth tremendous clout. Suddenly, to be a teen was trendy.

In 1967, Time lauded the new teenager as the "man of the year," proclaiming the blessings and hopes of and for the baby-boomer generation:

> Reared in a prolonged period of world peace, he has a unique sense of control over his own destiny. . . . science and the knowledge explosion have armed him with more tools to choose his life pattern than he can always use. Physical and intellectual mobility, personal and financial opportunity, a vista of change accelerating in every direction. Untold adventure and unlimited possibilities await this generation.[6]

Those boomer teens had been catered to by every segment of society. They had a sense that they were entitled. From the 1950s to the early 1970s, youth was power. These '60s teens had become a youth phenomenon that would prove to be a sociological and demographic aberration, appearing to be a permanent part of the American landscape. The great size of the baby-boomer generation also encouraged a sort of subliminal illusion, a generation that had mystically stepped outside time, one that was forever to remain young and idealistic; however, as baby boomers left high school, the teenage culture lost its size and energy.

Steppenwolfe's song, "Born To Be Wild," reflects the sentiments and mind-set of the baby boomers. In the great collision of generations, the '60s youth created their own world, a counterculture. The '60s youth saw through the contradictions and hypocrisies of their parents' generation. But it was the egotistical conceit of the baby boomers that demanded, "We want the world, and we want it now!"

The generation gap widened as "Don't trust anyone over thirty" became the slogan of the youth conspiracy. In reckless radical abandonment, '60s youth protested against the Vietnam War, sexual repression, racism and individual repression. They were anti-establishment, anti-traditional values, anti-morality and anti-anything else that was the norm. They believed in instant nonstop gratification, personal liberation, sexual freedom, drug-induced spirituality, long hair, rock music, peace, understanding and free love.

> The boomer ethos remained a deliberate antithesis to everything from their parents' generation, spiritualism over science, gratification over patience, negativism over positivism, rebellion over conformity, rage over friendliness, self over community. . . . The boomers' mixture of high self-esteem and selective indulgence has at once repelled and fascinated other generations, giving boomers a reputation for total self-obsession, a grating arrogance—and for transcendent cultural wisdom.[7]

We are the people our parents warned us about!

Psychedelic Counterculture

Avant-garde rock superstar Jimi Hendrix asked a generation the provocative question, "Are you experienced?" Enticing youth into a mystical world of psychedelic experience, Hendrix's music encompassed the anger, anarchy and raw energy of the '60s. Rock groups like the Strawberry Alarm Clock, Iron Butterfly, Vanilla Fudge and the Lemon Pipers ushered in psychedelic sights and sounds.

LSD, marijuana and other drugs became the spaceship launching youth into a new uncharted frontier. The LSD trip was supposed to expand consciousness, producing a heightened state of awareness to venture into the unknown while removing systems of control. Youth believed that psychedelic drugs opened their minds to a world of fresh perceptions while intensifying social consciousness. Newsweek writes, "the magic word was 'trip.'" The "ultimate trip" was a term used to describe a far-out destination, as far as possible from home and now.[8]

The psychedelic counterculture created a world where words — like mind-blowing, psychotic reaction, groovy, acid head, acid rock, trippin', stoned, paranoia, freaked out, spaced out, get high — characterized the trip of ecstasy and enlightenment. In The Electric Kool-Aid Acid Test, author Tom Wolfe chronicles the '60s journey into excess, describing the recreational and experimental use of LSD and other mind-altering drugs, while traveling on the bus. "The 'bus' is perhaps the artifact of the entire psychedelic era, the very embodiment of the trip."[9] The '60s generation would boldly go where no generation had gone before.

A Sgt. Pepper Landscape

In 1969, nearly a half a million young people gathered on a six hundred acre farm near Woodstock, New York, for the Woodstock Rock Music Festival. Woodstock represented the huge celebration and liberation of an entire generation, and the word would become synonymous with the turbulent '60s and its generation, the "Woodstock Nation."

As the youth counterculture movement was reaching mass momentum, the Beatles came out with their monstrously successful "Sgt. Pepper" album, which was immediately hailed as a monumental, ground-breaking rock masterpiece by music experts and youth alike, capturing the ongoing sexual, social and moral revolution.

Author Annie Gottlieb declared the boomer generation "a tribe with its roots in a time, rather than a place or a race."[10] First wave or last, boomers recall the time of the 1960s, a decade they remember more fondly than other generations.

The baby boomer youth's sense of generational identity and peer power was distinctively Beatle-oriented, Sgt. Pepper inspired. The Beatles' musical tapestry — from "Lucy in the Sky with Diamonds", "Strawberry Fields Forever," and "Come Together" to "Revolution" — mesmerized a generation of youth. The Beatles became the musical and cultural force that shaped, defined and identified the '60s generation.

The Surreal 60s

The Summer of 1967, known as the "Summer of Love," was a pivotal event in the '60s movement. As 70,000 youth would collectively gather for "be-in" demonstrations and celebrations in Washington, D.C. and New York's Central Park, San Francisco's Haight-Ashbury district became the new mecca of hippiedom and flower power.

These were the revolutionary the free speech and protest movement at Berkeley, the Vietnam War, '67 Summer of Love, flower power, love beads, hippies, be-ins, race riots in Detroit, LSD. Guru Timothy Leary advised youth to "turn on, tune in and drop out."

The youth of the '60s would see their utopian world of peace and love begin to crumble. The year 1968 exploded with violence, and rage was everywhere; blood flowed in the streets of Chicago, and the assassinations of Martin Luther King and Bobby Kennedy shook the country. Suddenly, life was complicated and scary. Time magazine writes, "1968 was a knife blade that severed past from future, then from now. The '60s had their crisp, brutal simplicities which co-existed in surreal stage craft with hallucinations and mirages, masterpieces of illusion and self-delusion. Many of the young, for example, cherished the illusion that they were a part of 'the revolution,' a force of history that would overthrow the power structure in the U.S. However, the dream would continue to unravel as the Chicago riot and later Kent State and Jackson State massacres in the days of rage in 1970 ensued."[11]

Ironically, the '60s was the best and worst of times, representing a time period of high expectations, extreme change, irrational optimism and a generation preoccupied with unbridled hedonism in an era of good times and fun. Idealism permeated the atmosphere where our utopian fantasy world seemed immune to pain or problems. The flip side of the '60s is a much darker scenario that emerged only in retrospect as sociologists and other experts analyzed it.

> The '60s might have been a time of tantalizing glimpses of the new Jerusalem. But it was also a time when the system — that collection of values that provide guidelines for societies as well as individuals — was assaulted and mauled. As one center of authority after another was discredited under the new left offensive, we radicals claimed that we murdered to create. But while we wanted a revolution, we didn't have a plan. The decade ended with a big bang that made society into a collection of splinter organizations, special interest groups and newly minted minorities.[12]

This created the fragmenting of America; everyone is totally obsessed with self-interest and the new morality that rationalizes everybody's actions, and nobody takes responsibility for anything.

Baby boomers are unaware of the '60s' destructive philosophical connection between themselves (now parents) and that of their children (the current generation). By the early '70s, the radiant optimism of the '60s turned into a dark, cynical pessimism.

As Bob Dylan sang, "How does it feel to be on your own, a

complete unknown, with no direction home? Like a rolling stone." That described the feelings of a generation whose ideal world was slipping away as the late '60s was a period of time that is characterized by delusion, distortion, excess and destruction.

Generational Cycles: The ’60s Effect

What the '60s generation did in excess, the present generation has taken to extreme excess.

Baby Busters (Born 1965-1983) are the second largest generation in American history and represent a totally different youth experience than any previous generation.

The term "youth culture" has come to describe not only a culture of young people, but also a culture that is preoccupied with being youthful, refusing to grow up. The mass media and marketing experts continually feed and fuel the perpetual youth cultural mind-set, appealing both to baby boomer parents and their teens. Promoting a culture of entitlements, limitless expectations, of immediate self-gratification and constant self-indulgences—a Peter Pan world that resists the process of maturity and adulthood. A society that embraces the egoism of youth and spurns maturity is a youth culture, even though it's pushing fifty.

2

The MTV Generation: The Radical Baby Busters

To what, then, can I compare the people of this generation? What are they like? They are like children sitting in the marketplace and calling out to each other: "We played the flute for you, and you did not dance; we sang a dirge, and you did not cry" (Luke 7:31-32 NIV).

The Radical Baby Busters (1965-1983)

Only twenty years after being obsessed with youth, Americans have now become preoccupied with aging. For the first time in history, American elders outnumber American teens. Enter the baby buster generation, those born from 1965 to present, getting their name from the marked decrease in the birthrate from the boomer generation. In the 1990s, these teens constitute a smaller percentage of the population, seven percent compared to ten percent in 1970.

Almost as suddenly as they became this highly visible center of attention and power in society, teenagers have reverted to anonymity and the old search for identity.[1] When the experience of one generation differs greatly from that of the preceding generation, social change becomes the norm. The boomers' youth experience was the wonder years, where good times seemed to be everywhere. In total contrast, today's generational youth experience could be described as "growing up cynical," where teens view everything as one big rip-off.

Boomer Teens versus Teens Today

When comparing the '60s teens to youth of today, it appears to be a study in contrasts; on the surface, these teens appear to be totally opposite to their counterparts. The paradox is that even though the experience of the '60s generation differs greatly from the baby busters, in many ways these groups are alike. There is definitely a link between the two generations.

Baby busters get their identity from what they are *not* as much as from what they are. They are constantly compared to boomers. Today's teens are fewer in number, politically conservative, not socially innovative or assertive. When reality doesn't meet expectations, they avoid reality, are more cynical and appear to be more apathetic about social issues. They are career-minded and materialistic; success is defined as getting better jobs, getting more and better things. They are a quieter generation, definitely not radical; they will go through life being noted for their contrast to the boomer generation.

The boomer teens were liberals, social activists and idealists, constantly protesting and crusading for their causes. They were radicals who were going to change the world and make love, not money.

The boomer teens of the '60s set in motion an avalanche of social and moral change that is being deeply felt by the current generations. The more we understand the '60s era — its hopes, dreams, disasters and pain — the better we will understand how and why the present generation came to be at risk.

The decade of the '60s has been called a "hinge of history" because so much changed as a result. It was the functional pivot for two generations. "In many ways, the '60s generation owed its orientation and ideology to the '40s generation. The boomers were a reaction to their parents and what they stood for. In like fashion, the kids of the '90s owe their orientation and ideology to the '60s generation, only this time as a consequence rather than a reaction."[2]

The irony of this present baby-buster generation is even though they are considered quieter and more passive, definitely not the radical teens of the '60s, in many ways their behavior is even more radical — skyrocketing suicide rates, epidemic drug abuse, rampant sexual activity, exploding violence, runaways and school dropouts.

Practically every society recognizes a discreet coming-of-age moment (or rite of passage) separating the dependence of youth from the independence of adulthood. This moment is critical in creating generations; any sharp contrast between the experiences of youth and rising adults may fix critical differences in the identity of that generation for a lifetime.[3]

African-American Baby Boomers

A much overlooked segment of the baby-boomer population is the African-American boomers. African-American baby boomers were born in poverty, and many have tended to remain at much lower income levels than white baby boomers. "In 1965, blacks represented 11.6 percent of the total population but accounted for 24 percent of the fatalities in Vietnam."[4]

African-American baby boomers obviously did not have the same experience as their white counterparts. While "wonder years" could describe the white baby-boomer youth experience, growing up alienated could describe the black-boomer youth experience. The two words that have characterized the white baby boomer are *expectations* and *entitlement*. The two words that could best describe the black experience would be *exploitation* and *oppression*.

African-American boomers experienced a world of hostility, injustice and racism. They did not have the opportunities or the privileges of the white baby boomers.

Nothing to Rebel Against

One reason '60s youth seemed so much more radical than today's youth is due to changing social values.

In the '60s, premarital sex was viewed as morally wrong by the culture. Young people were admonished by parents, educators, politicians and the rest of society to abstain from premarital sex. Today society not only tolerates but condones and encourages youth to have safe sex, since they're going to have sex anyway. Teens today have nothing to rebel against because now everything is accepted and viewed as permissible as long as it's your choice. Youth sex, abortion and responsible drinking are now life-style choices. What was considered radical teenage rebellion twenty-five years ago by popular culture is now considered moral behavior.

Today's youth must go to much greater extremes to get our attention. As a result teen homicides, suicides and satanic involvement have increased dramatically. Teens today must be so much more radical and shocking in their behavior to be considered rebellious.

Boomer Barometer

The baby boomers have been the barometer for our popular culture for the past three decades, whether in fashion, life-style or drugs of choice. The baby boomers are the largest generation ever to move through our society. They have had a tremendous impact and influence on cultural trends, changing tastes and values for the last thirty years; they are the trend setters.[5] Author and boomer expert Landon Jones says, "At every stage in their lives, baby boomers change the nature of the life stage they enter and force the nation to devote extraordinary attention to the problems and needs of the baby boomer generation."[6] If the boomers are the cultural barometer for our society, then the youth culture today reflects the depth of their effect.

The Drug Connection

The pervasive drug abuse among today's teens had its roots in the late '60s. The Summer of 1967 was a pivotal year for the emergence of the drug culture. The Beatles' "Sgt. Pepper's Lonely Hearts Club Band" was released, an album that Newsweek referred to as a drug-drenched album that would become the watershed for the drug movement in America.

> As the boomers became the first generation to grow up amidst widespread availability and use of drugs, now recreational drug use burst onto the American scene for the first time in the twentieth century. Recent research studies show baby boomers are most likely to be addicted. It's not just drug addiction, but all types of

> addictions that are widespread among them, including those involving achievement, power, material thoughts and images.[7]

In *Do You Believe in Magic?* author Annie Gottlieb describes the '60s teens' excessive drug use as "a greed for ecstasy, an impatience with the mundane, a mistrust of the efficacy of effort. For those who took a shortcut to magic, it's been hard to learn patience, persistence, discipline, to endure exile in the ordinary."[8] The boomers' philosophy was a quick-fix mentality, but with continual gratification. Teens today whose boomer parents used drugs are twice as likely to use drugs.

Author Fran Sciacca writes:

> The '60s generation needs to recognize the consequences of our past actions and take responsibility for the current generation in crisis. The collapse of the '60s social agenda created a new watershed out of which three mainstreams flowed — three avenues of attempted emotional and intellectual exit or escape from the decade of illusion; irrational optimism, hedonism and mysticism. Those three streams have grown into raging torrents into which today's youth are currently rafting without caution.[9]

These factors have created the conditions that have put the present generation — and our nation — at risk.

Love Generation Disaster

The lyrics of a popular song during the '60s reflected our relationship attitude: "If you can't be with the one you love, love the one you're with." We were in the midst of a sexual revolution as traditional moral values began to collapse. Sexual activity among teens and college students became the alternative accepted life-style.

In the '70s as baby boomers began to marry, the national divorce rate doubled. By the end of the first decade of baby-boomer marriages, it tripled. "Fifty-two percent of all baby boomers are now divorced by age thirty-four. This is five times the rate of our parents' generation at the same age." [10]

The boomer parents have become a moral mirror image of a self-absorbed, morally bankrupt, decadent culture.

The destructive consequences of the moral disaster of the '60s have become the legacy of today's youth. The late '60s may have created a signpost in history, but the decade fractured countless relationships as well. Author Annie Gottlieb's comments are chilling:

"If the right wing gets to write history, they will put us down not as the 'Love Generation,' but as the generation that destroyed the American family. They will point to the soaring rates of divorce, venereal disease, teen pregnancy and abortion as an [aftermath] of the '60s." Through misguided naivete and blinding idealism, "we truly believed that the family had to be torn apart to free love.... and the first step was to tear ourselves free from our parents."[11]

The boomers have set in motion a relationship disaster that is having a devastating effect on the current generation of youth. Today's teens are five times more sexually active than the radical boomer teens twenty-five years ago.

Premarital Sex Explosion

In the late '60s and early '70s, the rise of sexual activity among teens began to increase significantly. In 1971, 40 percent of all baby-boomer teens had experienced sexual intercourse by age nineteen. During the past twenty years, teen sex has risen dramatically. In 1992, 86 percent of teen boys and 75 percent of teen girls had been sexually involved by age nineteen, and the rates are still climbing.

The average age for boomer teens' first sexual encounter in 1971 was age seventeen for girls and age sixteen for guys. In 1992, the average had gone to age fifteen for girls and fourteen for guys. During 1971, nearly 300,000 teen girls became pregnant, compared with over one million in 1991.[12] In 1979, only 2 percent of fifteen-year-old girls said they'd had sex; today, 33 percent have. Sexual activity among teens today has increased 500 percent since 1965.

We have the most sexually active generation in history. Each year over one million teenage girls will get pregnant. Many of those (65 percent) will get pregnant a second time by the time they are nineteen. Forty percent of all fifteen-year-olds are sexually active. Twenty-five percent (one out of four) of teens have had five different sexual partners by age sixteen.[13]

Teens' concepts of love and their relationships have been profoundly affected by the generation before them. Much of what they have seen has been self-gratifying and noncommittal. They're feeling the pain and disillusionment of the '60s sexual revolution.

Television and Rock

The baby boomers were the first generation to be raised on television. By the time the average baby boomer reached the age of eighteen, he or she had seen over twenty thousand hours of TV, with more time spent viewing than in school or even with their parents. Television shaped their concept of reality and their attitudes, values, expectations and behavior. The baby boomers were the first "Television-Rock" generation, as these twin forces would shape, define and become as much their identity as anything.

The American dream was constantly shown to the '60s teens as we saw the ideal and perfect family's life: *The Adventures of Ozzie and Harriet, Father Knows Best, The Donna Reed Show* and *Leave It to Beaver.* Life was so innocent and simplistic; happiness was not something you had to search for — it was everywhere. Problems were very few, and the ones we saw were always quickly and neatly resolved. These model families always knew just what to do; major conflict or confrontation was nonexistent. Negative feelings such as anger, sadness, frustration and depression were not part of the scene. These shows always ended with everyone being close and happy; everything was fine and life was wonderful. The image of the happy, close, problem-free family was promoted, and the reality of human nature with its full range of human emotions was suppressed or removed. So a generation of kids grew up angry at this denial of their real selves, alienated from their feelings and unable to express or deal with conflicts or solve problems.

Today, we have the MTV generation as teens watch four hours of [illegible]on a day. The major themes are sexual, violent and [illegible] powerfully affecting the way a generation thinks and [illegible] was considered highly controversial twenty years ago i[illegible]dered boring. These teens are not easily moved; TV sh[illegible] movies are expected to have a certain number of killings and [illegible]ual encounters are to be considered interesting.

As boomers become elderly, they will listen to the rock music they grew up with. Youth today go to concerts with their boomer parents to see old '60s groups. Paul McCartney, the Grateful Dead, the Rolling Stones and other groups are in vogue with many teens today. Also, former Woodstockers and '60s rock 'n' rollers go for some of the radical rock groups today as they listen to their teens' music. This is probably the first time in history that parents and teens like some of the same music. As rock music was the major catalyst for the youth movement of the '60s, it's still a major social force for youth today, reflecting the attitudes and life-style of the youth culture.

The Big Chill Generation

Baby boomers, especially young boomers, have been taking their lives more frequently than any generation in history. In the past two decades, suicide among teenagers has tripled. The exceptionally high suicide rate among teens today began with the baby boomers in the mid-'70s and has remained a constant tragedy for the present generation. During the last seven years, more than five thousand teen deaths a year were suicides, while the nation's suicide rate has remained level over the same period.[14]

In a recent survey by *USA Today*, people were asked to describe their lives. Baby boomers were most likely to say their lives are getting harder and they are not as happy or having as much fun as they think they should. *The Big Chill,* a movie about a baby-boomer reunion, began with a funeral for a fellow boomer who committed suicide in mid-life. *The Big Chill* has captured the disillusionment, disappointment and frustration of the baby boomers and the '60s dream that went wrong. Boredom, cynicism and depression describe the general feelings of many baby boomers now in their '30s and '40s.

The American Psychiatric Association says that as many as one-third of baby boomers are more depressed and stressed than any other segment of population.[15] Recent national research reveals that baby boomers are ten times as likely to be depressed as their parents and grandparents. The only other facet of the population that has equally high depression levels are American teenagers. Still, teens today are eight times more likely to attempt suicide than teens of twenty years ago. This deadly connection reflects a despair and frustration among parents and teens.

The Boomer Mentality

The baby boomers were the focus of an entire society while growing up, and because of this constant attention and concern, they developed a distinctive mind-set. In Landon Jones's classic work on the baby boomers, *Great Expectations*, he says expectations, more than any other single sociological or psychological influence, bind boomers together. These ultra-high expectations have helped create the unrealistic expectations about success and relationships. The boomer generation had been conditioned with these lofty expectations that were too glorious, so noble and impossible to reach. The result was mass disillusionment and discontent.

The other factor that profoundly affected the boomers' attitudes about life was what Daniel Yankelovich referred to as the "psychology of entitlement." What other generations considered privileges, the baby boomers perceive as rights.[16] Entitlement says we can have it all. Immediate entertainment says we can enjoy it all now. Enlightenment says we can know it all. The excessive expectations combined with an ultra sense of entitlements and continual gratification have helped produce the "baby-boomer blues." Never has a generation been more disillusioned and disappointed than the baby boomers.

Born into greater prosperity than any other generation or group before it, advantage and opportunity abounded for these boomer teens because they were the most educated generation in history. "We baby boomers were raised to believe we deserved a college education, we deserved a great marriage with good children, a car and a beautiful home in the suburbs. We deserved not just the pursuit of happiness, we deserved to be happy."[17] The present generation of youth has been deeply affected by the baby-boomer sense of entitlement. The problem is the expectancy level of the current generation usually exceeds the expectations of the previous generation.

Following World War II, each generation has surpassed the previous one in terms of economic affluence, job opportunities, overall prosperity and growth. However, due to economic uncertainties, a society in transition to high-tech industry, scaling down, mergers, restructuring of the job market and economy, and more college graduates competing for fewer jobs, baby busters face the disappointment of downward mobility. For the first time since World War II the current generation will not have the income opportunity or life-style that their parents enjoyed. If their parents' house were on the market, they wouldn't be able to afford it. What happens when society is unable to fulfill the high expectations of the current generation of youth, when the American Dream becomes the American Nightmare?

The boomer generation always expected more — more happiness, more intimacy, more pleasure — goals that can be extremely difficult to achieve, thus setting them up for maximum disappointment.

> As they approach mid-life many baby boomers feel trapped by their lives. They are still searching for clear values and life purposes. But while they are suspended between their dreams and ultimate life directions, many feel stuck in boring dead-end jobs, financial problems, stagnant dating relationships, meaningless marriages and unfulfilling life-styles.[18]
>
> Today's youth still have a sense of entitlement, even though they have not been the focus of society like the boomers. In fact, this has actually increased their sense of entitlement because they've felt slighted compared to the '60s teens. They have also been constantly surrounded by an affluent culture. Materialism and greed permeates our culture; teens see multimillion-dollar contracts for athletes and the lavish life-styles of rock and movie stars, whether they are from the suburbs or the inner city. They feel entitled to interesting and fulfilling work without supervision or menial tasks, yet they don't have any realistic notion about how to get those extraordinary privileges. They simply expect them.
>
> Criminologists and law enforcement officials cite as the major cause of juvenile crime a feeling of entitlement that "society owes me." Youth may feel a growing anger and betrayal by the society around them due to continued unrealistic expectations that will exceed our culture's ability to fulfill. This could create a dangerous atmosphere of random violence as youth

will begin to lash out at anything and everything around them.

Thirty Years of Excesses

These values questions — about how we've chosen to live our lives and how that has affected our children, about the nagging sense that unrestrained personal freedom and materialism yield only greater hungers and lonelier nights — have been quiet American obsessions for some time now, the source of deep, vexing national anxiety.

Everyone gets to act out. There are no consequences; everything is rationalized. Mass excesses and indulgences of popular culture have run their course. The thirty-year spree has caused a monster hangover and produced a deadly generational cycle.

Authors William Strauss and Neil Howe point out in *Generations*: "By almost any standard of social pathology, the boomers is a generation of worsening trends. During the 1970s the incidence of serious youth crime grew twice as fast as the number of youth. Criminals born in 1958 . . . were 80 percent more likely than criminals born in 1945 to commit multiple crimes, and 80 percent more likely to send their victims to the hospital or morgue."[19]

Multi-Generational Scope

The generational cycle that is in motion has profoundly affected two generations: the current generation of teens and the baby-boomer generation and even those children who will be teens during the next decade. This multi-generational effect is influencing the lives of over one hundred million Americans. *Many youth and adults today are experiencing deep unresolved conflict.*

For the boomer generation, more pleasure and more gratification is the antidote for guilt. We've exchanged rationalization for responsibility, convenience for commitment, self-love for the needs of others, instant gratification for long-range happiness and a marketable image for true character.

Four Significant Questions

Youth are asking many questions today. However, there are four paramount questions that encompass their critical needs and fears, ultimately determining their expectations, motivations and behavior. How they answer these questions will profoundly impact their lives.

1. *Is it real?* Pseudo-relationships, manufactured identities, media images and moral confusion pervade the youth culture, creating a landscape of illusion. *Are the relationships I'm involved in real? Is the person I see in the mirror real? Is what's really important in my life real?* Everything and everyone around them is a mirage; the closer they get to it, they realize there's nothing there. Focusing on their fears to fulfill their needs always produces a false sense of reality. Teens tend to see what they want to see. The line between fantasy and reality becomes increasingly blurred as stresses, fears and needs intensify. Youth are searching for something that is real in this culture of illusion.

2. *Will it last?* In a culture of instant gratification, everything is constantly changing. Relationships today are noncommittal, short term and disposable. Youth have experienced momentary fulfillment through multiple relationships, radical parties, material gratification and even the sexual experience. Youth are desperate for something or someone that will last — something that will endure, that will stand when everything else walks away or fades.

3. *Who'll stop the pain?* Enormous pressures and unprecedented situations have produced a vast potential for pain among teens. If teens believe something to be real when it is fantasy, their pain is intensified greatly. Youth attempt to escape or anesthetize their pain through drugs, alcohol, sex, self-gratifying pleasures, violence and even suicide. A certain amount of pain is inevitable, even necessary. How youth deal with their pain determines their success and happiness. By confronting their pain, they develop commitment, courage, intimacy and emotional maturity. Also, pain teaches teens to be sensitive and compassionate to the needs and pain of others. Too many youth are trapped in a perpetuating cycle of pain created by bad choices based on their fears.

4. *Can I make a difference?* The major goal of many youth today is self-preservation (survival) or self-gratification and the pursuit of pleasure. This generation is one without a unifying cause; the only cause seems to be noncommitment. Teens become so distracted by the trivial, the irrelevant and the absurd that they can't focus on what's significant, meaningful and critically important.

In an increasingly high-tech, high-powered, complex culture, feelings of inadequacy and lack of control over their lives are magnified. Youth need a sense of destiny, to feel that they are influencing and impacting their world. Nothing is more frustrating to teens than to sense that they don't count or can't make a difference. There is a deep desire among youth to take control of their lives and determine their future.

In short, life is made into a nonstop, state-of-the-art commercial—a prepackaged, self-indulgent, self-gratifying fantasy.

"Life does seem to get more insane as the century comes around. Things get more nuts and surreal in life, and eventually reality will pass Batman by."

Tim Burton
Batman Director

"Here we are now entertain us."

Nirvana

"The most profound problem with popular culture isn't its immediate impact on a few vulnerable and dangerous individuals but its long term cumulative effect on the rest of society. The most disturbing concerns go beyond mass media and popular culture roles in provoking a handful of specific crimes. But rather involve its pervasive influence in creating a general climate of violence and cultural self indulgence."

Michael Medved
Hollywood vs. America

Chapter 3

Illusions of Reality: The Media Maze

And do not be conformed to this world, but be transformed by the renewing of your mind, that you may prove what is that good and acceptable and perfect will of God (Rom. 12:2 NKJ).

Never in history have youth been exposed to so much, so fast. Powerful images of love and hate, pain and pleasure, success and failure, life and death captivate their senses, coming at them at a faster and faster rate. What is fantasy? What is reality?

Your perception of reality is critical to understanding yourself and others, and in making choices. That perception and your beliefs are a result of information you receive and experiences you have. What you see shapes what you think, especially if what you see appeals to a need, either real or perceived.

Our perception of reality is greatly determined by the needs and fears we have. Teens today live in an image-oriented society where, as the commercial says, "Image is everything." The media have saturated youth with provocative images, appealing to their vulnerable emotional needs and exploiting their fears.

Fantasy or illusion is only the appearance of reality—false, deceptive, delusional. When young people focus on their fears in an attempt to meet their needs, reality becomes distorted. A distorted perception of relationships, identity, meaning and happiness will produce fantasy or an "illusional life-style." This false sense of reality is fed by endless, enticing media images, that exploit needs and fears and accelerate the need for immediate, continual gratification.

If youth believe someone or something to be real when it is not, then every choice they make from that moment will be wrong. A false perception will greatly increase the pain and frustration in their lives.

In this media-image age, youth's view of the world is shaped by the information they receive and the means by which they receive it. Television is the window to our world for today's teens; much of what they see presents a distorted view of reality.

Teens live in an increasingly dangerous and stressful world of failing relationships, pressures at home and school, fear and lack of security. When teens are engulfed by these constant pressures, they are much more prone to fantasy. The impact of fantasy on this generation is evident. When confronted with reality, many of today's teens postpone it, ignore it and ultimately avoid it. We live in a society that deceives itself daily about choices, success, relationships, identity, future happiness and what's really important.

By the time the average American teen has graduated from high school, he or she has spent twenty-four thousand hours watching television compared to twelve thousand learning in a classroom. This is having a powerful effect on their attitudes, expectations and their decisions. Because the youth culture is a massive consumer market that represents major dollars, media executives go to great lengths to showcase their perception of what youth deem important; they are not so much concerned with the happiness or fulfillment of teens as with their purchasing power. Much entertainment is designed not for fun or pleasure but for profits, to develop committed customers.

The media's economic survival depends on the youth market. Youth, in turn, need the media for direction and development in a society where once-stable social institutions — family, school and the church — do not shape the youth culture as powerfully as they once did. Thus, we have a codependent relationship between media and youth.

Created in the Image of TV

Television emerged in the 1950s and immediately became the most pervasive, persuasive mode of communication to hit planet earth. Its massive social influence on the American scene has been deeply felt for the last forty years. *Watching American,* a groundbreaking scientific study, is the first research on how social issues have been presented on television throughout its history. Professor Stanley Rothman, who conducted the research, states, "If one examines public attitudes on certain issues, it is quite clear in many cases that the changes came to television before they came to change public opinion." The study goes on to say that TV has helped shape the way Americans behave, or think they should: "The television agenda reflects a morality of sexual permissiveness and perversion, widespread violence, suspicion of authority, contempt for business and yuppie liberalism."[1]

Originally, TV reflected traditional moral, social, and political values. More recently, beginning in the late '60s and early '70s, television has become dominated by "advocacy" programs that directly reflect the values of television's creative leaders, who are clearly indifferent to and even cynical about religion.

Ninety-three percent of the media hierarchy say they never or seldom attend religious services, and the vast majority of these say God plays no role in society today. In fact, the influence of religion (Christianity) and God on society is considered detrimental by television leaders.

According to television's creators, they are not just in it for money. They have a specific agenda to move the audience toward their own vision of the "good society." As the authors of *Watching America* point out, this is a vision where homosexual behavior and extramarital sexual activity are not only accepted as normal but are encouraged as legitimate choices of personal life-style. The social and moral change television has brought about and continues to bring about is so subtle as to be nearly imperceptible and yet massive enough to be undeniable.

The authors of *Watching America* argue, "The uneasiness many people feel about television stems from the sense that the medium is changing our lives in ways we cannot measure and may not even notice." The television society has created its own image.

The Gradual Effect

There is a vast contrast between the programs of the '50s and the programs of the '90s. Research notes that a distinct change took place in the philosophical view of television and movies in the mid-'60s. If media executives had attempted to show '90s material in the '50s, there would have been a nationwide public outcry. However, subtle change occurring over a period of time prepares us to accept what was previously unacceptable and even bizarre. We've become familiar, comfortable and desensitized to reality.

When we are exposed to something over and over again, it eventually becomes part of our mind-set. This process has been used for years as one of the most effective learning techniques for students. Through the media, youth are continually exposed to thousands of mesmerizing images everyday. If a picture is worth a thousand words, what happens when the picture moves and talks or sings and can be seen from every imaginable angle and dimension?

"Joseph Goebbels, Nazi propagandist minister for Hitler, said if a lie is told often enough, it will be believed as the truth."[2] He theorized that when a lie is big enough, bold enough and spoken often enough, people will believe it, no matter how incredible it is. When fantasy is shown enough, it becomes engraved in our lives as reality.

The Flattery Factor

All of us respond to people who tell us what we want to hear, even if it isn't true. Television's commercial communication must appeal to our egos in order to be successful. It must address our need to feel good about ourselves and our lives if it is to get our attention.

Youth must be told what they want to hear about themselves. They very quickly reject anything that is negative or critical, even if it is true. Television advertising tells teens what they want to hear: "You are a special person." The mass manipulation of a generation impedes the ability of today's youth to make significant choices.

The media is a major catalyst in the altering of reality. Constantly reinforced by high credibility and state-of-the-art marketing techniques, fantasy can become the perceived reality of a society. Substituting fantasy in any area of life can be a deadly illusion.

Creating an Illusion

In creating an illusion or fantasy, the media appeals to three basic premises:

1. Meeting a basic desire or need that is presently unfulfilled.
2. The "grass is greener" syndrome, which says you should have a better life than you have now.
3. Life is boring and depressing, but it could be fun and exciting all the time.

Because this generation has been inundated with so many images, they cannot separate fantasy from reality. The media has created a fantasy land where life is constantly moving from one exciting experience to another. When reality is too painful and too stressful, fantasy becomes an inviting alternative for teens.

Dr. Gary Collins describes the defense mechanisms of the mind and how our minds don't always handle pressure in logical and efficient ways.

Ego Defense Mechanisms. These are ways of thinking that automatically protect our minds from experiencing anxiety and depression, and from recognizing danger. But when these defense mechanisms keep us from working to remove or reduce pressures, they prevent us from coping and confronting.[3]

Some of these defenses are:

- *Denial of Reality*—the refusal to be aware of threatening topics, to admit weakness, to face criticism, to admit danger or to look at unpleasant sights.
- *Rationalization*—the seeking of logical or socially approved justification for one's actions or beliefs.
- *Projection*—shifting blame for one's own shortcomings or mistakes.
- *Emotional Isolation*—detaching oneself emotionally from a painful or threatening situation, avoiding associations that invoke anxieties, guilt or fear.
- *Repression*—the convenient forgetting of things that would be painful, traumatic or threatening.
- *Fantasy Formation*—a subordination of reality in favor of a fantasy world peopled by fantasy people, in fantasy relationships and situations.[4]

Rooted firmly in reality, creative fantasy can be an asset.

However, retreating into magic or wishful thinking, coupled with fantasized sensual gratification can plunge youth into obsessive and dangerous behavior. Addiction to these perceptual defenses can inhibit a mature orientation to reality.

Illusions Projected by TV

Here are four basic illusions depicted over and over to young people by television:

First Illusion. Based on the need for intimacy, sex and love have become synonymous. Premarital sexual activity among teens is presented as normal behavior, preparing teens for lasting and fulfilling relationships. This premise is demonstrated by the ease with which people flow in and out of relationships and beds. The implied message for teens is that if you're not sexually active, you're really out of it, abnormal or weird. The media has helped create feelings of inadequacy in teens by promoting relationships that are based solely on sexual involvement.

The American Academy of Pediatrics research states that teenagers will view on TV approximately fourteen thousand sexual references and innuendos per year. Of those, only 150 even remotely refer to sexual responsibility, birth control or abstinence. Of the sexual activity shown, 85 percent is outside the commitment of marriage, in premarital and extramarital affairs.[5]

The *Journal of Communication* reports that television portrays six times more extramarital sex than sex between spouses. Ninety-four percent of the sexual encounters on soap operas are between people not married to each other.[6] Josh McDowell in his outstanding book, *Why Wait?* says, "TV never shows youth the pain or consequences for their actions. Rarely on TV does anyone pay the price for illicit sex. You only do that in real life."[7]

Youth see sensual images advertising everything from Levi's 501 jeans to Caress soap. Gorgeous girls and handsome hunks, in a series of captivating scenes with mood-enhancing music, create the illusion of relationships they can never actually supply or fulfill, which only intensifies youth's desperation. Teens are transported from the repetitive, boring rituals of existence to romantic fantasy. What is implied is that if you use this cologne or that toothpaste, you can have exciting and fulfilling relationships. When teen sexuality is based on fantasy, the consequences can be devastating.

Second Illusion. Alcohol consumption is shown as the best way to interact socially. If you want friends, you drink; if you want a beautiful girl or handsome guy, you drink; if you want to have a good time, you drink; if you want to be successful, you drink. These alluring commercials say, "The night was made for Michelob! You can have it all! It doesn't get any better than this. When you've said Bud, you've said it all." They imply that if you miss this moment, if you don't do it now, you've missed it all! In the advertisements, everyone is always happy, laughing and drinking, having fun together. Television creates a sense of immediacy among youth that promotes an instant quick-fix mentality, concerned only for the immediate now, even if the choice they are making in the present will devastate them later. Rarely ever do they show teens that are drinking not having fun, nor do they show teens who have been killed or seriously injured in an alcohol-related car accident.

The number-one drug abused among teens is alcohol. The number-one cause of death among teens is alcohol-related car accidents; more than eight thousand youths are killed each year. The National Institute on Alcohol Abuse states there are 3.3 million teenage alcoholics in the U.S., yet alcohol is the socially accepted drug of Americans.[8]

I've often heard parents say, "I would rather my kids drink, as long as they're not doing the really dangerous drugs." That is a fantasy that can be fatal.

Third Illusion. Acts of violence and lawlessness are acceptable solutions to problems. High-tech media is looking for new creative ways to kill using the most graphic and chilling methods. Youth see TV and movie heroes in *Rambo, Die Hard, Robo Cop* and *Total Recall* kicking down doors, shooting, punching, slashing, ripping, maiming and laying waste to everything and everyone in their path in order to achieve their purpose. They are in control and have power. This appeals tremendously to teens who feel their lives are out of control or are being controlled by others.

Newsweek says of the exploding violence in our culture, "America's addiction to make-believe violence is like any other addiction; it takes more and more to accomplish less and less."[9]

The average teen by the age of eighteen has seen forty thousand murders and two hundred thousand violent acts — rape, robberies, knifings and countless other crimes — according to Thomas Radecki, research director for the National Coalition on Television Violence.[10]

More than three thousand studies have linked television violence to aggressive or violent behavior in young people. Violence among teens is becoming an epidemic, homicide has increased 400 percent since 1950.[11] Youths fourteen to twenty-four years old account for over half of the nation's arrests. In a study of youth gangs in Los Angeles one of the major factors cited as contributing to deviant behavior was "media sensationalism."[12]

The Fourth Illusion. The marketing of happiness by the youth-oriented media strategically connects the consumption of products with relationships, identity and happiness. Identity and intimacy are packaged commodities; youth think they can find meaning by acquiring things. In this kind of setting, identity and intimacy turn into marketable commodities.

In actuality the "consumer media" only deepens teens' need for relationships and intensifies their identity crisis by creating even more needs—and not fulfilling them. "The dominant spirituality of this generation is the spirituality of consumerism. Today's youth believe they can find happiness by buying it, driving it, wearing it or drinking it."[13]

Popular culture has decided to let the consumer market dictate the cultural landscape of adolescent life. The consumer-oriented media has forged a powerful emotional and economic tie with the youth culture by implying they will fill youth's needs and solve their problems by consumption itself.

Consuming Madness

Every day, Americans find temporary comfort and, at most, fleeting happiness by purchasing more things. Youth are flooded with the consumer's message that says consumption is the cure-all. If you're depressed, buy some new clothes. If you're bored, take in a movie or rent a video. If you're hungry, head for a restaurant. More and more youth and adults buy something to create a social event.

The youth-oriented media has constructed a consumer mind-set where buying appears to be the answer. The media emphasizes novelty, excitement and glamour by endlessly reciting the magical formulas for youthfulness; the key is trendy consumerism.

Youth see "perfect Hollywood people" and ideal situations that distort reality and call teens' attention to their imperfections and real life. Most of them could never measure up to the perfect images they see; the result is deeper insecurity and inferiority.

Combine teen vulnerability with spending power unlike anything popular culture has ever seen, and you have a market ripe for the picking. "According to Teenage Research Unlimited $57 billion of their own money is spent on products ranging from clothes to music to food. Teenage girls spend $62 a week while teenage boys spend $69 a week."[14] Media advertising experts go after the youth market with sensual, creative, high-energy ads that communicate a "gotta have it" message that is extremely manipulating and exploitive.

Television ads create unrealistic expectations, feelings of inadequacy and a false hope for many youth by trivializing the depth of their pain. The consumer-oriented electronic media appeals to and exploits youth's needs for identity, intimacy and meaning. Acceptance by their peers and the opposite sex and a sense of significance are all offered to youth through the purchasing of more things.

The power of mass communications depends on the electronic media's capacity for creating illusion and "emotion" in their desired relationships, not actually fulfilling or supplying such relationships. The media fuels and enhances an illusion of intimacy and a "media identity" for many youth today.

Thus, we have the mass marketing of the emotional needs and fears of teens. The song says, "Can't buy me love," but we still believe we can.

Mass Marketing Emotions

The rise of the entertainment industry during the last thirty years parallels the decline of the family. The media and the peer group have become the surrogate parents; they've shaped the mind-set and life-style for today's youth culture.

To a great extent, the electronic media has filled the void created by the erosion of authority and relationships within the family and local institutions such as school and church.

From the '50s to the present, the media has redefined and reshaped the youth culture according to the latest trends in fashion, language, leisure activities, life-style and especially electronic media consumption, which is a way of life in America.

Television advertising has constructed an artificial world for youth that leaves them frustrated and disillusioned. Many young people are anchored in this specialized media fantasy world, a youth subculture that gives their lives superficial meaning but at the same time distances them from reality and significance. Today's consumer media is far more market sensitive to generational change and cultural trends than any media of the past. These television ads effectively exploit the youth culture while offering a panacea for all their problems; they capitalize on their desires and discontent.

Sociologist Herbert Marcuse states: "The apathetic state of the youth today is in part a product of the advertising techniques of American television. This is an increasingly passionless generation. We have let youth encounter reality through the media. We have jaded them with so much artificially generated excitement that it has become difficult for them to find anything to be authentically enthusiastic about. Even sex, supposedly one of life's most exotic and thrilling experiences, has been stripped of its mystery in our overly sensual culture."[15]

Television projects a sense of immediacy that offers them what they want now; the media defines and distorts youth's sense of time and reality. The commercialization of America has made life a nonstop advertisement to purchase certain products.

Shock Entertainment

What happens when a culture becomes so progressively decadent that what was once shocking is considered normal? That culture crosses over a dangerous line where its moral consciousness is seriously impaired, where perversion and depravity become the norm.

Time says, "The '90s in America are destined to be the 'Filth Decade.' Words and ideas formerly on the fringe have engulfed the cultural mainstream. It's a four-letter word out there in rock and rap, in movies and on television, in comedy clubs and for real life. America is a foul-mouthed, X-rated pop culture!"[16] Smut that was considered extreme has become part of the entertainment landscape in America and threatens the moral fabric of our society. The media must raise the level of sleaze to new heights to maintain their audience. In the '90s, perversion will not be perceived as wrong. It will be considered enlightened and sophisticated, in the same manner that previous moral taboos are becoming in vogue for today's youth.

This shock-effect entertainment is producing an unshockable generation. Youth today have been exposed to so much obscenity that it takes much more to move, excite and entertain them. Their response is, "Impress me, entertain me, if you can." Sex, which previously had a certain mystique and wonderment for youth, has become boring, just another aerobic activity.

Competition for high television ratings is another factor driving TV programming and movies to extreme raunchiness; television today offers scores of options to the viewer through cable channels. The remote control device gives the television viewer instant access to literally scores of viewing options. This contributes to boredom, restlessness, shorter attention spans and a jadedness among youth and adults.

The shows are breaking new ground in immorality. Youth will see programming become increasingly risqué. The entertainment media will continue to escalate violence, sexual perversion and the bizarre of the occult to maintain audience ratings.

Superficial Society

An image-oriented culture is more concerned with a surface appearance; it's not how much depth a person has, but how much stuff they appear to have. The media appeals to the shallowness of human nature; we're afraid to look too deep inside because we might find nothing.

The media feeds this superficial life-style that emphasizes style, not substance, creating a marked superficiality among young people. A myriad of artificial images with dazzling special effects that flash, glitter and sparkle help produce fantasy relationships and pseudo-significance. Beneath the glitz and glamour is nothing but emptiness.

The average American family watches 8.7 hours of television each day; this leaves no time for meaningful interaction and communication between teens and parents. The family doesn't talk; they watch TV rather than develop strong family relationships. In a superficial culture, commitment, character and integrity are sacrificed to noncommitment, shallowness and deception. Youth quickly learn how to develop surface-only relationships and how to project the appropriate image.

The Image Generation

Through the rise of the electronic media, we have become a visually stimulated, image-oriented society. On TV we see thirty-second spots with twenty cuts. The commercials reflect the speed, variety and high-tech sophistication of modern communications where creating a mood with images is more marketable than delivering reality.

We watch rapidly changing visual images, as many as 1,200 different slick, state-of-the-art production shots every hour. The average length of a shot on network television is 3.5 seconds; the average in a commercial is 2.5 seconds. This image-inundation has produced the electronic media generation—hyper-bored and constantly watching.

A Passive Generation

The media has conditioned youth to watch rather than do — a spectator mind-set. The decline in motivation, discipline and achievement in schools is traced to a characteristic passivity (apathy) among youth today. Television offers easy instant solutions to problems and pain, taken care of in thirty- to sixty-minute time spans—no determination, patience or personal initiative required. One research study shows conclusively that children and teens who watch more television have decreased academic skills. Creativity, initiative and other learning skills (reading, writing and problem-solving and communication competencies) are adversely affected. [17]

Also, television implies to young people that they aren't necessary. If they don't show up, it doesn't really matter; their contribution or presence is irrelevant, thus they are irrelevant. You watch, you buy; thus, you are. Such a mentality breeds apathy.

Delightful Distractions

The mass media age has created fascinating and mesmerizing distractions that effectively keep youth from thinking about what's really important in life. These hypnotic images divert their attention from reflecting too deeply about themselves or other people, reality or the pain and problems of life. This generation has become so entertainment-oriented that a happy life must be a continually exhilarating entertainment experience. This produces a shallow, superficial and impatient mind-set, where style and image become more important than substance and character.

Youth are constantly looking for the ultimate entertainment and experience. In a world of nonstop distractions, the mass media redefines culture as a perpetual circus of entertainment where youth become addicted to the entertainment drug, which further separates them from reality.

In this electronic media-constructed fantasy world, distractions are a way of life for youth; reality becomes unpleasant and undesirable. Young people are enchanted by these entertainment distractions where reality is avoided.

Fantasy-Oriented Culture

The media has created a fantasy culture:

1. *Fantasy Culture* — When a culture becomes technically advanced and morally confused, the result is fantasy.

2. *Fantasy Culture* — Believes in "magical wishful thinking" that no matter what choice we make, everything will have a happy ending.

3. *Fantasy Culture* — Is self-absorbed, self-indulgent, addicted to pleasure consumption and immediate gratification. Anything that's not fun, exciting and instantly fulfilling is irrelevant and trivial.

4. *Fantasy Culture* — The electronic media has created a "fantasy mentality" where popular culture is mesmerized, obsessed and fascinated by multiplying images, moods and illusions. The media wants to make you feel rather than think. An image-oriented culture produces mass manipulation and self-deception.

5. *Fantasy Culture* — Where unrealistic expectations exceed reality, and the result is disappointment, disillusionment and

discontent, which fuels more fantasy.

6. *Fantasy Culture* — Massive stress, uncertainty, fears of relationships and the future, with unprecedented situations and failures create an avoidance, postponement and escape of pain. When reality becomes fearful, depressing and boring, fantasy becomes a desirable necessity.

7. *Fantasy Culture* — Electronic media uses state-of-the-art marketing techniques that are based on two premises: giving people what they want and creating needs they don't yet realize they have.

8. *Fantasy Culture* — Promises to fulfill our emotional needs for intimacy, identity, a sense of significance and ultimate happiness by exploiting our fears which creates an "illusion of reality."

In *1984*, Orwell stated that people are controlled by inflicting pain. In *Brave New World,* Huxley stated that they are controlled by inflicting pleasure. In short, Orwell feared that what we *hate* will ruin us; Huxley feared that what we *love* will ruin us. In this distracted media culture, Huxley feared the truth would be drowned in a sea of irrelevance. Entertainment becomes a noble pursuit, the ultimate cause and cure for our boredom and emptiness; as Neil Postman says, "we are amusing ourselves to death" as youth and adults pursue entertainment as the key to meaning and fulfillment.[18]

"Change is avalanching upon our heads and most people are grossly unprepared to cope with it. The result is mass disorientation, shattering stress, fear and future shock on an enormous scale."

Alvin Toffler
Future Shock

"Toto, I don't think we're in Kansas anymore."

Dorothy in *The Wizard of Oz*

Chapter 4

Change Is Changing: The High-Tech Explosion

Jesus Christ is the same yesterday, today, and forever (Heb. 13:8 NKJ).

Change has always been with us; we feel it in our lives and we see it in the culture around us. It's been said that the only thing that's permanent is change. Throughout history, each generation has experienced change to some degree. With each century, the gradual changes have happened at a little faster rate and have been more significant.

For the last two hundred years, Western culture has seen drastic changes. With each successive generation, change is becoming more extreme and mounting with unimaginable force. During the last forty years, North America has experienced change socially, morally, environmentally and technologically, at a faster rate than ever before. No one has felt this change more deeply than America's youth. They have been thrust into a rapidly changing and impersonal world without the security structures of past generations. The American high school student may be the most significant casualty of the technological age.[1]

Change Fast Forward

Nothing affects our lives more than change; sometimes it's good, sometimes it's devastating, depending on how we adapt and cope with it. The lyrics of a recent popular song describe the feelings of today's youth, as change comes crashing down upon their world: "In these uncertain times, there's a yearning undefined." [2]

In a world that's constantly changing, certainty becomes uncertain.

When change occurs in a shorter span of time, our ability to adapt becomes greatly impaired. "Shock occurs when we are confronted with something both unexpected and apparently unmanageable."[3] The youth culture is colliding with a high-tech society, and the effect of these changes could have a cataclysmic effect.

Alvin Toffler said that we have released a totally new social force, a stream of change so accelerated that it influences our sense of time, revolutionizes the tempo of daily life and affects the very way we experience the world around us.[4] This accelerated change is a psychological and social force that is profoundly affecting youth.

Accelerated change has impaired the way youth respond and relate to situations, pressures and problems that confront them. When their frame of reference (their security or reality base) changes drastically to something they've never experienced before, they become disoriented. As youth face rising pressures without a previous personal frame of reference, mass emotional upheaval could occur. Youth are experiencing culture shock and high-tech shock simultaneously. This makes them especially vulnerable and unprepared for a world racing to the year 2000.

The Frog in the Kettle

In *The Frog in the Kettle,* researcher and social analyst George Barna describes the social and moral change in America as "having a disarming effect because it is more evolutionary than revolutionary." Each day brings an incremental shift in some fundamental aspect, a small ripple that we often overlook because we are on guard only for tidal waves. Social scientists tell us that if we could stand back and measure the rate of change in modern America, we would discover that things are changing at a faster pace than ever before. However, because most of us are so immersed in a daily struggle for survival and preoccupied with the possibility of wealth and happiness, we plant ourselves in the short term. Thus, the numerous changes that are reshaping our everyday reality and eroding our Christian culture go unnoticed and unanswered.[5] This is having a powerful effect on today's youth, the way they experience reality, their sense of commitment, their ability to adapt and cope and their perception of time.

Emotional Acceleration

Emotional acceleration occurs when our culture prematurely exposes children and teens to the pressures and problems of an adult world without adequate emotional development or preparation. Adulthood pressures prematurely intruding on the youth culture have a bizarre effect on the roles of adults, teens and children. We have ten-year-olds who have experienced so much so fast they are no longer children but little adults. Imagine that ten-year-olds were allowed to drive. Even with specially equipped cars, can you imagine the confusion and devastation that would occur on America's highways?

Extreme social and moral change is robbing youth of meaningful roles in our society and has produced a sociological distortion where they feel unnecessary and irrelevant. It is difficult for teens to develop a sense of purpose and significance without being needed, listened to and taken seriously. Also, the unpredictability arising from unique situations magnifies their anxiety, confusion and perception of reality. Confronted by a threatening high-tech culture with a seemingly insurmountable and uncertain scenario of "neo-change," youth become apathetic—no shock, no rage, no tears, only uninvolvement, boredom and noncommitment. Today's teens feel culturally displaced; their once-privileged position in society, where they had special recognition and protection as an adolescent, is no longer there. Their passage into adulthood has become imperiled.

Change causes more stress in our lives than any other factor. Of the over forty major stress-related events or situations listed on the Holmes Rake Scale of Stress Ratings, change was the primary source in nearly every situation listed. "When things start changing outside you, you are going to have a parallel change taking place on the inside," says Christopher Wright of the Institute of Human Affairs.[6]

Today's teens are exposed to more pressure and change than any previous generation. The teenage girl who cannot cope with the pressures and mounting complexity of daily life will choose sexual activity, even pregnancy, as an alternative. She will experience immediate relief, even momentary satisfaction. Only later will she realize she has intensified her pain and stress. For the teenage guy struggling for identity in a stress-drenched world, drugs appear to be the great escape, the ultimate solution.

While the stress level for youth has risen dramatically, the security structures have disintegrated. What happens when what was previously secure has become insecure? What happens when family, school and societal environments — where youth formerly received protection, guidance and nurturing — change from stress reducing to stress producing?

This harsh scenario has rendered teens more vulnerable to stress than ever before. The vanishing of these security structures represent major social change in how we view youth and their diminishing role in society. These factors have caused this generation to be displaced. This high-stressed, fast-changing atmosphere, that is constantly creating new demands and new situations, has caused a general feeling among youth of being out of control of their lives.

Change in Relationships

Alvin Toffler defines *transience* as "the rate at which relationships turn over." Relationships that once lasted for long spans of time now have much shorter life expectancies; the loss of permanence in relationships has made youth insecure. When the world around them is rapidly changing, the need for meaningful relationships becomes even greater. However, due to the fragmented family in America through divorce, step-families, single-parent families and physical and emotional abuse, youth feel disconnected. The rate at which people move in and out of youth's lives gives rise to a new restlessness, uncertainty and anger.

Contemporary culture develops a throwaway mentality in relationships where people get used up quickly and relationships are terminated. These disposable relationships coupled with the fast-changing landscape around youth have created a generational discontinuity, where youth and adults become isolated and alienated from each other's worlds. This breakdown in teen-adult relationships continues and the pace of life accelerates as youth's sense of disconnectedness deepens.

Change in Schools

School environments have undergone drastic change in the last twenty years. Once our schools were a safe haven where teens could grow academically, emotionally and socially. It was a place where they could be teenagers; it was a safe and secure place to be. A popular song in the '60s, "Be True to Your School," characterized this fun, secure period, describing loyalty and commitment to each other and the excitement of school.

Schools have become breeding grounds for violence, drug use, gangs and crime. You walk on a junior or senior high campus in many places in America and you see security police, and metal detectors checking for weapons.

As many as 2.5 million U.S. teens carry guns, knives, razors or clubs, according to the Centers for Disease Control. Up to 250,000 guns are carried into schools each day. Gunfire has turned many playgrounds into battlegrounds. One in five high school-age kids (one in three boys) has carried some type of weapon to school in the last month. Across the U.S., in rural townships, urban inner cities and suburban communities, kids with guns are turning the once-placid school experience into a frightening, bloody shootout.[7]

This explosive, deadly atmosphere has turned education into an afterthought in some schools, where the first concern is learning to survive.[8] Being in school has become a fearful experience for many youth today, where hostility, frustration and the fear of the unexpected reign supreme. For the last twenty years, every succeeding graduating class has scored lower in achievement, motivation and discipline than the class before, and has shown marked increases in destructive behaviors.

In the past thirty years, the problems in schools ranged from running in the halls and talking and chewing gum in class to being tardy and shooting spitballs. Today, those problems in schools have been replaced by rape, murder, automatic weapons, teacher assault, shootings, stabbings, arson, gang warfare and drug traffic. Every day 180,000 young people stay home from school because they fear violence. School violence contributes to loss of family control, perpetuates the attitude that violence solves problems and teaches disregard for human life.

Our schools reflect the stresses and problems of the rest of our society. Youth must cope with the frustration of trying to prepare for their future vocation in school settings that hinder rather than facilitate learning. Couple that with a culture whose value system has turned upside down and is constantly changing, and the youth's sense of insecurity is magnified. All told, today's teens live in a bizarre warp of too much freedom and pressure at a stage of their lives when neither is appropriate, when pressure makes them brittle and freedom's just another word for everything to lose.

Fifties vs Nineties Experience

Recently on CBS's "Eye to Eye", they did a special segment focusing on the 1950s. They showed educational films from the '50s about family life, teen dating, peer pressure, manners etc., to a group of high school students on a Miami, Florida campus composed of Hispanic, Black and White teens. As I watched, I laughed. I grew up during the '50s, and these films were so hokie and corny, I couldn't believe it. But what was more shocking was the unexpected response of these 1990s students. They did not laugh or make fun of these incredibly corny films, instead they were totally mesmerized by them. The students were asked later what they thought about the films. These high school students, one after another said, "I wish it could be like that today." The innocence, simplicity, security and safety of the 1950s, (except of course without the prejudice and racism), is something today's youth know nothing about but would give anything to experience. Students today said, "I'm afraid of getting shot, raped or getting AIDS."

The '90s experience reflects a very different world, one of lost innocence, violence, insecurities and moral confusion—total contrast to the '50s.

Blizzard of Information

Young people are being engulfed by a sea of information that promises to rapidly increase as we approach the year 2000. The invasion of technology into their world and the mass of information they are being exposed to daily have dramatically changed the way they think and live. This flood of information and technology has become a major social force in contemporary society. Personal computers, cable TV, laser discs, satellite dishes, voice mail, fax machines, VCRs, compact discs, cellular telephones and other electronic gadgets have revolutionized our life-styles.

The flow of information seems endless and is growing as today's youth are exposed to 1,600 commercial messages per day. The average home receives more than one thousand pieces of unsolicited mail during the year. There are over ten thousand magazines published in America, complementing six thousand radio stations and four hundred television stations with a viewing access of twenty-four to sixty cable channels. The number of books in top libraries doubles every fourteen years.[9]

This glut of information has helped produce the most overstimulated society in history, interfering with youth's ability to distinguish between the trivial and the significant. Fantasy and reality become blurred in this age of information. We have become a "culture of trivial pursuit" where youth live for the things that don't really matter and don't pursue the things that do. The amount of available information now doubles every five years and soon it will be doubling every four. That's an incredible amount of information; however, that volume will be just 3 percent of what we will have access to by the year 2010.[10]

Experts tell us that to survive in the workplace today and even to function in society, we are forced to assimilate a body of knowledge that is increasing by the minute and is obsolete within a year. They also predict we will experience another high-tech information explosion during the coming quarter century. Think of the millions of youth who, in the next five to ten years, will be grossly unprepared for a high-tech job market that becomes more complex each day.

We have created what author Richard Wurman refers to as "information anxiety," the ever-widening gap between what we understand and what we think we should understand.[11] Youth need to be able to separate the important and relevant information from the insignificant. This, however, is becoming increasingly difficult with a continual barrage of information. The attempt to stay current is creating more anxiety, stress and confusion among teens.

Exploding Choices

Young people's decisions define and determine their relationships and sense of identity. There are many more critical choices for today's teens than for any previous generations. The choices teens make during their high school years are critical in determining who they are, shaping their happiness and success for the rest of their lives. Teens are confronted with a mine field of crucial decisions about relationships, identity, teen pressures and the direction of their lives. Too many teens base their decisions on their fears— fears of rejection, failure, insignificance, inadequacies, and the future — which always distort reality. This fear-distorted perception of reality produces wrong choices that set in motion a devastating and destructive cause-and-effect cycle.

In *Mega Trends,* noted author John Naisbitt states, "We have gone from a chocolate and vanilla to a Baskin Robbins society where everything comes in at least thirty one different flavors." As he explains, "In the past, we lived in a clearly defined either/or society. All of our choices including moral choices were simple. Either you drove a Chevy or Ford. Either you were married or you weren't, most were. Either you had sex when you were married or you didn't have sex at all."[12]

But now we live in a multiple-option era; now there are so many choices that the issue of right and wrong has become irrelevant. What makes something right today is the fact that you choose to do it. This multiple-option society has made it much more difficult for youth to make significant choices.

Accelerated Choices

Teens today are confronted with more critical choices at a younger age with less guidance to make those choices. Young people eleven to fourteen years of age need to decide: Should I have sex? Am I going to drink or do drugs? Should I join a gang? Am I going to stay in school? Should I carry a gun to school? Two generations ago, some of these decisions weren't even considered by college-age adults—A generation ago, high school students made these decisions. Now, they're being made in junior high, says Dr. Victor Stursbugen of the American Academy of Pediatrics Research.[14]

Some of the choices our youth are making now are not only going to have a powerful effect on their own lives but on the generation that follows. Also, as the rate of change continues to accelerate, so will the complexity of choices for our youth. Youth are having to make faster decisions while the decisions are more difficult than ever. These factors combine to create mass disorientation and distortion of reality.

Pursuit of Leisure

In this increasingly high-tech, high-stress, complex, ever-changing society, youth pursue their leisure time to make their lives meaningful. Americans' quest for leisure experiences reveals what is really a priority in our culture. We are a "fun culture," driven by our insatiable appetite for leisure activity.

The decade of the '90s will be characterized by this relentless pursuit of leisure as other areas for youth — relationships, occupations and other social interaction — become disappointing and disillusioning, failing to provide contentment or satisfaction. To satisfy our hunger for multiple experiences, we allocate shorter blocks of time for any single leisure activity. "As a nation, we believe that the more different experiences we have, the more likely we will be to find fulfillment."[14]

The expectation level for youth has been tremendously affected by the emergence of the leisure revolution. Teens today not only expect the "leisure experience," they feel it is their right to have it. Teens today have experienced more leisure activities during their adolescent years than most adults experienced in their entire lifetime seventy-five years earlier.

There is nothing wrong or evil with enjoying leisure activities or entertainment unless it becomes the ultimate goal in life — our reason for living. The leisure, fun-oriented culture has produced a "Disneyland life-style" where teens have more amusements than any generation in history. Youth even feel like everything they do in life must be entertaining to be meaningful and fulfilling. If it's not, something is wrong. Gorging themselves on the leisure menu has only magnified youth's feelings of boredom, confusion and meaningless drift. This leisure-addicted life-style has increased the desire to escape reality for many youth.

Leisure in our culture has become the ultimate numbing drug. "Leisure desperation" is attempting to fill the void in our lives with more amusements, entertainment and fun. Leisure is the delight of our culture, and youth think it's the answer to their needs and problems.

A fun-oriented culture is not concerned with reality or long-range consequences, only with having fun now! Anything that is not exciting, fun and instantly gratifying is irrelevant and unimportant. The mass pursuit of leisure has caused a loss of perspective, more confusion and frustration in the youth culture when it comes to scheduling their time.

Teens today are on a constant leisure trip with unprecedented amusements and high-tech entertainment, yet many are more addicted, less content, more aimless and desperate than ever.

The media has helped create this leisure-consumption atmosphere in the youth culture where youth from every social background are affected — black and Hispanic youths from inner city ghettos as well as white youths in suburban and rural America. Poverty-level youths are exposed to these lavish, exorbitant leisure life-styles through the media. They see it and believe they can have it, and they must have it. The leisure dream cuts across every socioeconomic background of America.

As contemporary culture becomes more technologically advanced, socially fragmented and morally disoriented, the leisure entertainment experience becomes the dominant life-style.

Technical Leisure

The need and desire for leisure in the '90s and beyond will reach new heights as the pressures, complexities and discontent of a high-tech nation continue to increase, creating even greater demand for new leisure experiences.

Fantasy and leisure go hand in hand; both are vital outlets. However, the need for escape will become even greater as change continues to occur and our relationships become less secure.

Addiction to the fantasy leisure experience will become widespread among youth and adults in the '90s.

The Leisure Identity

"During the past decade or so, we initiated a transition related to our primary source of personal identity. Many years ago, our identity was a reflection of our family heritage. More recently, it became a reflection of our salaries and careers. Increasingly, adults and youth are pointing to their life-style with an emphasis upon their 'leisure activities' as the best indicator of who they are and what they stand and live for."[15]

Youth rush headlong to buy the latest album, see the hottest movie, wear the trendiest styles or get the latest athletic shoe. All of these products are purchased to enhance the experience of leisure. Teens work at purchasing those things conducive to enjoyment — cars, clothes, stereos, CDs, movies, eating out, Walkmans, athletic shoes, concerts — to make the good times even better.

The leisure monster gets bigger; it threatens to overwhelm youth as their appetite increases. Amusements, variety and pleasure beckon teens; in the end, they are left dissatisfied. The monster gets bigger, and youth become slaves to the consumption of leisure entertainment products to fill the need for identity, intimacy and meaning. *Every culture that becomes totally obsessed with leisure and fun loses its cultural purpose and identity as cultural confusion and deception abound.*

Virtual Reality

Imagine experiencing a walk on Mars, revisiting a childhood experience or rocketing into a future world or a faraway, unexplored galaxy. Researchers are perfecting the computer-created world of virtual reality. Also called "cyberspace," or simply VR, this emerging technology allows people, wearing high-tech gadgetry reminiscent of *Total Recall,* to enter computer-generated worlds where you can literally experience your imagination. VR can give a person the ability and experience of time travel, at least in their minds, exploring their wildest imaginations and fantasies. Standard virtual-reality gear includes a helmet with built-in video displays and a data glove studded with sensors. It also includes head gear with 3-D sights and sounds. These components are wired to a computer that tracks hand and head movements and adjusts visuals and sound accordingly.

Virtual reality is already being touted by medical professionals, biochemists, research technologists, NASA engineers and neurological doctors as a major advancement for medical, psychological and scientific breakthroughs. However, there is a downside. Some could use virtual reality to escape further into a fantasy world that makes them even less able to deal with the real world, producing "fantasy freaks" who never want to live in reality. VR could be the "electronic LSD" of the future. VR has been labeled "new edge," one step beyond the cutting edge. There's already a new subculture growing around VR ideas: "cyberpunks" or the "avant tech." There is a new nongeographic, computer-linked culture emerging, and VR is on the "new edge." "It's a celebration and warning to people entering the future that it'll be very hard to determine what is real and what is illusion."[16]

Dangers of a High-Tech Society

The emergence of this highly technological world will pose several dangers to us as a society, especially for young people. Here are some dangers that will characterize our high-tech society:

Predetermined Behavior. The more complex society becomes, the more the government must be in control of the actions and behavior of the masses. For a technological society to function more effectively, the unpredictability of human emotion must be stifled and unbridled enthusiasm must be suppressed. Adolescence is a highly emotional period of life where youth experience intense emotions and behavior.

In a technological society spontaneity, enthusiasm and youth's energetic craziness are unnecessary and unplanned and therefore not permitted. The capacity for youth to express their feelings when they experience them and to do the unexpected are God-given qualities. Spontaneity, enthusiasm and emotional unpredictability are vital to their development. They need the freedom to express emotions such as compassion, reaction and excitement. These qualities become liabilities in a predetermined, predictable techno-society. "The worst sin of a machine or computer is to be unpredictable. Therefore, spontaneity is not permitted. In a world of technology, it is too dangerous."[17]

Cloned personalities. "High-tech society is not ultimately concerned about what makes each individual unique but rather what makes us identical, what can be computerized, standardized and systemized."[18] Cloned society is also not interested in what is on the inside, the spiritual capacity. Genetic cloning is in theory the exact physical reproduction of a person.

People are special because of their individual differences, but techno-society is not interested in the uniqueness of each person; everybody is reduced to a computer number, and youth become just another face in mass humanity. Youth lose their individuality and distinctiveness in this setting. Also, the cloned society is not concerned with the personal touch or intimate connection between youth and adults that is so critical. Technological society further separates and isolates to effectively categorize every person. Youth who lose their individuality lose their identity.

Techno-Morality. What happens to morality in a technological society? Jacques Ellul says that we develop a technological morality—a morality that accepts as right whatever is technologically possible. If abortions are technologically possible and if the techniques for abortion are scientifically and medically sound, then technological society reasons, why not?[19]

Biblical morality in a high-tech society becomes outdated and irrelevant; spiritual values and commitment have no place in a technological society. The gospel has no place in this society since it works to deepen our moral capacity and conviction. Techno-morality is based on society's advancement and human intellectual potential; this new enlightenment leaves youth with no moral sense of right and wrong.

This robs youth of moral conviction and values and their spiritual relationship to Jesus. The immorality and breakdown of moral standards that is plaguing today's society is a result of a moral vacuum. A culture cannot live long in a moral vacuum; it must have morality. Technology expands to fill the vacuum because technology creates its own new morality which is totally opposed to Christian faith.

Manipulated Choices. Technological society determines what youth perceive as reality. This is an "age of manipulation." Highly effective technologies of exploitation, which are becoming more advanced every day, determine youth's choices and attitudes. Technologically sophisticated cultures are conditioned to accept belief systems, behaviors and values that would have been rejected by previous generations.

Technological media-created fantasies continually shown to youth as reality combined with the reinforcement of wishful thinking about themselves cause youth to lose their ability to distinguish between fantasy and reality.

High-tech culture increases the anxieties, fears and impermanence of relationships among youth, making them very vulnerable and susceptible to manipulation. In this setting, youth are robbed of their ability to choose and make meaningful decisions. Technological society chooses for them, for only *they* know what's best.

"Every society reproduces its culture — its norms, its underlying assumptions, its modes of organizing experience — in the individual, in the form of personality."

Christopher Lasch
The Culture of Narcissism

The reckless relativistic philosophy creates the aboliting of guilt for ones actions, which ultimately abolishes the conscience as well.

Cultural Christianity must create its own personal concept of God to justify its lifestyle, to determine its own morality, to become its own god.

Chapter 5

Redefining the Truth: The Moral Dilemma

> Beware lest anyone cheat you through philosophy and empty deceit, according to the tradition of men, according to the basic principles of the world, and not according to Christ (Col. 2:8 NKJ).

During the turbulent '60s, the social and moral foundations of America began to crumble as the basis for right and wrong was lost in the flood of secular humanism, which has become the dominant philosophy of America today. We have two generations that are being profoundly affected by this assault on biblical truth. From the '60s generation the present generation has inherited self-absorption and moral relativism as the driving philosophies of life.

Renowned theologian Francis Schaffer says, "*This change in the concept of the way we come to knowledge and truth is the most crucial problem, as I understand it, facing Christianity today.*"[1] The '60s failure transformed normal adolescent egocentricity into a perpetual state-of-adolescence indulgence, and self-gratifying pursuits into a full-time career.

The current generation of youth is drowning in a sea of moral confusion with no concept of truth or moral direction. An array of social forces is converging on today's young people, and they have no secure, stable foundation on which to stand. The new way of defining truth and the moral drift that has taken place during the last thirty years has gathered momentum and will hit with massive force during the '90s.

Values Vertigo

Confronted with all these pressures, youth are now experiencing "values vertigo." When a pilot has vertigo, his equilibrium is "reversed." What he reads on the instrument panel is totally opposite to what he feels. Vertigo so alters your sense of reality that you believe something to be false when it is actually true. In this disoriented and confused state of mind, you believe up is down and down is up.

We have an entire generation that is experiencing values vertigo. Youth today are morally flying upside down, yet they feel they are right side up, and the consequences are devastating. Their frame of reference is cracked and distorted by the humanistic philosophies of our culture.

What Is a Philosophy?

A philosophy is defined as a set of values or beliefs of a culture or an individual, our concept of truth or what we believe to be reality. Our philosophy of life is the basis for our choices and actions, everything we do, and our belief system. If your philosophy is based upon a lie, then the result will be destructive to you and to those around you.

The anti-Christian philosophies of Western culture have greatly affected the choices, attitudes and behavior of today's youth. They have drastically influenced the way youth view truth, which affects the way they view morality.

Christianity's belief system is not based on man's intellect, opinions, life-styles, abilities or the social and moral trends or changes of contemporary society. Christianity is founded on God's divine, eternal truths, as revealed through Jesus Christ and biblical teachings, revealing God's character, nature and principles of wisdom. Christianity is the ultimate love story of the redemption of fallen humanity, through the reconciling mercy and love of God in Jesus Christ.

Cultural Christianity

Popular culture has created a "cultural Christianity" based upon man's definition or concept of God, which in reality is pseudo-Christianity — a self-centered, self-gratifying religion without God's purity, truth or power. Every imaginable life-style is being accepted; promiscuous, bizarre, perverted and dangerous behaviors are not only tolerated but encouraged, and viewed as normal. America today is deeply entrenched in a decadent, post-Christian cultural climate.

What is alarming and disturbing is that popular culture is making a greater impact on the church than the church is making on the culture. Most of the churches in America today are more a reflection of the life-style and morality of popular culture than the life-style and teaching of Jesus Christ. In this new "enlightened" society, God is defined by our personal morality.

"The evangelical church in America has become a moral mirror image of the larger secular culture. We have created the illusion of separateness by developing a religious subculture complete with its own agenda, marketing techniques and industries. Under close inspection it becomes clear that we are as self-indulgent as the larger secular culture."[2]

"This secularization is a serious deviation from God's plans for His people and constitutes large-scale spiritual decay. This places the next generation at risk more than all the ills of society combined."[3]

Four Major Philosophies

Let's examine the four major philosophies that have powerfully shaped the mind-set of today's youth culture and have created the current social and moral atmosphere. To fully understand young people's mentality and behavior, we must understand their belief system.

Relativism. Relativism is the philosophy of personal choice. It espouses no absolute truth. Everything is relative; therefore, there is no wrong choice or life-style. There are so many options and situations today, the issue of right and wrong has become irrelevant.

Rarely, if ever, in American history have questions of morality been so troubling for young people. It's not easy to make moral decisions today. Truth is complicated, and often the whole truth cannot be known, says *U.S. News and World Report*.[4]

The baby-boomer teens assaulted the traditional value system in the late '60s, rebelling against long-held moral standards and certain accepted behavior. Suddenly, every authority structure from family and school to government was being shaken by this wave of radical teens. Youth began to think in a new dimension; multiple-choice morality was in vogue. With the relativistic mentality of "do your own thing," moral standards became personal preferences, and what made something right was that you chose to do it.

The power of choice was youth power. The '60s youth said, "It's our choice to do drugs; it's our choice to protest; it's our choice to have sex." Their choice made it right! "What was unique was that they were making a choice to have a good time in your face. In the context of the times, it was an unusual and liberating thing to do."[3]

Youth today say, "Premarital sex is right for me, abortion is right for me, doing drugs is right for me, cheating and stealing is right for me." This power of personal choice has become the new morality of the day, the foundation of the social and moral revolution. Baby-boomer youth, now parents, have powerfully shaped the values and attitudes of today's teen.

"Another destructive legacy of the '60s is the tendency to look to self for moral absolutes. Kids started looking inward for survival and comfort. When the basis for truth and morality shifts gradually from outside ourselves to inside ourselves, we, rather than God, have become the final authority for all areas of our personal lives."[5] We answer to no one but ourselves. Personal liberation and a feelings-oriented life-style determine the new enlightened morality.

Immorality, the conscious violation of accepted standards, was the standard of the '60s. Yet by definition immorality still admits the existence of some standard, somewhere. It is a small step from immorality to amorality — the prevailing principle of the previous two decades. The belief that no moral standards exist abides as the moral mentor of youth today. The "immorality stage" says, "Certain things are right and wrong, but I don't care!" The next and final stage is amorality, which says, "There's no such thing as right and wrong!"[6]

The Relativist Mind-Set—The personal liberation philosophy from the '60s — preoccupation with self and the present, and the shift in the basis for truth and morality from external absolutes to internal feelings — and situational ethics are rampant in America's popular culture.

The basis for relativism is pride that says, "I have a right to choose whatever I want, and I don't have to answer to anyone." There's always a reason or excuse for our actions. This philosophy of personal choice attempts to eradicate guilt and absolve us of any responsibility for our behavior.

Right is wrong and wrong is right; evil is good and good is evil — it's all relative. This reckless philosophy creates freedom without responsibility and actions without consequences, which produces more guilt, confusion and pain.

Professor Allan Bloom, author of *The Closing of the American Mind,* says that "malignant relativism is destroying the ideas of moral truth, wisdom and greatness in America today. The intellectual and moral crisis we face is a direct result of rampant relativism on our campuses."[7]

To truly understand the character of a generation is to know that which reveals their values. From the core values spring forth attitudes and morals, reflecting what we love and hold dearest. George Barna writes:

> To the typical baby buster . . . there is no such thing as absolute truth. Statistically 75 percent claim that absolute truth does not exist, that all truth is relative and personal. This view is supported by their belief that everything in life is negotiable. In this way of viewing the world, since there are no absolutes, all decisions and realities can be debated until an accommodation is reached between the parties involved.[8]

This type of experience-oriented negotiated reality is made possible by the attitude that you cannot trust anything of which you do not personally have a first-hand knowledge or experience. Nearly 75 percent of the buster generation believes that nothing can be known for certain except the things that you experience in your own life.

The moral ambiguity of the '70s and '80s can be traced directly to the immorality of the '60s, when a generation decided they would be autonomous. Intoxicated with personal gratification and existentialism's appeal of creating our own moment, we cut ourselves away from the past and felt no responsibility for the future. Popular culture became detached from history itself, a generation lost in time.[9]

The relative mind-set says believing in absolute or moral truth will stifle our creativity, smother our individuality and rob us of our quest for new truth. The philosophy of relativism has created a generation without a conscience.

The so-called new, enlightened, relativistic morality has created a moral vacuum in our society, where confusion, disillusion and uncertainty reign. It's said that nature abhors a vacuum. Nothing has filled the void that is now swallowing up young people at a frightening rate.

Narcissism. Historian Christopher Lasch has argued that we "live in an era of narcissism distinguished by a fear of intimacy, pseudo self-insight, loss of historical time and self-absorption."[10]

The boomer generation of the '60s definitely characterizes the rise of narcissism in America. For more than a decade, the battle cry was "If it feels good, do it." Immediate self-gratification, constant self-indulgence, and arrogant self-centeredness characterized the '60s as narcissism (self-love) became the guiding philosophy and self-fulfillment the ultimate goal.

Looking Out for Number One was a best-selling book; advertisements feeding self-absorption — "You deserve a break today," "Have it your way," "I love what you do for me" — accurately describe our culture's preoccupation with itself: Nothing or nobody is more important or entitled than "I." This obsession with self has pervaded every facet of our society, especially affecting our youth, how they view themselves and how they relate to others.

One of the developmental characteristics of adolescence is a concern for self to the exclusion of others. But, narcissism is more than the inability to acknowledge that there are concerns other than your own; it is the subtle attempt to make yourself the center of the universe.[11]

Self-centered youth can't see anybody but themselves; they are so absorbed by their own needs, problems and desires, they become insensitive and unconcerned about the needs and problems of others. This self-centeredness is a deeply entrenched emotional characteristic of adolescence. However, when it has been accepted by our narcissistic culture as normal, youth develop manipulating, controlling and exploiting attitudes.

Self-love creates a deep fear of commitment or intimacy in relationships because we're committed only to ourselves. We fear the very things we bring to relationships — manipulation, phoniness and greed. Youth don't trust themselves; how can they trust anybody else?

J. McDowell says, "Young people's problems limit their freedom to love others; they simply can't take their eyes off their own problems to help others, because of the magnitude of their own problems. The cause of their self-centeredness is self-hurt, not just self-love."[12] Due to the devastated family and a multitude of overwhelming teen pressures and situations, many youth are obsessed with themselves, not so much because of self-love, but because of their need for survival.

The exaltation of self has created not only a totally unrealistic perspective for youth but also a false identity. Self-absorbed youth tend to overestimate themselves and view themselves as more valuable and important than others. Their own evaluation of themselves and their false sense of superiority interfere with every relationship they have. However, their preoccupation with self doesn't just mean feeling superior; it also means feeling inferior. When youth feel inadequate and lack confidence, they are constantly focused on themselves and their insecurities.

Self-centered, self-indulgent youth feel that life owes them happiness and fulfillment. They believe that their existence should be effortless and without frustration. Narcissistic individuals are always disillusioned because their expectations for themselves and life are too grand and unique. Self-love is one of the major causes of depression and disappointment for youth today. Cultural disappointment is the result of cultural narcissism.

Existentialism. Existentialism is the non-rational, non-logical, unexplainable pursuit of experience. In other words, there is no reason or logic for our *actions* or experience. All our experiences are an attempt to find meaning. However, to the existentialist, meaning has nothing to do with facts; therefore, truth and meaning are themselves meaningless and illogical.

Youth today are becoming obsessed with the experience-centered life-style. Noted author and speaker Winkie Pratney describes the adolescent experience mind-set: "Thousands of youth think that truth can only be found in personal experience. They think the world has no meaning outside themselves. This way reality can become whatever you want it to be; there is no reality outside your own mind."[13]

Youth are driven by the social need for acceptance by their peers, and the boredom of everyday routine causes them to seek "on the edge" experiences. The need for social interaction and sense of belonging compel youth to attempt radical, wild and sometimes dangerous experiences.

The "party philosophy" is a way of life for contemporary youth, who live for the "weekend experience" or the next opportunity to get wasted! "Fight for the right to party" is the battle cry of North American youth. Shoot for the rush, the high, get wasted—the maximum thrill experience. Be a party animal! The ultimate goal in life is pleasure, and youth pursue the pleasure experience at all costs. Youth have sniffed transmission fluid and used crack cocaine and other exotic drugs in their search for the most exciting experience.

Another social experience that has become a major goal of youth is materialism. The materialism experience — to acquire, to possess — is about more than status symbols. For today's youth, it has become the happiness-fulfillment experience.

How youth relate to the opposite sex is crucial in determining their value and significance as a person. Their need for intimacy and affection make the sexual experience look very exciting and enticing. Due to the disintegrating family, and surface relationships, youth become especially susceptible to the sexual encounter. "Youth easily mistake a relationship of experience for a relationship of quality."[14] It is easy for them to become involved with someone from the opposite sex and suddenly experience intimacy so powerful and overwhelming that everything else in life seems dull and insignificant. The sexual experience can become addictive for youth because they are using a physical action — sex — to fulfill emotional needs.

Their experience produces an erotic cycle; once they've experienced sex, it increases their sexual capacity and desire for continued involvement. Hence, they fall victim to the ultimate illusion of love. Our overly sensual culture has promoted and encouraged sexual activity by telling youth to have responsible, safe sex, setting up an entire generation for the illusion of love.

Youth are looking for a spiritual experience, something supernatural, something powerful to fill the spiritual vacuum and emptiness in their lives. The movie *Ghost* was an enormous box office hit, one of the all-time most successful motion pictures. The movie touched a spiritual nerve in our society. *Ghost* was about a girl making contact with her dead boyfriend through a medium or channeler. Youth are fascinated and intrigued by the unknown, the magical, the darker side of the supernatural experience. The current upsurge in the mystical, the bizarre, the magical is due to their quest for spiritual fulfillment.

In *Psychology Today,* an article entitled "The Vampire Craze in the Computer Age" describes the current rise in our culture's preoccupation with the occult. Our fascination with vampires seems to be part of a deep disenchantment or boredom with science and rationalism, a feeling reflected in our society's growing interest in mysticism, spirituality and belief in the psychic and paranormal experience.[15]

The vampire craze and other occult phenomena reflect a deep desire for religious substance among youth. This bizarre desire is a hunger for the marvelous; "the vampire is another side of our culture that needs a voice."[16] Youth are very susceptible to the wrong spiritual experience. Spiritual deception is not only dangerous, it can be disastrous.

There has been tremendous interest in the near-death experience of people who were actually pronounced dead. They describe feelings of floating, of peace, a sensation of being out of the body, seeing a great light, walking down a long corridor, etc. In the movie *Flatliners* a group of medical students conduct experiments to see how long they can sustain medically induced death before revival, because they are curious about the unknown and want to know what happens after death.

Through the New Age movement, millions are involved in spirit channeling, astral projection or soul travel; the out-of-the-body experiences, crystal power, mental telepathy and reincarnation point to the obsession with supernatural experiences.

Nihilism. Nihilism is the philosophy of futility and despair, based on the premise that everything is meaningless and chaotic. It is also the final stage of desperation for youth who have tried the other philosophies that have left them unfulfilled and disillusioned.

The suicide note left by a sixteen-year-old girl graphically describes the fatal desperation that is epidemic among youth today: "If only someone would have smiled at me today, I could have made it." The suicide rate has jumped 300 percent since 1960, making suicide the second leading cause of death among teens.

Despair cuts across all socioeconomic differences in the youth culture. In the inner cities of America, black youth experience despair and hopelessness as they see their dreams unfulfilled by a system that seems to ignore their pain. There is an undercurrent of frustration and anger below the surface of the youth culture, especially in the inner cities of America. The black male adolescent is ten times more likely to be murdered than his white counterparts.

Newsweek describes America's lost tribe of teen runaways in a heart-ripping article entitled "Somebody Else's Kids." "There are more than a million of them on the streets of our major cities and most of us would like to believe that they are all other people's kids. They are prostitutes (male and female), drug addicts and thieves. Most act like hard cases, posing as predators so they will appear less like prey. But for every new wave of runaways, playing it tough becomes an increasing deadly game."[17]

Youth consume relationships, products, entertainment and the latest trends, only to find boredom, futility and a new level of despair. Their quest for truth and meaning gets lost in a culture that intensifies their despair by offering momentary contentment, projecting an illusion of truth. Like a drug addict looking for another fix, youth run to what the culture says is meaningful, only to find when they "come down" that they are more discontent and more desperate than ever.

Redefining the Truth: The Moral Dilemma

In a relativistic culture, everyone creates, shapes and defines their own morality; the result is a moral crisis.

Popular culture has influenced and impacted the morality and life-style of this generation more than has the church.

It's not your fault. There is always someone else to blame. Unfortunately, that is a formula for social gridlock: the irresistible search for someone or something to blame colliding with the unmoveable unwillingness to accept personal responsibility. Victimism is reshaping the fabric of American society, including employment policies, and, in an increasingly Orwellian emphasis on "sensitivity" in language. This culture of victims has produced an ominous result: the decay of the American Character.

Charles J. Sykes
A Nation of Victims

Chapter 6

Personal Liberation Philosophy: The Moral Crisis

For it is written: "I will destroy the wisdom of the wise, and bring to nothing the understanding of the prudent" (1 Cor. 1:19 NKJ).

Social historical research indicates that from 1966 to 1974, Americans succumbed to a whirlwind barrage of attacks on pro-child, pro-family, pro-traditional morality and values, replacing these with a cluster of social values that may be called "Personal Liberation Ideology" (PLI).[1] Many social analysts have asserted that it was specifically during the mid-'60s and early '70s that a dangerous and destructive value system came to prominence within America. When a culture has lost its moral sanity, right and wrong must constantly be redefined to meet individual desires.

Before 1966, Personal Liberation Ideology had exerted effectively no influence on the American public. But by that time PLI had acquired such power and legitimacy that millions of Americans accepted it as conventional thinking concerning such vital issues as child rearing, marriage, family life, divorce, sexuality, moral choices and life-styles.[2] The '60s youth movement was the breeding ground for the Personal Liberation Ideology that has become the guiding philosophical force in today's liberated culture.

By 1968, the well-respected social analyst Vance Packard insisted in his classic book, *The Sexual Wilderness*, that "disarray in moral concepts was rapidly becoming manifest in American society." Packard noted that by 1967 in America there was no longer a general or national moral consensus about sexual morality and that millions were confused about the issue.[3] This "new liberated enlightened morality" is a total antithesis and diametrically opposed to the teachings of Jesus Christ.

Since there is no moral consensus in the '90s, everyone determines their own personal moral code. And, of course, being morally right today must "be convenient and feel good." All choices are now made based on personal desires, personal liberation and a personally defined, self-indulgent morality. Popular culture advocates and promotes the "credit card mentality," which is a life-style of continual indulgence and instant gratification without restraints or responsibility for our actions. This cultural mind-set seeks the postponement of pain, the escape of consequences and the denial of reality.

The Self-Esteem Movement

The PLI movement ushered in the new pop psychology/therapeutic mind-set where the focus of the culture became "self." Thus began the pursuit of personal gratification and the development of personal potential through the latest self-help techniques of self-realization, self-interest, self-indulgence and self-esteem in an attempt to gain self-fulfillment. This insatiable quest for liberation, gratification and esteem has become the ultimate goal for millions of teens and adults.

The basis of the personal liberation philosophy is rooted in a totally self-centered, self-obsessed attitude where personal freedom, personal choice and personal happiness become the all-consuming life-style of the entire self-oriented culture.

The "self-esteem" philosophy is defined as the fulfillment of a person's emotional needs and desires without any constraints, obligations or commitments to anyone or anything except self — without any guilt. The "New Age" human potential movement uses psycho-babble terms like *self-actualization, self-awareness* and *self-realization,* which is really self-worship. These PLI attitudes and life-styles have produced a morally decadent culture, which creates chaos and confusion, with devastating and destructive consequences.

In describing popular culture's preoccupation with itself, *Newsweek* in a recent cover article entitled "The Curse of Self-Esteem" stated: "Self-esteem is the model and key principle for analyzing almost every problem in American society. Self-esteem is clearly a product of today's restless, relentless search for ever more fundamental and unifying laws of nature. Self-esteem is the quirk of social science, a way to make sense of the wildly proliferating addictions and dependencies...jostling for air time on [the talk-show circut]. Now, self-esteem is a 'transcendent addiction,' a state that seems to underlie and diagnose afflictions as diverse as bulimia, anorexia and performance anxiety. As the distinction between therapy and the rest of American life has eroded, the concept of self-esteem has established itself in almost every area of our society. Even churches have discovered that low self-esteem is a less offensive phrase to congregations than sin."

The self-esteem concept can be dangerous when it becomes an excuse for total self-indulgence, without regard for anyone else, where everything is measured in terms of "how it makes you feel about yourself."

The lack of self-esteem has been blamed for almost everything: depression, social despair, brutal violence, addiction, moral irresponsibility, educational failures, the problems of the inner city and our dysfunctional society.

The self-help, feel-good movement is the new gospel for young people today rather than spiritual commitment and the development of godly attributes. These self-esteem gurus believe that every social and personal problem plaguing our nation today can be attributed to the effects of low self-esteem and inhibited self-gratification. From cradle to grave, Americans are urged to feel good and reach their full potential, even at the expense of everyone else. We have become a "culture of obnoxious self-flattery."[4]

Moral Immorality

The relativistic culture is one that creates, shapes and defines its own reality and morality, where moral absolutes are a thing of the past. In this "do your own thing" atmosphere, individuals are not responsible to or committed to anything or anyone, unless it's personally beneficial or gratifying, all without any guilt.

A person's morality determines their perception or concept of God and dictates their life-style. If they live a self-obsessed, sinful life-style, it's rationalized and justified. They even tack God on the end of their immoral actions as though He understands and blesses their depraved behavior. Moral absolutes and Christian commitment are viewed as oppressive, outdated and irrelevant, an unnecessary burden and an impediment to the nobler goals of self-realization, freedom of choice, moral liberation and self-fulfillment.

According to Sartre, in a relativistic society "the outcome of our choices carries no moral weight. . . . Because there are no moral absolutes, there are no value-associated reasons to make one decision over another."[5]

Renowned theologian Carl Henry says, "Our generation is lost to the truth of God, to the reality of divine revelation, to the content of God's will, to the power of His redemption, and to the authority of His word. Paganism is now more deeply entrenched than in the recent past and holds a firmer grip on Western society."[6]

The Secular Wasteland

Swiss theologian Emil Brunner describes *secular cultures technology* as: "the product of the man who wants to redeem himself by rising above nature, who wants to gather life into his hand, who wants to owe his existence to nobody but himself, who wants to create a world after his own image, an artificial world which is entirely his creation. Behind the terrifying, crazy tempo of technical evolution, there is all of the insatiability of 'secularized' man who, not believing in God or eternal life, wants to snatch as much of the world within his lifetime as he can."[7]

Youth are morally bankrupt, disoriented and emotionally devastated. They think, *Why is it so hard to be happy? I just don't understand. It's so confusing.*

The current disillusionment, irrelevance and lack of truth and power of organized Christianity, combined with personal liberation life-styles, have left a path of devastation and a shattering inner emptiness — a void in the human soul. Liberated and enlightened man has no way to meet the deepest fathoms of his need. Jesus Christ is Lord of the universe and is still the answer in this desperate, desolate humanistic secular wasteland.

The Trivialization of Sex

Despite the booming increase in sexually transmitted diseases and the rising specter of AIDS, sexual activity among teens is at an all-time high and still increasing. Sex has become part of the consumer society, where we have created a "frantic sexuality."

If there are two words that describe the sexual mind-set of today's youth, they are *tolerance* and *entitlement.* Nowhere are the effects of the sexual revolution more dramatically evident than in teenagers' sense of entitlement to make their own choices about sex and in their tolerance of all kinds of sexual behavior, so long as they meet the current peer norms. This is in sharp contrast to the youth of earlier generations who, for the most part, respected and attempted to adhere to a biblical morality; the concept of entitlement to sex was nonexistent.

Teens using condoms are now viewed as mature and responsible. They believe they have found a way to enjoy safe sex. Our sex-oriented culture, through safe sex, is sanctioning and endorsing sexual activity among teens. The safe-sex message advocates and promotes the use of condoms as the answer to our sexual problems. For teens today, the question is not *if* you engage in premarital sex, but only a question of *when.* Sexual abstinence is viewed as outdated, unrealistic and insensitive—out of touch with reality and the needs of teens.

Promoting "safe sex" rather than sex within marriage implies that sex is a purely physical action. If you use a condom, you will experience a protective, healthy and fulfilling encounter. Sex was designed by God to be a three-dimensional act involving body, soul and spirit, reflecting Christ's relationship of love to the church. Using a condom will not protect teens from emotional and spiritual consequences and pain. I have talked with hundreds of teens on high school campuses all over America as they candidly shared their frustration, anger and desperation over disillusioning sexual relationships that were supposedly "safe sex." They were not pregnant, did not have AIDS or any other sexually transmitted diseases, and yet felt emotionally shattered and deeply depressed.

The Sexual Revulsion

U.S. News and World Report listed nine major historical hidden turning points that were true watersheds in human affairs. The decline and fall of chastity is listed as a major turning point in America. "The belief that moral decency required a girl to remain a virgin until marriage held sway in America for much of U.S. history. Then, in the 1960s and 1970s, chastity all but died as a mainstream ideal."[8] Popular culture increasingly saw sex as just one of life's pleasures, one that now could be easily separated not only from procreation, but also from marriage, and emotional and spiritual commitment, thanks to the pill. This was an unprecedented pivotal event in American history.[9]

On one hand, sex was trivialized, stripped and robbed of its beauty, sacredness and meaningful intimacy; on the other it was viewed as something of critical and utmost importance, something to be pursued with unswerving perseverance, as if sex alone was the key to love and happiness. Ironically, promiscuous, premarital sex does not prepare teens for meaningful, fulfilling relationships; instead, it produces desperate, destructive relationships based on sex. This sexual culture has created a "relationship revulsion."

Having sex today, as a teen, is considered normal; if you don't have sex, you're viewed as abnormal and uncool. Popular entertainers and sports personalities further fuel this attitude by advocating the use of condoms among hip, sexually active youth.

Promiscuous sex unleashes powerful psychological, emotional and spiritual forces that have a destructive effect on teens' lives and relationships. Sexually active teens have deep feelings of guilt, betrayal, self-hatred, fear, anger, rejection, loneliness, disillusionment and bitterness. The rampant sexual promiscuity is a symptom of a much deeper problem—the need for intimacy, identity, security and spiritual commitment.

Syndicated columnist Cal Thomas says, "Now it seems we approach sex and nearly everything else as we do microwave dinners, quick and pretty tasteless."[10] "Microwave sex" is more concerned with immediate self-gratification; in this context, true love and sex have nothing to do with each other. The ultimate irony is that "safe sex" is actually more dangerous, producing more destructive relationships based solely on sex, not love. Popular culture is more concerned that teens discover their sexuality through immediate gratification than through Christian morality with long-range happiness.

This enlightened, progressive-liberated society is creating a deadly generational sexual cycle—setting up an entire generation for destructive relationships, with unimaginable emotional pain, disappointment and indifference. This produces apathetic, detached, unemotional relationships where there is no joy, no tears, no anger, no excitement, no commitment and no love — only unquenchable sexual lust. Lust can't wait to get; love can't wait to give.

Having "safe sex" is like having a "safe trip" on LSD—one moment it's ecstasy and the next it's a horrible nightmare. The goal of sexual personal gratification has become the end in itself, and we lose something very special as a result—committed, intimate, lasting love.

The Safe Sex Band-Aid Approach

There are built-in cause-and-effect consequences to irresponsible promiscuous sexual behavior. Society has decided to ignore the emotional, psychological and spiritual consequences of approaching premarital sex without true love, commitment, biblical perspective or accountability. A surface-oriented culture always focuses on the symptom of the problem rather than the problem itself.

The excessive, rampant sexuality in our culture is indicative of our inability to experience real security and true intimacy in relationships. "A teen who had been involved sexually with several guys wrote: 'It is far easier to bare your bottom than to bare your soul.'"[11]

Emotional fulfillment is the goal, and sex becomes the means although sexual gratification will not produce emotional happiness. But when you're a teen desperate for intimacy with another person, it seems reasonable. The responsible safe-sex mind-set is producing a totally irresponsible generation whose only concept of relationships and love will be entirely from a sexual, self-gratifying, self-centered perspective.

Safe sex is the quick-fix Band-Aid approach to a culture that has lost its moral sanity and spiritual convictions. Popular culture is committing slow relationship suicide, where a generation becomes sexually addicted, emotionally exploited and relationship-dead.

Safe-sex advocates believe that using a condom makes young people responsible, mature persons. That's like saying that using a clean needle makes a heroin user a responsible addict. The Centers for Disease Control recently stated that "it does not consider a person (teen) who has had 'only five' different sexual partners as being promiscuous."[12] Responsible sex is now characterized as having sex with multiple partners, as long as it's done safely using condoms or some other form of contraception.

A new national study by the Centers for Disease Control involving nearly twelve thousand students said, "By senior year, one in four high school students has had at least five sex partners." The current trend among teens, even with the recent AIDS threat, is having sex with more partners.

Teens who have multiple sexual partners are playing a deadly game of Russian roulette, where pulling the trigger once can result in HIV infection, and the more you pull the trigger, the more likely it is to fire.

Being a responsible person takes much more than using a condom or being sexually active. True responsibility means thinking about and being accountable for our choices and actions, and that takes self-control, emotional maturity, delayed gratification, moral commitments and self-sacrifice. The ultimate product is future happiness and success, not just instant sexual gratification and self-indulgence. The responsible safe-sex mentality is producing a sexually savvy but emotionally wasted and spiritually destitute generation.

Teen Pregnancy Phenomenon

> The skyrocketing teen pregnancy rate transcends racial and ethnic lines. Now one in sixteen teenage girls has a baby each year, up from one in twenty in 1986 — about 75 percent of these mothers are unmarried. Soon, one in three babies born in the U.S.A. for all age groups will have an unwed mother, an increase of 60 percent in the

last decade.[13]

The phenomenal rise of teen pregnancies has become an alarming trend that many experts say is putting our nation dangerously at risk. Social analysts are calling out-of-wedlock births a crisis more important than crime, drugs, gangs, poverty, illiteracy, welfare or homelessness because they actually contribute to these social problems.

No one can really measure the effect of two generations growing up together. But this explosion of children having children, entwined with the controversy of out-of-wedlock births, has created a social and moral crisis.

The teen pregnancy trend has set in motion a devastating cycle of generational poverty:

> Compared to their peers, teenagers who become mothers are more than twice as likely to live in low-income households. As much as three times as likely to have parents who dropped out of high school. Two times as likely to have a mother who was a teenage parent herself. . . . That link worries many who believe that teen pregnancies further widen the gap between society's have and have nots, for the groups with the highest poverty rates also have the highest birthrates. More than one in nine black teenagers and more than one in ten Hispanic give birth each year, compared with about one in twenty white teenagers. The largest increase in teen pregnancies was among Hispanic teens, from 1986 to 1992, rising a dramatic 34 percent. In the black community over 90 percent of births to black teens occur out of wedlock.[14]

Being young, uneducated, unemployed and pregnant is a formula for disaster.

"Although the teen birthrate is rising faster among whites and Hispanic teens, black teenagers remain the most likely of the three groups to have a child. We now have communities that are having new generations born every fifteen to eighteen years instead of twenty-five to thirty-six years," says Kristen Moore of the research group Child Trends Inc.[15] With shorter generations, communities don't have time to socialize kids and adequately prepare them for a positive transition into adulthood.

> The United States has the highest teen pregnancy rate among the industrialized countries of the world. When it comes to teen pregnancies, the U.S.A. looks more like a developing country than an industrialized one.[16]

The Myths of Sex Education Programs

Myth One. Family planning groups insist that comprehensive sex education and easy access to contraceptives does not encourage an increase in teenage sexual promiscuity. That's a myth. Numerous studies show that family planning endeavors do encourage both sexually active and inactive teens toward increased promiscuity.

Planned Parenthood's own study, conducted by Lou Harris and Associates, clearly shows that "comprehensive sex education programs significantly increase the percentage of teens becoming sexually active, while limited sex education classes discourage kids from becoming sexually active."[17]

The National Research Council, in a report titled "Risking the Future," points out that increased sexual activity in teens "is directly related to birth control information and other sex education information for adolescents."

In Planned Parenthood's *Family Planning Perspectives,* Dr. Deborah Dawson, a survey research consultant, concluded that "prior contraceptive education increases the odds of starting intercourse (at the age of fourteen) by a factor of 1.5." A factor of 1.5 might not seem like much, but in actuality it is a staggering 50 percent increase. A random survey of four hundred family physicians and psychiatrists has shown that "81 percent believed there was an increase of sexual involvement among teenagers due to increased availability of contraceptives."[18]

Myth Two. Family planners have contended for years that comprehensive sex education, including easy access to contraceptives and free abortions, will solve the problem of teen pregnancy in this country. This myth is the heart of Planned Parenthood and of advocates for school-based clinics. Numerous studies reveal that family planning methods and comprehensive sex education produce a dramatic increase in teen pregnancy.

Even Planned Parenthood admits that school-based sex education programs are not reducing pregnancies as had been hoped. In her article, "The Effects of Sex Education on Adolescent Intercourse Contraception and Pregnancy in the U.S." in *Family Planning Perspectives*, Dr. Deborah Dawson says this:

> The National Survey of Family Growth data revealed no significant relationship between exposure to sex education and the risk of premarital pregnancy among sexually active teenagers — a finding that calls into serious question the argument that formal sex education is an effective tool for reducing adolescent pregnancy.[19]

Dr. Dawson was forced to admit that the existing data do not yet constitute compelling evidence that sex education programs are effective in increasing teenage contraceptive use and reducing adolescent pregnancy.

The family planning groups and comprehensive sex education curricula have failed in the U.S. We have ended up with the wrong results because we started with the wrong premises.

Wrong Premise: Sex education reduces pregnancies.

Wrong Results: Increased sexual activity, increased pregnancies, increased abortions.[20]

The AIDS Generations

In this sexually charged atmosphere where each year in America more than one million teenage girls become pregnant and over three million teens contract a sexually transmitted disease (that's one out of every seven teens), more teens are having sex and at younger ages than ever. In recent research findings from a Centers for Disease Control Survey released, the following percentages of high schoolers who said they've had sex were revealed: freshmen—40 percent; sophomores—48 percent; juniors—57 percent; seniors—75 percent.[21]

Today's promiscuous environment, combined with youth feelings of invincibility and immortality and the attitude that "it will never happen to me," is producing skyrocketing teen sexual activity and diseases. Statistics indicate that the number of AIDS cases among teens is doubling every fourteen months. Teens are now emerging as the fastest-growing segment of HIV-infected persons in America. Health officials estimate that there are thousands of teens infected with the AIDS virus who don't know it. Experts are predicting that a wave of infection of the teen population will be the next crisis in the AIDS epidemic. "It's this see-it-to-believe-it attitude that could be fatal," says author Jeanne Blake, whose book *Risky Times* addresses the dangers of AIDS among teens. In essence, "it's a death wish," says Blake.[22]

Research experts in numerous major studies, where teens were surveyed and their identities remained anonymous, found that as many as 40 percent of male teens did not use condoms correctly in the highly excitable moment of sexual passion. Combined with the 20 to 25 percent leakage or failure rate of condoms, this means as many as 60 to 65 percent are using "safe sex methods" that in reality are not safe at all.

The AIDS virus can go undetected during the incubation period for as long as three to five years. Currently, one out of four AIDS patients is twenty to twenty-nine years old; many of these were in high school when they were infected. The Centers for Disease Control says AIDS is the sixth leading cause of death for fifteen- to twenty-four-year-olds.[23]

The World Health Organization is projecting that more than four million people in North America will be infected with the AIDS virus by 1995.[24] With the rampant spread of AIDS and other sexually transmitted diseases, having sex as a teen today has become a deadly choice where living fast may mean dying young. The AIDS threat hangs over the youth culture like an executioner's sword, ready to fall at any time.

The Gay Nation

Homosexuality twenty years ago was viewed as illegal, depraved and perverted. It is now not only tolerated but accepted and approved by an understanding society as the enlightened and trendy morality of a progressive culture. According to a recent Gallup poll, nearly 50 percent of all adults believe that homosexual relations between consenting adults should be legal, up from 33 percent in 1987.[25]

The Gay Movement has gathered unbelievable momentum during the past twenty years and has become a major force in the American culture. The homosexual life-style has infiltrated every aspect of contemporary culture. In a matter of two decades, the homosexual movement has powerfully transformed the nation's perception of homosexuality, homosexual behavior and homosexual attitudes. Making giant strides toward disassociating homosexual behavior from sin, degradation, perversion, sexual disease (AIDS), and identifying being gay as an alternate sexual preference and life-style, the "gay mentality" believes sexual orientation has nothing to do with outdated biblical teachings in determining a person's morality, character or choice as a human being.

Movie stars, other entertainers and athletes have publicly acknowledged their homosexuality, "coming out of the closet." All three extremely popular talk show hosts—Oprah Winfrey, Phil Donahue and Geraldo Rivera—are pro-gay sympathizers, who advocate alternative life-styles and diverse sexual preferences as morally individual rights. *USA Today* says, "Rivera's show is the most sensitive to the gay population, even more than Phil Donahue."[26] This positive, tremendous media exposure from three individuals who are much admired and respected, has resulted in increased sensitivity to and acceptance of gay life-styles by the public.

Some of the major Christian denominations—the Presbyterian Church, the Episcopal Church and the United Methodist Church—are rethinking the rules of sexual conduct. We also have the ordination of gay and lesbian ministers, homosexual marriages and homosexual adoption, homosexual police, gay military, gay lawyers and so on.

The National Gay and Lesbian Task Force has become a major political entity. *Newsweek* in a feature article, "The Future of Gay America," said, "The '90s reflect a new spirit of anger, activism and political clout for gays." *USA Today* did a cover story entitled "Queer Nation," which is the national militant homosexual group that fights gay oppression. Queer Nation prides itself on "anything goes" with an "in-your-face" attitude. "It has become a way for us to address lesbian-gay specific issues that were not AIDS focused," says Alan Klein, one of the founders of Queer Nation. "Queer Nation is a multicultural, direct action group dedicated to fighting homophobia, queer invisibility and all forms of oppression that a queer may face. It reflects the pent-up rage and anger that many gay and lesbians feel."[27]

We now have a major homosexual subculture across America that is becoming more militant, more powerful by the day. Perversion is now tolerated and accepted by mainstream culture.

It should be noted that from a Christian perspective we do not endorse or advocate any hateful attitudes or violent actions toward homosexuals or lesbians. However, we do not approve of these life-styles because they are defined as deviant and perverse acts from a biblical perspective.

As Christians, we should be compassionate and caring, but we cannot condone their behavior, even though our so-called enlightened society considers gay life-styles as progressive, predetermined and personal sexual orientation.

Sexual Orientation Is Genetic?

The scientific community in what researchers are calling a breakthrough study that supposedly could determine sexual orientation are attempting to prove there is a "gay gene" that predetermines homosexuality.[28] However, they still haven't identified a sexual orientation gene and previous major studies claiming links between genes and homosexual behavior have been debunked in the scientific community.[29]

The Genetic Link Theory would make homosexuality no longer a personal choice or a behavioral aberration or a sin. Rather, you are born gay or created by God to be gay or bisexual or heterosexual. This latest inconclusive research theorizes that certain genes could not only determine homosexuality but also could indicate drug or alcohol addictions and even identify genetic predisposition to criminal behavior.

This research is attempting to remove any guilt or responsibility for our life-style choices. It totally rejects all biblical teaching concerning moral choices and certain immoral behavior. This new enlightened culture seeks to further fuel liberated life-styles and denounces any moral responsibilities or restraints.

Lesbianism Is Chic

On a recent cover of *Newsweek Magazine*, two very attractive lesbian women are embracing each other. For the first time lesbians were featured on the cover of a national magazine.

"Suddenly lesbianism is in vogue and totally trendy in the '90s.

As now, during the dawning of the 'Gay '90s,' these women are stepping front and center from Hollywood studios to the political arena in Washington; from bestseller lists to the top of the music charts. Superstars such as pop singer k.d. lang, tennis great Martina Navratilova and comedian Rosie O'Donnell have all come out to proclaim their lesbian life-styles." From every facet of society lesbians are boldly out of the closet and in your face.[30]

The media and the political left are promoting the "Gay Agenda," which is now considered to be politically correct. "Everywhere you look there are positive lesbian images in the media. This 'lesbian is chic' is going from shocking the straight culture to hopefully gaining mainstream acceptance."[31] In this new enlightened society, lesbianism is a matter of sexual orientation or personal choice, not to be limited by outdated, oppressive biblical morality.

Prime time hit TV shows such as *Rosanne* and *Seinfeld* portray lesbians as normal. These programs, as well as talk shows hosted by Geraldo Rivera, Arsenio Hall and Oprah Winfrey, are all applauded by lesbians as progressive and positive to their cause.

Lesbians would love for Northampton, Massachusetts, to become a microcosm for the rest of America. It has become a mecca for lesbians; it's estimated that as many as ten thousand of its thirty thousand residents are homosexual women.

Abortion the Terminator

Since January 1973, when the Supreme Court of the U.S. legalized abortions, nearly thirty million babies have been slaughtered in the "Silent Holocaust." Each year, 1.5 million babies are aborted; over four hundred thousand teen abortions occur every year in America.[32]

Pro-abortionists advocate the woman's personal right to terminate an unwanted pregnancy, arguing that it is her body and that the fetus is not a human being; therefore, abortion is not murder, but rather an exercise of the fundamental right of a woman to determine whether she wants a baby or not.

This self-seeking, self-centered mind-set believes having a baby would interfere with a person's capacity for personal gratification and self-fulfillment. Therefore, the only commitment they must have is to themselves, an all-consuming self-love. Research indicates that 95 percent of all abortions are performed simply for convenience.[33] Abortion has become the nation's means for birth control and self-worship.

So, millions of women, under the facade of morality and the noble-sounding guise of "pro-choice liberation," choose a self-absorbed life-style for themselves and cruel calculated murder for millions of babies. The pro-abortionists rationalize and justify their actions as enlightened, progressive and their God-given right to choose. God abhors that choice!

The abortion mentality has produced a coldheartedness as brutality and cruelty to one another pervades our society. Abortion has created a destructive ripple effect as the value of human life has drastically decreased. The pro-choice abortionist sends a message to youth that self-interest and self-indulgence are to be pursued at anyone's expense.

Human life has become cheap today as respect, sanctity and sacredness have disappeared, replaced by an atmosphere of selfishness, violence, murder and abuse that are exploding in our hardened self-centered culture. Abortion subconsciously degrades and devalues every human being in society.

Based on the number of abortions each year since 1973, beginning with the year 1990 and for the next twenty years, there will be 1.5 million missing high school seniors. Each year young people won't graduate with their classmates, won't fall in love, get married or have children. They won't become doctors, lawyers, ministers, teachers, fathers or mothers or anything else. They are the "missing non-generation" of youth that never got a chance to choose, the generation that never was.

The Helpless Minority

Recently, *USA Today* revealed the shocking rise in infant murders in America: "The teddy bear was supposed to bring three-month-old Christopher Otten happiness. Instead, it was used to kill him. More children are being murdered than ever before. Murders of children, one year old and under, have more than doubled since 1973, according to FBI data. Child murder is 'a perversion of human values,' says Dr. Charles Clegg, medical director at College Hospital in California. Experts say hundreds of infant/child murders may go undetected. There are people in our culture who, instead of valuing good, idealize the power of evil. The rise in child murders reflects a fundamental change in U.S. mores (morality) that has produced a generation that is less patient, less caring, less compassionate with children, and quicker to explode in rage and violence. Latest research from the Children's Defense Fund says, 'USA's children are falling further behind on health, education, family support and love. Every thirty-two seconds a baby is born into poverty, every two and a half hours one of our children is murdered.'"[34]

America's most disadvantaged and helpless minority is its children. Recent covers of *Time, Newsweek* and *U.S. News and World Report*, focusing on this dangerous trend read: "Save the Children," "Where Have All the Children Gone?," "Do We Care About Our Kids?" and "Innocence Lost." We have a neglected, abused and angry generation of children who will unleash their rage at a culture that has betrayed them.

Where Have All the Heroes Gone?

Author Dr. George Roche says, "We know, at least, that what sets the hero apart is some extraordinary achievement, not for applause or money or self-exaltation. Whatever this feat, it is such as to be recognized at once by everyone as a good and noble thing; and somehow, the achieving of it seems larger than life. We have been struggling frantically, merely to achieve the ordinary: that measure of happiness each of us is supposedly entitled to. The hero, in contrast, overcomes the ordinary and attains greatness by serving some great good. The hero seeks not happiness but goodness, and his fulfillment lies in achieving it. His reward is in knowing he did what was right and true."[35]

Real heroism requires courage. It entails peril, danger or pain. Heroes are distinguished by valor or enterprise in danger or fortitude of suffering. The hero causes us to reexamine our values, attitudes and goals, and challenges us to rise above the obstacles we face. In a world of moral chaos, superficial love, senseless violence, materialistic addictions and rampant self-centered life-styles, where have all the heroes gone?

A recent major landmark survey reveals, "The majority of us (70 percent) believe that America has no living heroes today. Nearly 80 percent say that our children/teens have no meaningful role models."[36]

Hero worship in the U.S. has fallen on hard times. The lack of positive, moral role models reflects the moral and spiritual deterioration that began in the '60s. Ethical problems from every direction seem to be hounding our heroes today in sports, entertainment, religion and politics. Television, movie and rock stars, politicians, preachers and star athletes haven't been quite the same since Watergate, according to social observers.

Basketball superstar Magic Johnson's recent announcement that he had the HIV virus sent shock waves across America and the world. This is symptomatic of our times. Johnson admitted to having casual sex with literally hundreds of women over the last ten years. Johnson says, "As I traveled around the NBA cities, I was never at a loss for female companionship; after I arrived in L.A. in 1979, I did my best to accommodate as many women as I could, most of them through unprotected sex."[37]

Time, in a feature story on the "Promiscuous World of Pro Sports," states, "We look at an institution so influenced by images of virility, masculinity, potency and sensuality that sex and sports have almost become synonymous."[38] For the pro-athletes in football, basketball and baseball who care to indulge themselves, there is a flourishing groupie subculture readily available. These groupies are always ready to offer sports pros recreational sex, no questions asked. The notion that athletic prowess and sexual attraction go together filters down to every budding jock who swaggers across a junior or senior high campus.[39]

Recently, America has been rocked by scandals: baseball's Pete Rose's gambling addiction and imprisonment; Olympian gold medalist Ben Johnson's steroids; pro-football's Lyle Alzado's steroids and claim that 70 percent of NFL players use steroids; baseball's Wade Boggs's adulterous sexual addictions; Gary Hart's and Ted Kennedy's sexual escapades; Jimmy Swaggart's and Jim Bakker's sex scandals and fraudulent activities; Judge Clarence Thomas's sexual allegations debacle; D.C. Mayor Marion Barry's drug addiction and adulterous affairs; and former heavyweight champion Mike Tyson, convicted of raping eighteen-year-old Miss Black America.

We are in what experts are calling the post-heroic era, a time when there are no heroes because we have ceased to believe in anything strongly enough to be impressed by its attainment. Heroism is a microcosm of the character of our culture, the mirror that reflects our beliefs and convictions. The obvious vacuum of heroes constitutes a swelling denial of value, morality and purpose to human life, setting us adrift in an empty existence without meaning or hope. Andrea Sarti said, "It is an unhappy country that has no heroes."[40]

Heroes represent what we really stand for and believe in. This hero-less world suggests that we stand for nothing and believe in nothing. The absent hero is a tragic symptom of the moral confusion and cultural decline. The depth of who we are is reflected in our heroes. Sadly, we have become a very superficial, artificial and hollow culture. Dr. George Roche says, "A world without heroes is uninhabitable by humans."[41]

Today s Anti-Heroes

Our role models today have grown more violent, sensual and irreverent. There was a time when TV and movie heroes needed a cause before committing acts of violence and mayhem. In the 1990s, because we don't believe in our institutions anymore, our TV and movie heroes are loners, violent, even renegades. They are cynical about everything, self-interested, almost never involved in a team effort, capable of expressing themselves with only brute force, sophisticated weapons and an amazing ability to kill and destroy. Sylvester Stallone (*Rambo*), Clint Eastwood (*Dirty Harry*), Arnold Schwarzenegger (*Terminator*) and Steven Seagall (*Marked for Death*) all play anti-social, violent loners.

These male anti-heroes are characterized and admired for their ability to produce massive, high-tech violence and widespread destruction with an ever-increasing body count. Death and devastation have become synonymous with the character of male anti-heroes of today. Frighteningly, violence has become a major part of Americans' real life as well as their fantasy life. In a comprehensive survey, "one in four Americans say that they've acted on their violent impulses. An equal number think that they'll do so at some time in the future. Every seventh person you pass on the street in America is carrying a weapon, either on their person or in their car."[42]

Social experts say the anti-hero came out of the '60s anti-establishment, counterculture movement, which accelerated and intensified following Watergate in 1973. Anti-heroes do not believe in a personal God or in any spiritual purpose or identity, even though on the surface they give a token pseudo-allegiance to their concept of God.

The most important, most popular and most powerful people in American culture are entertainers, musical performers, TV and movie stars and pro-athletes. Today's concept of a hero is based as much on media hype, media image and media exposure as anything. The rich, the glamorous, the talented and their ability to perform have created the "popular hero."

Those who follow the anti-hero philosophy pursue the hedonistic, self-indulgent, self-fulfilling life-style, gorging themselves on their own lusts and deceiving themselves with their grandiose self-flattery and self-worship, believing the end justifies the means. They indulge in whatever it takes to achieve self-gratification, running from one exhilarating happiness fix to the next. Self-sacrifice, self-denial, self-control and delayed gratification are considered uncool, outmoded and undesirable qualities.

The "anti-hero" mind-set also creates a nihilistic-futile life-style that dismisses all purpose and meaning as illusion. We become just another "irrelevant particle" or "helpless pawn" in the vast universe, unable to shape our own fates or determine our ultimate destinies. Anti-heroes are unable to distinguish between right and wrong or fantasy and reality. They really believe that good and evil have no meaning or are relative and therefore nonexistent.

The anti-hero life-style is a totally self-absorbed, subtle yet hostile rebellion against God, an irreverent denial of spiritual truth and morality, discounting it as unenlightened-obsolete absurdity. It is essential to the anti-hero's belief that all religion be meaningless and that Christianity in particular be untrue. Here is the summation of cultural anti-heroism: nothing is sacred.

Anti-heroes are glorified as modern-day heroes when in reality they are exceptionally skilled, tremendously gifted and highly paid performers. These TV, movie, rock and sports stars should not qualify as heroes. Despite dynamic personalities and spectacular performances, there is nothing heroic in doing what one is paid mind-boggling multimillion-dollar salaries to do.

Society has exalted these people to such elite status that we have trivialized the rest of our culture. We have communicated to youth that financial status and personal achievement is more important than serving humanity. Today, most of the TV, movie, rock and sports superstar anti-heroes promote and display a life-style that is a total contradiction to the moral principles and life-style taught by Jesus Christ. These anti-heroes aren't spiritual, moral, loyal or humble and are not committed to anything except themselves.

The Madonna Phenomenon. ABC's *Nightline* featured an interview with the controversial superstar Madonna on the *Justify My Love* video and scored the highest ratings of 1990. The program drew nearly twice as many viewers as other programs featuring stories about Iraqi troops surrounding the U.S. Embassy, U.S. citizens taken hostage, the first video out of Baghdad, and D.C. Mayor Barry's arrest.[43] Madonna's mystique captivates this generation. She is a cultural phenomenon reflecting the sensuous, irreverent and perverted life-style that is in vogue in today's anti-hero world. Being sexy and erotic is considered important, desirable and powerful in our "over-aroused" culture.

Madonna and other rock stars are cultural heroes who create their own moral standards. Madonna says, "I think you can be a very sexual person and also a very spiritual person."[44] Alienated and rebelling from her traditional religious background, Madonna combines sexual immorality with perverse-erotic rituals and music to create a "sexual spirituality," which mocks biblical morality.

Rock heroes Michael Jackson, Prince, Paula Abdul, George Michael, Janet Jackson and Van Halen all promote sensual, lusty messages, encouraging sexual immorality, perversion and liberated life-styles in state-of-the-art erotic music videos featuring blitzes of seductive images.

Today's anti-heroes are defined as rich, sexy, powerful, attractive, popular, immoral, charismatic and cool. Sex is power, and the "anti-hero" is a seductive force in this sexually driven culture. Madonna says, "Power is a great aphrodisiac and I'm a very powerful person."[45]

The State of American Morality

Yesterday's certainties have vanished, lost in an ever-increasing moral maze where every choice is rationalized and justified. Unpredictability and chaos have become the norm.

There is no absolute moral standard; there is no black and white anymore, only a "gray" mind-set. This moral vacuum produces an even more extreme effect, where good is evil and evil is good. This relativistic philosophy exalts radical individualism, which celebrates and embraces personal choice, personal liberation, personal fulfillment and personal morality as the new cultural authority. We answer to no one but ourselves.

"Adults and youth in the 1990s have more of both freedom and doubt, and of depression, too, than did any previous generation."[46]

We can no longer distinguish, or maybe no longer want to distinguish, between right and wrong. A commercial perfectly describes the new moral mind-set — total indulgence, zero guilt. "The number one rationalization in America is 'If everybody's doing it, why shouldn't I? If everybody is breaking the rules, am I a complete idiot to play by them myself?'"[47]

This generation is grappling with the consequences of their new freedom to define their own moral codes. Research expert George Barna says, "Relativistic self-interest and self-indulgence will be the cornerstone of the 21st-century philosophy."[48] Two thousand Americans from across the country participated in the most in-depth survey of what Americans really believe that has ever been conducted. No research had been completed on what Americans privately think, feel and believe—on what we really believe, as opposed to what we think we're supposed to believe. Here are some shocking findings listed in the book *The Day America Told The Truth*:

1. At this time, America has no leaders and especially no moral leadership. Americans believe, across the board, that our current political, religious and business leaders have failed miserably and completely. Our void in leadership, moral and otherwise, has reached a critical stage. We still want leadership; we just can't seem to find it.

2. Americans are making up their own rules, their own laws. In effect, we're all making up our own moral codes. Only 13 percent of us believe in all of the Ten Commandments. Forty percent of us believe in five of the Ten Commandments. We choose which laws of God

we believe in, a selective morality. There is very little respect for the law; we have become the law unto ourselves.

3. Lying has become an integral part of the American culture, a trait of the American character. We lie and don't even think about it. We lie for no reason; 91 percent lie regularly and mostly to the people closest to us. The majority of us find it hard to get through a week without lying. "Lying has become a way of gaining power over other people."[49]

Here are ten extraordinary commandments for the 1990s. These are the commandments, the rules, that most people actually live by. The percentage of people who live by each commandment is included.

- I just don't see the point in observing the Sabbath (77 percent).
- I will steal from those who won't really miss it (74 percent).
- I will lie when it suits me, so long as it doesn't cause any real damage (64 percent).
- I will drink and drive if I feel that I can handle it. I know my limits (56 percent).
- I will cheat on my spouse; after all, given the chance, he or she will do the same (55 percent).
- I will procrastinate at work and do absolutely nothing about one full day in every five. It's standard operating procedure (50 percent).
- I will put my sexual partner at risk of AIDS and other sexually transmitted diseases. I sleep around, but who doesn't? (All too many adults and teens are willing, and will even say that they are willing, to risk infecting their sexual partners with a disease that is killing them. They seem to value their own sexual pleasure and gratification more than they value someone's life.) (45 percent).
- I will use recreational drugs (40 percent).
- I will cheat on my taxes—to a point (30 percent).
- Technically, I may have committed date rape, but I know that she wanted it; 20 percent have been date-raped.

Americans of the '90s stand alone in a way unknown to any previous generation. When we want to answer a question of right and wrong, we ask ourselves. The overwhelming majority of adults and teens (93 percent) said that they and nobody else determine what is and what isn't moral in their lives. They base their decisions on their own experience and on their daily whims and personal desires.[50]

This personally defined and secular-shaped morality has created a scenario of illusion, confusion, despair and meaningless life-styles. The neo-existentialist of the '90s says, "I am, therefore, I am not!"

The sexual revolution of the '60s has turned into the "sexual revulsion" of the '90s. Having "safe sex" is like having a safe trip on LSD—one moment it's ecstasy and the next it's a horrible nightmare.

We have an entire generation of youth who do not relate Christian principles to sexual behavior or relationships.

Chapter 7

Love-Starved: The Relationship Vacuum

There is no fear in love; but perfect love casts out fear, because fear involves torment. But he who fears has not been made perfect in love (1 John 4:18 NKJ).

Real Love

As we see the enormous problems confronting the youth culture today, many so-called experts are groping for solutions. I'm constantly asked, "What do you see as the greatest problem facing teens today? Is it drugs, violence, AIDS, suicide, pregnancies, gangs, crime?"—the list goes on.

My reply always surprises people when I say that these are not the actual problems but are only symptoms of a much deeper problem. We have approached these youth problems like a poorly treated poisonous snake bite. We put a Band-Aid over the wound. We've only dealt with the surface symptoms; the poison is still in the system and unless action is taken, the victim will die.

Real love is "other-person centered," always reaching out and giving away. This love is compassionate, sensitive, understanding and unselfish.

Motivating Needs

Powerful needs and fears motivate young people in every choice they make, ultimately determining their actions, beliefs and lifestyles.

Youth need meaningful relationships. Nothing affects their lives more than relationships with family, peers and the opposite sex. The need to love and be loved is crucial for young people. It affects every facet of their life. There isn't anything they wouldn't do to experience real love.

Kim was a high school senior and was voted class favorite at a large suburban high school in America. One day, during a visit to her doctor, she received some devastating news: she had leukemia in its advanced stages and maybe had a year to live.

Kim's world suddenly came crashing down around her. She began taking chemotherapy treatments, and her hair fell out until she was completely bald. She said, "God, why is this happening to me? I don't want to go back to school anymore. I don't want kids to feel sorry for me, or laugh at me, or be afraid to come talk to me—I'm still the same person." God began to speak to Kim's heart about kids on her campus who were hurting. They were teens who were from broken homes, teens who were doing drugs, young people who were lonely and felt ripped off. She said, "I can help those kids."

Kim got a wig to cover her baldness and went back to school. One day she saw a girl sitting alone in the cafeteria; this girl was insignificant, invisible on a campus of two thousand teens. She was a loner, one of those kids who doesn't fit; she didn't have the latest fashions or what is considered "campus beauty." Kim walked over to the girl and asked her if she could sit down. The girl was so shocked that anybody would want to go out of their way to be seen with her; she said nervously, "Sure."

Kim said, "I've seen you sitting here all year long, and I want to apologize to you for not coming over before now. I want to be your friend; if you need someone to talk to or if you're in trouble and need somebody, I want to be there for you." Kim shared about how Jesus was helping her deal with her disease and directing her life.

This girl sat there in shock that someone was taking time for her. Big tears began rolling down her face as she said, "Kim, you'll never know what this means to me. I had the pills and I was going to take my life. I thought if I wasn't back at school on Monday, nobody would know or really care. Kim, you showed me there is someone who cares, and I know there is someone else just like me." Kim is making a difference, and her disease is in remission at this writing.

In a recent research study, it was found that the highest-achieving teens were those who reached out to help those around them. Other-centered love is always focused on the needs, problems and pain of others rather than self.

Real love is *unconditional.* Most love today is conditional, and youth are not into the sacrifice and pain of real commitment. Unconditional love is committed no matter what; it loves you when you fail, it loves when you don't look good, when you're not lovable; it loves when it's tough; it loves when everyone else walks away. This is the essence of God's love; it is agape love—a love totally different from any other love we know.

Commitment to Jesus is the foundation of any genuinely loving relationship. Radically, this love is commitment; without it, our lives become desperately empty.

Another dimension of unconditional love is intimacy. True intimacy is the revealing of oneself to another person, "being able to be totally transparent with at least one person, to remove all masks and disguises we hide behind without fear of rejection, and to be known and loved for who we are."[1] Young people find it extremely difficult to be intimate with someone because their lack of identity and their fear of rejection prevent anyone from getting too close.

Trust is a vital part of any meaningful relationship. Without it, the relationship will self-destruct. Youth need someone to believe in, someone they can always depend on and someone who'll be loyal. There is deep distrust among teens concerning relationships, due to revolving relationships in the family. They have been disillusioned by people who said they would be there for them but were not. As a result, young people look for trapdoors and escape hatches in their relationships. They don't get too attached because they are afraid that person might not be there for them someday.

Decisional Love

Decisional love is a conscious act of one's will to love that is not based on emotions. It allows us to make unselfish choices regardless of our feelings or the situation. Decisional love *always* chooses to love.

Youth today, due to the promotion of sensual love, believe love is a feeling, warm fuzzies, a rush of emotion, goose bumps and butterflies. While love can cause us to feel all these things, they do not necessarily signify love. Emotions can be deceptive and fleeting; our feelings are constantly subject to change. Feeling-based love is a very temperamental love, and the only dependable thing about it is that you can never depend on it.

A family in Southern California had a big, ugly, Heinz 57-type dog named Gladys. This dog was always getting into trouble, chewing up everything in sight; she barked at night and kept the family awake.

Finally, Dad had had enough. He said, "I am sick and tired of this worthless dog; she is a constant nuisance; I would sell her for two dollars." The little four-year-old girl put her arms around Gladys and protested boldly, "Daddy, you can't sell her. I love her. She's so sweet; she's worth a million dollars."

That night when everyone was asleep, a fire broke out in the lower part of the two-story house. Gladys always slept downstairs. She smelled the smoke and sensed danger and began barking, trying to wake up the family; but nobody was waking up. So she climbed the staircase and ran into the room where the teenage boy was. Barking, she jumped into his bed and licked him in the face.

Immediately, he jumped from the bed to wake up the rest of the family. In moments, everybody was up and running downstairs. By then, flames and smoke were everywhere as they got quickly out of the house. As they stood at the end of the driveway watching their house engulfed in flames, Gladys strutted with pride.

Then, Gladys didn't see the four-year-old because she was wrapped in blankets and there was so much confusion with fire trucks and firemen on the scene. The dog ran back into the burning house, thinking the four-year-old girl was still inside. The family saw what was happening and screamed, "Gladys, no!" But she knew where she was going—to save the little girl.

They watched in horror and amazement as the dog ran into the house that was now an inferno. Gladys never came out again. The next day, in sorrow, they walked back through the burned-out house. They came to the area where the little four-year-old's room was and saw the hardly recognizable, charred remains of a big, old, ugly dog named Gladys. Gladys showed what unconditional, committed, real love is all about. This kind of love is a risk, but it's the kind of love we all want.

The fear of rejection is the basis for most relationships among teens today. This fear totally distorts their concept of healthy relationships and creates an illusion of love.

If Love

"If love" is widespread among youth. "If love" says, "*I love you if*—if you do this or you don't do that. As long as you do what I want you to and as long as this relationship benefits me, I love you."

Here are some classic "if love" statements:

- If you're going to be friends with her, you can forget our friendship.
- Hey, are you with us? We've got some good stuff. If you drink this or snort that, we're buddies; if you don't—later.
- If you really love me, go to bed with me and prove you love me.
- If you let me borrow your car this weekend . . .

We've all heard similar statements from people who said they really loved us. "If love" is the ultimate self-seeking love that says, "How can I use you?" "If love" is conditional; it always comes with strings attached, because you must always perform and meet expectations to receive another's love. "If love" is a manipulating love that uses the emotional blackmail of guilt and fear to exploit you.

Recently, after a presentation I gave at a high school, a young and attractive fifteen-year-old girl with tears streaming down her cheeks approached me. This scene is repeated hundreds of times as I speak in schools across the country.

Kelly said, "Eric, you were talking about "if" love. I guess that's the kind of love I have. I've been going with this guy for the last year and I really love him. We've gone all the way, and now I'm pregnant.

"I'm afraid I'll have to continue to meet his conditions for him to stay. I wonder now if he really loves me; now I'm scared he'll walk away when I need him the most. Eric, I feel so desperate, I feel ripped off. I feel trapped. I feel used and alone."

"If love" relationships are a very frustrating and scary place to live. Nobody wants to be committed to someone who is only committed to themselves, to have given them everything you are as a person only to have them take your love and throw it down and walk away.

Vacuum of Love

The need for real love has created a vacuum to be filled with fantasy relationships based on sexual activity. Youth are using sex to try to meet their needs for real love and commitment. Sex is such a powerful experience that once youth get involved, they've set in motion a cycle where their relationships are dependent on sexual involvement and everything revolves around the physical or sexual encounter. Everything else in the relationship becomes secondary and boring.

Sex first appears to fulfill their need for affection, security and identity. The problem is when youth use sex to fulfill emotional needs, the result is increased confusion and a magnified need for love.

Sexual promiscuity is cited as a major factor contributing to the exceptionally high teen suicide rate today. The tremendous increase in sexual activity, beginning at a much earlier age among teens, increases frustration and emotional pain and makes finding real love later on much tougher. Youth don't realize that having sex is a three-dimensional act, involving the emotional and spiritual aspects as well as the physical dimensions of their being. Sex was originally designed and intended by God for marriage, to be a wonderful, exciting and fulfilling consummation of a couple's love and commitment to each other—the merging of body, soul and spirit between a man and woman.

The first dimension is obvious. It's the physical dimension where two people become one physically. The second dimension is the emotional or soul dimension. This aspect represents the real you as a person; your feelings, needs, fears and desires become one with another person. The third dimension is the spiritual dimension, the one in which two people become one spiritually. If one of these three dimensions is missing, youth will always experience an incomplete and unfulfilling relationship. As youth use sex to fulfill their emotional needs, their feelings of guilt, anger and desperation are increased.

Easy Love

There's another illusion of love that has increased the adolescent pain; it's called "easy love." Easy love is a noncommittal love that loves only when it's easy, convenient and fun. Easy love says as long as this relationship doesn't cost me too much, as long as there's no pain, risk or commitment, then I'll love you. Easy love lives for the moment; it goes for instant gratification—the rush, the thrill, the high of the now—while sacrificing real happiness in the future.

Easy love doesn't want to deal with reality and problems, or think about the consequences of its actions. Don't tell me about the pain of next year or even next month; I just want to party now. For youth today, instant gratification is too slow. They are going for immediate instant gratification, and it's keeping them from experiencing ultimate gratification.

Here are some "easy love" statements:

- Easy love says when you look in the mirror and don't like who you see, fake it!
- If you do something tonight that you'll regret in the morning, sleep late.
- If all else fails, lower your standards; everybody else does!
- It'll never happen to me!
- Everybody's committed to something; I'm committed to being uncommitted.
- I'll love you forever . . . maybe.

Easy love goes for mediocrity rather than striving for excellence. It's much easier. Easy love wears a mask. It's easier to go along with the crowd than to take a stand; it allows other people to control your life.

I'll never forget a certain inner city school assembly in a major city in America. I remember walking into the principal's office; he nervously introduced himself and was obviously in total panic about the assembly.

He said, almost hyperventilating, "Eric, we're glad to have you here at our school; however . . ." He paused, looking very troubled. "I want to prepare you for our student body. At the last assembly presentation we had, there was a riot; some kids pulled guns and there was shooting. They charged the platform; it was total chaos!"

At that point, I wished I could have disappeared. I wanted to be anywhere but there. I was looking for any kind of encouragement. At that moment, he said, "There's a door to your right off the stage; if there's any trouble in this assembly, don't stop to talk; run out that door." There was my encouraging word.

To say I was slightly apprehensive is the understatement of the year — I was scared to death!

The walls on this tough campus had gang graffiti and radical slogans scrawled all over them. I especially remember a statement that stood out in bold red letters: "Who'll stop the pain?" That statement screamed with desperation, and I realized these teens were really no different than any other young people. The culture that surrounded them was different, but the needs and the pain were the same.

The students' response was overwhelming—the atmosphere was electric; there were moments when you could have heard a pin drop. Immediately following the assembly, scores of youth in this tough, inner-city school crowded around me, wanting to talk.

This gang leader — six foot three, 220 pounds of leather and chains, and another two feet of Mohawk haircut — wanted to talk to me. He said, "Hey, Eric, I want to talk to you, man!" His voice was impatient and slightly angry. "I was in your assembly," he said. "I didn't want to hear anything you had to say. Hey, if that's what you think, Eric, that's your thing; but I don't need this. I'm the radical dude on this turf, man. I'm a gang leader. I fight and I do drugs because they expect me to. That's who I am, and that's the way it is.

"But you said something that got to me. You said, 'Have you ever been in the middle of a crowd and felt alone?'" Then he said, "That's me. I looked in the mirror and it scared me. I saw somebody I didn't know. I've become what they want me to be. They say, 'You're our leader,' so I fight and I do drugs. Now, I wonder which of them are really committed to me and which of them are just using me." He said, "How can I be real?" I shared with him about the reality of Jesus Christ. He said, "I don't care what it takes; if I can look in the mirror and feel good about who I am, it's worth it!"

That hard-nosed gang leader made a decision that day to follow Christ and really be radical. He came out of the gang and became a student leader on the campus, reaching out to help other kids.

Illusions of Love

"If love," the self-seeking conditional love, and noncommittal "easy" love have become a way of thinking among youth today. Both are based on the fear of rejection and the insecurity that have created illusions of love. Youth are caught in a false sense of security because fears always distort reality. Love that is based on fear only produces more insecurity, rejection and fantasy.

Youth get trapped in a cycle of desperation, going from one bad relationship to another because they've never dealt with the root cause of their problems.

Josh McDowell says, "Our main problem today is not sexual, it's relational. We have embarked on a false quest for intimacy because we haven't understood what real intimacy is all about. We have allowed our culture to dictate to us that the only way you can find intimacy is through physical or sexual experiences. I am convinced that most youth use sex as a means of achieving intimacy. They don't want sex as much as they want closeness and commitment with another human being."[2]

There isn't anything that so profoundly, powerfully, impacts and affects young people's lives, either positively or negatively, as relationships.

Control Freaks

The need to be in control and the desire to have power over other people is a driving force in popular culture. Young people today are obsessed with and addicted to controlling, manipulating and exploiting relationships. The powerful fears of teens — the fear of rejection, the fear of vulnerability, the fear of being criticized, ridiculed, ignored or disappointed, the fear of being displaced and not being in control create the compulsive control freak.

In youth's relationships with their peers or the opposite sex, they must be "in control" for their sense of security, identity and significance. As a result, there are five major motivations and benefits that help keep control freaks in charge. Controlling helps them:

1. meet their needs.
2. repel and avoid their fears and prevents out-of-control

situations.
3. fulfill their expectations.
4. stay apart and maintain their current "secure control system."
5. feel in control of their own lives by controlling the lives of others.

Many youth are caught up in the destructive control game, either being in control or being controlled. Both mind-sets become very addicting and produce excesses, distortion and emotional devastation. The girl or guy that must be in constant control in a relationship to feel confident, secure and fulfilled, the person in the peer group that manipulates, uses and must be in emotional control of others to verify and enhance their self-esteem — these are the controllers. Each time they successfully control you, control freaks confirm their sense of being in control and achieving a certain goal in attempting to meet their needs. This produces a titillating side effect, an exhilarating emotional power rush, that can be even more fulfilling and reinforcing than the outcome itself. The psychological and emotional charge confirms control freaks' belief that they can get whatever they want by controlling and that they should be in control.

For many teens, sex is a powerful controlling force or tool they use to manipulate and dominate their victims.

Control means power, and these two attributes will close the gap between a need and its fulfillment, a desire and its satisfaction, or a wish and its realization; by controlling, they experience tremendous gratification and a deeper need to be in constant control.

Why Teens Get Involved Sexually

Wrong Perception of Love. Youth crave real love and affection. The problem is they often have a distorted view of what real love is; their perception of love will greatly affect their relationships. Some youth equate sex with love. While sex is an important part of real love between two people in a marriage relationship, there is much sex without love when youth believe love is a physical action rather than a commitment.

Self-centered and non-committal loves, "if" and "easy," permeate our culture making them instantly accessible. Both of these loves are based on the wrong motives and will lead to sexual involvement, heartbreak and more confusion for young people.

Everybody's Doing It. Nothing exerts more pressure and influence on youth than their peers. Since everybody's doing it, it must be right. Also, when a culture has lost its moral convictions, the sexual life-style for youth is not only accepted as normal but something to be pursued. As one young person commented, "We feel inadequate and unaccepted if we don't live up to our friends' standards where sex is concerned." The pressure by society and the peer group for youth to have sex is enormous. If youth don't stand for something, they'll fall for everything.

Being cool is the goal of teens. Whatever it takes to be considered "radically in" is the driving force behind youth actions. Being sexually active has become a status symbol on campus today. If you're doing it, you're cool; if you're not, what's your problem? Youth constantly strive to live up to everybody else's expectations; having sex is expected and is definitely cool.

Loss of Perspective. The most recent national research from the Guttmacher Institute found that virginity is less common among teenage girls than ever before. The studies stated that today 60 percent of teen girls, age fifteen to nineteen, were sexually experienced, up from 48 percent in 1982 and 30 percent in 1972. The National Survey of Family Growth said that over seven out of ten teens — 75 percent — have had sex by age eighteen.[3]

A generation ago, virginity was highly valued. It was important to maintain one's sexual purity for marriage. Virginity in today's youth culture signifies inexperience, ineptitude and inadequacy. "Society and youth's peers value sexual experience and do not value sexual inexperience."[4] In a culture of "trivial pursuit," we live for the things that do not really matter and do not pursue the things that do.

Insecurity. Young people crave acceptance and security; this often leads to premarital sex. A teen who feels unloved and lacking identity will use sex to feel loved and secure. However, the temporary feeling vanishes as quickly as the sexual encounter, leaving behind intensified feelings of rejection and insecurity. Youth fears create an illusion of love and security that never really existed. Insecurity has been defined as putting your trust in something or someone that can be taken from you or leave.

Premarital sex is the ultimate expression of insecurity among teens; most teen relationships are based on the fear of rejection and insecurity.

Over-aroused Culture. The mass media in America have created an erotic and sensual atmosphere in which teens see a distorted view of love. Sex in the media is shown as this exciting and fulfilling lifestyle. Constant eroticism in a society produces a level of stimulation so high that it can never be fulfilled sexually, and it takes more and more to arouse and satisfy.

Premarital sex for teens is now the norm in popular culture, promoted as the key to responsible, fulfilling relationships — as long as you have safe sex. This is causing more destruction, emotional devastation, and the inability for teens to distinguish between fantasy (sex) and reality (love).

We have produced a generation of hyper-sexed youth, which will only lead to more illusion, confusion and empty relationships.

Boredom and Curiosity. Youth have experienced and been exposed to so much today, they tend to be bored with life very quickly. They're looking for the radical, thrill, rush experience. Sex greatly appeals to their need for excitement. Curiosity is basic to human nature; the mystique of sex and the desire to know what it feels like draws youth like a magnet.

Boredom and curiosity are inextricably linked together because boredom feeds curiosity. When the boredom factor is high, the curiosity factor gets even higher. The need to experience the exciting and discover the unknown combine to be a captivating force. Even if the experience may be destructive, many youth are willing to experiment anyway.

Panic Mentality. The fear of not finding the right mate or never getting married, coupled with the feeling that time is running out, equals sheer panic and desperation. Teens see their friends going steady and some about to get married. They feel like they are going to miss out, so they push the panic button and make choices based on the fear of uncertainty, of missing out.

The irony is so many of their friends are experiencing unnecessary pain and disillusionment. The reality is they are not really missing out; there's plenty of time, but there's also plenty of pain. Getting pregnant as a teen is like being grounded for eighteen years; the only thing they're missing out on is life.

Fear of Rejection. There is nothing more devastating for youth than to feel the pain of rejection. The need to love and be loved is so critical for youth that they will do anything for the approval and love of someone they care about. Teenage girls especially are looking for affection, security and someone to love them for who they are. So, they get involved sexually, looking for love, only to find deeper rejection than before. This creates deep anger and resentment toward the person who rejected and used them, which negatively affects future relationships unless resolved.

Youth fears are always based on legitimate emotional needs for love; the problem is when they focus on their fears in order to meet those needs. For every need, there is a fear that produces fantasy relationships.

Pressure from the Opposite Sex. When a teenager really cares about someone, they feel a certain allegiance and even an obligation to have sex with them, especially when a teen couple is going steady or have been dating for an extended period. This creates a certain emotional bonding and commitment to that person. More often than not, a boy may be very convincing when he asks the girl to prove her love by having sex with him, making the girl feel if she doesn't have sex, she doesn't really love him. This is performance-based conditional love; lust can't wait to get, but real love can't wait to give.

Teens in relationships also may feel, "I owe it to the person to have sex because they've really done a lot for me; I can at least repay them by having sex with them." Another pressure point is the fear of losing their boyfriend or girlfriend if they don't have sex. The fear of not having a date or a steady relationship can cause teens to do anything, including having sex, to save the relationship. The line "If you don't have sex with me, we'll have to break up," strikes horror in the heart of an insecure and desperate teen. When a girl or boy becomes a teen's whole world, they are terrified to be without that person.

Relationships Without a Biblical Basis. This sexually oriented, morally relativistic society defines what are acceptable and normal relationships for young people today. The problem is, none of it relates to biblical principles but to the supposedly new enlightenment and personally liberating life-styles. The result is an epidemic of sexually based relationships without any regard for biblical morality.

As *Time* magazine states in a feature article, "Kids, Sex and Values," society says "Just do it; just say no; just wear a condom; just be safe."[5] Young people are being bombarded with an array of confusing mixed messages concerning sexual values and critical choices they must make, and youth are more sexually active than ever (at younger ages) and more confused.

Good Kids Aren't Saying No To Sex. We have an entire generation of youth who do not relate Christian principles to sexual behavior or relationships. Several major research studies revealed that six out of every ten evangelical church youth are now sexually active. According to numerous studies of teenage sexuality, American youth encreasingly believe that sexual behavior is merely a matter of personal choice, rather than Christian principles.

In very disturbing new research it was found that these factors did not deter or immunize teens from sexual involvement

- church involvement
- high grade averages
- sex education
- high self-esteem
- two parents at home

"This is very depressing," says Dr, Michael Benson, a North Western University Researcher. "These are results a lot of people don't want to hear."[6] However it should be noted that in recent surveys there are growing numbers of youth who would like to have an abstinence message, and that it's okay to wait to have sex. North American Christian teenagers are giving in to cultural life-styles that are opposed to Christian beliefs in numbers unparalleled in history."

Sexual Generation Cycles. The baby-boomer teens of the '60s became the first sexually liberated generation that advocated sexual freedom and expression as the key to real love. Their sexually oriented life-style and philosophy has had a profound impact on the mind-set of today's teens and their concept of relationships. Many of the baby-boomer teens are parents of our current youth generation. Teens who were raised permissively often become self-indulging parents, and self-indulging parents often seem indifferent to their children. Their children and teens often will go to negative extremes in their behavior to seek attention. It is a way of crying out, "Hey, I'm here. Does anybody care?"[7]

The '60s teens set in motion a "sexual cycle" that has gathered massive momentum over the last twenty years and has become a sexual monster that is growing, affecting millions of teens. The heartache and pain generated by their parents is now being mirrored in the lives of the teens. Youth today are experiencing more sex and less love than ever as the sexual revolution of the '60s has turned into the "sexual revulsion" of the '90s. The current relationship maze among adults in our society has magnified the need for real love among teens.

Loneliness. Loneliness is becoming more widespread in America as nearly five in ten Americans admit in a national survey to frequent or occasional feelings of intense loneliness.

The loneliest people in America are high school girls, says a recent national study. Josh McDowell said, "What some people think is a desire for sex is really a reaction to loneliness."[8] Loneliness is one of the most painful emotions youth can experience. Sex cannot eliminate loneliness, only temporarily displace it for a while, as many youth find out. True loneliness is breaking up with the person they thought would always be there, which causes them to get involved in another destructive relationship or to isolate themselves and avoid relationships.

Fragmented Families. A vast number of teenagers come from broken homes. Youth's attitudes about love and their perspectives on relationships have been shaped and developed by their families.

A broken home is a major influence in teenage sexual involvement. For instance, "only one teenager in five (20 percent) whose parents are separated or divorced report that their parents' attitudes about sex affect them positively."[9] Research has shown that teens whose parents are divorced or separated are twice as likely to have sexual relations than teens whose parents are still together.

Josh McDowell lists four ways in which broken homes can lead to premarital sex:

> 1. A lack of value structure results from a void of positive adult role models if Mom and Dad are unforgiving, unaccepting and mean to each other. In this environment, teens' concepts of right and wrong disappear.
>
> 2. Influence and pressure from peers becomes stronger than that in the home. When closeness and sharing that should take place in the home is replaced by guilt, anger and isolation, sexual escape looks

inviting.

3. The lack of security in the home may motivate a teen to look for intimacy in irrational ways.

4. Divorce greatly affects a child's or teen's self-image. Feelings of rejection and guilt arising from a divorce may cause a teen to seek a boost in his or her self-image through sex.[10]

Need for Intimacy. Josh McDowell cites the overwhelming need for intimacy as the major reason teens are having premarital sex today. Young people desire closeness and affection with a person to whom they can trust their innermost feelings, dreams and hopes. Young people use sex as a means to experience intimacy. Real intimacy is an emotional and spiritual bonding with another person. Teens often experience intimacy on only one level, the physical, exploiting their own emotional and spiritual being. Sexual experience becomes a substitute for rather than an expression of intimacy.[11]

The desire for intimacy, security and affection makes youth vulnerable to "manufactured instant intimacy" that promises to alleviate their emotional pain. Youth are exploited by a culture that offers intimacy as another product to be purchased at the mall.

Our sex-saturated culture is producing a generation of youth who are the most sexually active and yet the most love starved ever, and the search continues.

Love-Starved: The Relationship Vacuum

Popular culture's obsession with looks has created an identity crisis among youth and adults where appearance and performance, not character, determines how much power we have and our worth as persons.

In a culture that celebrates self-actualization, self-absorption and instant gratification, the "self" becomes the center of the universe.

Chapter 8

The Cracked Mirror: The Identity Crisis

For the Lord does not see as man sees; for man looks at the outward appearance, but the Lord looks at the heart (1 Sam. 16:7 NKJ).

In counseling hundreds of teens after my assembly presentations junior and senior high schools across North America, it's very clear that many of them have a distorted view of who they are. They behave not in accordance with reality but with their perception of reality.

I'm always taken by surprise when some of the most popular, attractive and highest-achieving teens say to me: "I wish I was like her or him; I'm not attractive; I could never do that; I feel like such a failure; I don't know who I am anymore." If these are the feelings of some of the top students on our campuses, where does that leave the rest of the young people who would give anything to be just like them?

The Cry of Self-Hatred

Our self-concept is determined not only by how we view ourselves but how we think others perceive us. The Gallup organization cited low self-esteem to be the number one psychological problem in contemporary society.[1]

In a landmark study by Search Institute, *Five Cries of Youth,* more than seven thousand teens were surveyed focusing on a specific need cherished by youth and the underlying emotion expressed. The cry of self-hatred or low self-esteem was the number one emotion that dominated many youth.[2] These feelings of inadequacy, unimportance and distorted identity seriously affect the lives of three young people in five.

How youth see themselves has an incredible ripple effect on every choice they make, every relationship they have and their success or failure as persons. A young person's attitude toward himself has a profound influence on his attitudes toward God, his family, friends, the opposite sex and his future happiness.

Young people need to see their uniqueness and importance as individuals and understand who they really are. If the person they see in the mirror is distorted, then their perception of everyone and everything will be false. Many young people have a false sense of identity based upon a wrong perception of reality and of themselves.

Three-Dimensional Persons

God created us as three-dimensional beings, consisting of the physical dimension (the body), the emotional dimension (the soul) and the spiritual dimension (the spirit).

The physical facet is the most obvious dimension, encompassing our outward appearance and bodily needs of food, drink, sleep and shelter.

The emotional aspect is expressed by the feelings we have regarding relationships and situations. It also includes our personality type and temperament, which are the foundation for our basic motivations and our emotional responses such as guilt, anger, fear, love, joy and kindness.

The spiritual dimension is the most powerful and the least understood of all three, and it is the key to our fulfillment and happiness. We can experience temporary and apparent fulfillment from the physical and emotional facets of our being, but we will be fragmented and incomplete people without the spiritual commitment. Many youth are experiencing an identity crisis; unless they explore their own spiritual dimension, they will never really know who they are. It is the God dimension of our being that gives us identity; it doesn't mean that we know God, only that we are known by Him and have the capacity to know Him.

Most youth's identities are based solely on the physical and emotional levels of their being, with the greatest emphasis on the physical. This leaves them feeling fragmented, incomplete and insecure. To know who they are, they must know God's love, acceptance and forgiveness.

Causes that Shape and Affect Teens Self-Esteem

The Societal Factor. "Beautiful is better" is the prevailing attitude in America and especially in the youth culture. Starting from childhood, you must have a certain look to really be somebody. A recent study showed conclusively that teens and adults that were rated as above average in looks or considered strikingly good-looking made more money and had more friends and opportunities than the average- or below-average-looking person. We live in a society where human worth is determined by outward appearance, and this value judgment is magnified on junior and senior high school campuses.

Television, movies, music and media advertisements have helped produce this beautiful and handsome mind-set that rules the youth culture. The media has further confused youth concerning their identity by defining the most attractive and beautiful young people in America. This creates deeper feelings of inadequacy and inferiority.

We are an image-oriented culture that never gets below the surface to see who we really are, feeding the perpetual identity crisis among youth and mainstream culture.

A number of years ago in a mental institution just outside Boston, Massachusetts, a young girl known as Little Annie was locked in the dungeon. This institution was one of the more enlightened ones for the treatment of the mentally disturbed. However, the doctors felt that a dungeon was the only place for those who were hopelessly insane. In Little Annie's case, they saw no hope for her, so she was consigned to a living death in that small cage that received little light and even less hope.

An elderly nurse who worked at the institution was nearing

retirement. She felt that no one was hopeless with God's love, so she started taking her lunch into the dungeon and eating outside Little Annie's cage. She felt perhaps she could communicate God's love and hope to the little girl.

Little Annie was like an animal. Sometimes she would go into a rage and violently attack the person who came into her cage. At other times, she would withdraw into a catatonic state and completely ignore them. When the elderly nurse started visiting her, Little Annie gave no indication that she was even aware of her presence.

One day, the elderly nurse brought some brownies to the dungeon and left them outside the cage. Little Annie made no response, but when the nurse returned the next day, the brownies were gone. From that time on, the nurse brought brownies when she made her Thursday visit.

The change in Little Annie was so dramatic that the day came when this "hopeless case" was able to leave the institution. But Little Annie did not wish to leave. The nurse had reached out to her, had loved her and had known she was valuable. Little Annie felt she could help someone who was just like her, so she stayed to help others.

Many years later, Queen Victoria of England, while pinning England's highest award on a foreigner, asked Helen Keller, "How do you account for your remarkable accomplishments in life? How do you explain the fact that even though you were both blind and deaf, you were able to accomplish so much?"

Helen Keller said, "If it had not been for Annie Sullivan (Little Annie), the name of Helen Keller would have remained unknown." Little Annie — that crazy, insane, hopeless case locked in a dungeon — became the motivating person in the life of Helen Keller, who influenced millions because someone cared.[3]

The Parental Factor. Youth's relationships with their parents affect their view of God, their view of themselves, their ability to relate to others and how they love.

The positive or negative input teens receive from their parents has a tremendous impact on how they see themselves and others. "If a teen's parents were [and are] loving, nurturing and supportive, then they probably believe that God is loving, strong and dependable. They are probably secure and confident and are able to relate easily and care for other people. However, if your parents were harsh, demanding, critical and insensitive, you probably believe that God is also that way, and you may think you can never do enough to please Him."[4]

A young person's self-image is a reflection of their parents' attitudes and actions regarding them. Through the responses of their parents they learn who they are. A teen's sense of love and security is based on the acceptance, affection, approval and trust they received from their parents.

Parents who have a low or unhealthy self-esteem tend to be unloving, neglectful, unforgiving and condemning toward their teens, perpetuating the cycle of self-hatred. This creates a vicious cycle of pain and low self-worth among youth; they tend to love the way they were loved.

Parents who are loving, forgiving, understanding, accepting and godly, and who spend quality time with their teens, help them develop a dynamic sense of self-worth.

"All of us have formulated a mental image of ourselves based on the feelings of acceptance we received from our parents. A child-teen develops his sense of being as a worthwhile, capable, important and unique individual from the attention given him by his parents. He sees or feels himself reflected in their love, approval, acceptance and attention to his needs."[5]

The powerful factor that significantly affects a youth's self-esteem is an attitude of unconditional acceptance and love. This attitude is a constant; it is not something given or withdrawn based on a teen's performance, behavior or meeting conditions.

> If a teen has not experienced loving and strong parental modeling, then there will be a vacuum in his life. Virtually everything he does will be designed to accomplish two purposes: to gain the approval he so desperately wants, or to avoid pain.[6]

Due to the epidemic divorce rate, single-parent families, step-families, working mothers, and parents who spend less time communicating with their teens than parents in any other country in the industrialized world, youth see a distorted and confused image in the mirror.[7]

The Peer Factor. On a high school campus of two thousand teens, only five hundred make the social status of acceptance, leaving 1,500 teens on the outside looking in. This cruel and competitive system breeds feelings of inferiority and inadequacy. Every day youth ask themselves the painful and introspective questions: Will they like me? How do I look? Will I say the right thing? Will they think I'm cool or a jerk? "Teens become so self-conscious by other people's opinions and attitudes toward them that they cannot give sufficient or quality attention to other people's needs or pain. Their feelings of inadequacy prevent them from reaching out to love and care for others."[8]

ABC-TV did a feature story on the sudden increase in cosmetic plastic surgery among teens. These teens were wanting to improve their looks with nose jobs, lip enlargements and other facial surgery, also liposuction and breast enlargements. They ranged in age from fourteen to eighteen years old and actually were already very attractive. Most of the girls looked like beauty queens and yet felt they needed additional plastic surgery. They said they had to have a "certain look," and they weren't happy with what they saw. When the most attractive and popular students on a high school campus were asked if they were satisfied with their basic appearance, over 95 percent said they were not!

USA Today reported that by the age of thirteen, more than 60 percent of U.S. girls think they're fat — though few really are. Most already have been on a diet, says the largest study on middle-school kids and their attitudes about weight. The percentage of girls who perceive themselves as being fat increases as they get older, as 85 percent of high school girls believe they are fat.[9] Anorexics and bulimics (95 percent are teenage girls) are obsessed with being thin and have a fear of becoming fat. Anorexics will literally starve themselves. Even when an anorexic is dangerously thin, she looks in the mirror and still sees a fat person. Fear and emotional needs that are not being met create a distorted image and a fantasy identity.

Opposite Sex Approval. The ultimate measure of identity in the youth culture is based upon how desirable you are and how well you do with the opposite sex. Many young people feel incredible pressure to get a boyfriend or girlfriend no matter what it takes. Everyone's dating someone, going steady or with that certain person, or so it seems. Sex has tragically become the accepted norm and expected behavior in most teen relationships today. Everyone's having sex, and if you're not, you're viewed as out of touch, inadequate and uncool by the opposite sex. Insecure teens feel they need to have a relationship with a girl or boy in order to be fulfilled.

Wrong Assumptions

A youth's self-perception is usually based on wrong assumptions or beliefs. Wrong perceptions produce false beliefs about identity.

False Assumptions. Robert McGee, founder of Rapha Ministries, summarizes four false beliefs that are based on specific fears that can shape our self-concept and determine who we are and what we think we must do for acceptance. These four false assumptions can have devastating consequences and cause immense emotional pain when youth believe them to be a reality.

The Performance Trap. "I must meet certain standards to feel good about myself. If I don't meet these standards, I am a failure." This belief drives youth to succeed, manipulating others to achieve their goal; it also produces a perfectionism mentality and is based on the fear of failure.[10]

The Approval Addict. "I must have the approval of certain others to feel good about myself. If I do not have the approval of these people, something must be wrong with me." This belief causes youth to attempt to please others at any cost; it also causes them to withdraw from others to avoid disapproval and is based on the fear of rejection.[11]

The Blame Game. "Those who fail are unworthy of love and deserve to be blamed and condemned." This produces a tendency to punish others and also blame others as well as themselves for personal failure. This belief is based on the fear of punishment.

Feelings of Shame. "I am what I am; I cannot change; I am hopeless. I am simply a total of all my past failures and wrongs I have done." This belief is the result of a sense of shame, causing feelings of inferiority, isolation and hopelessness.[12]

These beliefs create an illusion of self, where young people behave not in accordance with reality but with their perception of reality.

Appearance Perfectionists. Appearance perfectionists define themselves by the image they present to the world. They believe the aspects of themselves that matter the most are the ones that other people see. Appearance perfectionists become obsessed with the way they look. They derive their sense of self-worth from controlling that which is visible to the eye. They are preoccupied with their weight, the size of their thighs or biceps, the clothes they wear, how their hair looks, their facial features and, most of all, the impression they make on other people through their appearance.[13]

The appearance perfectionists have concluded that looking good will make them feel happy, worthwhile, complete and in control; they unwittingly set themselves up for disappointment and failure. No matter how drastically they alter their appearance or how skillfully they maintain the image other people see, because their sense of self-worth is virtually non-existent or mostly negative, they are chronically insecure and dissatisfied with themselves.

As a result of growing up in a dysfunctional family where parents were extremely critical and judgmental, or perhaps being ridiculed and rejected by their peers or the opposite sex because of some imperfection, the appearance perfectionist came to believe the following: "My flaws and deficiencies are to blame for all the pain, criticism and unhappiness in my life. To be loved, accepted and rewarded, I must conceal my flaws and control the impression I make on other people; by making things perfect on the outside, I will prove I am a worthwhile valuable person and will never have to feel anxious or unhappy again. I am the image I create."[14]

For the appearance perfectionist, life is one continual beauty contest. The appearance mind-set defines your identity; what you wear and how you look determines who you are. This mentality only intensifies youth's feelings of insecurities, fears and low self-worth.

Appearance perfectionists still believe deep down that they are dangerously flawed and inherently unacceptable. As a result, nothing they see in the mirror or find reflected in other people's eyes ever completely convinces them that they are finally good enough. Driven to create an outward appearance of perfection, they can never achieve their goal because their perception of external reality is distorted by their deeply ingrained fears, insecurities and assumptions about themselves.

Performance Perfectionists. Performance perfectionists determine their sense of identity by what they achieve, accomplish or produce. They are driven by a powerful need to prove to themselves and others that they are valuable, capable, lovable people. Like all perfectionists when they look inside themselves, they see someone who is not as valuable, capable or lovable as they should be. They turn to external sources to supply them with the sense of self-worth they cannot generate internally. For the performance perfectionist, achieving rewards, recognition, praise, admiration and approval is that external source.[15]

Because ours is a highly competitive performance-oriented society, many people derive a sense of identity from what they accomplish, achieve or produce. We believe, "I am what I do. Consequently, the more I do and the better I do, the better I am."[16]

If you are what you do perfectly, then you also are what you fail to do perfectly. If you prove that you are a valuable, lovable, capable person by being the best, then each time you turn in a performance that is less than perfect and flawless, you have proven that you are not valuable, lovable and capable after all.[17]

Performance perfectionists are always driven to achieve more and more in less and less time. The compelling urge to prove their worth also creates strong fears of failure, prompting them to do whatever they can to avoid failure. They get trapped in a self-defeating cycle of failure, frustration and self-hatred.

Negative Traits of Low Self-Esteem and Insecurity

Over-emphasis on outward appearance. The latest fashion statement, "You are what you wear." Undue attention is concentrated on clothes and looks, which overcompensates for lack of inner security. Focusing on the outside keeps us from looking inside.

Condemning Self. Constantly self-critical statements like, "I can't do anything! It's all my fault!" Youth are continually preoccupied with their personal faults and inabilities and can't see their abilities.

Lack of Self-Confidence. Feelings of inferiority and inadequacy cause youth to fear attempting anything; they always feel somehow they'll blow it or mess it up, and "everybody will laugh at me or think I'm stupid."

Judgmental of Others. Youth who are critical of themselves find fault and criticize everyone and everything around them. Gossip makes them feel better about themselves at the expense of others.

Center of Attention. These individuals are an enigma. On the surface, they appear to be very secure and together. They are generally the super-athletes, top students, stars, musicians, beauty queens, performers and speakers who are the most popular, most talented, best looking and most outstanding youth on a campus.

However, in reality, they are very insecure and self-absorbed; they must be the center of attention and have the admiration, praise and applause of the crowd to be happy. Their security and identity is dependent on the adulation and attention of everyone. They must be in the spotlight, on center stage; if they are not, they feel threatened and can be very manipulative They are ego maniacs.

Wishful-Comparison Syndrome. Never satisfied with how they look or who they are, youth's frame of reference is each other. Comparing themselves can produce one of two negative responses. One is to feel superior, where they say, "I'm glad I don't look like that." The other response is to feel inferior, where they say, "I wish I could look or be like him or her. I'm a real loser." These attitudes cause feelings of pride and insensitivity, or envy or jealousy which produce bitterness.

Extreme Shyness. Feelings of inadequacy and lack of competence combined with the fear of what others think cause youth to withdraw, avoiding people and situations that require their participation or involvement. The fear of rejection and failure is too great a risk.

Overbearing Loudmouth. This person is constantly trying to impress others by what they've done, what they have or what they know. You can never top their accomplishments or stories; they can spend hours talking about themselves and how great they are. These people can be very obnoxious and offensive and will exploit anyone in order to look better. They come across very loud and arrogant, but must be in control to feel secure. They hide behind this apparent confidence and security, which is really a facade.

Beneath that tough, loud and domineering front is a very insecure and threatened person. All the noise and bravado covers their fears; their behavior can include extreme drug use, sexual conquest and fighting, but they are always the life of the party. These people feel they must always prove something to be accepted and liked, and even when they do they are still desperately insecure.

Inability to Love Others. It is very difficult for youth to love others when they don't like themselves. Teens can't be sensitive to the needs and problems of others when they feel worthless. Part of their capacity to experience real identity and acceptance comes from opening themselves to others by giving and caring.

Many teens are so wrapped up in themselves and their world, they cannot love others. Caught in an endless cycle of self-hatred, absorbed by their fears and inadequacies, they have tunnel vision, unable to see that the key is to give what you need.

Inability to Love God. Many youth reason, "If God created me, He must be mad for making someone like me." Also, their parents' negative attitudes and lack of love and understanding cause them to believe that God is unfair and unconcerned about them. They say, "If God is love, why is this happening to me?" And they blame God for their parents' divorce and other painful situations and disappointments of life. Their parents weren't there for them when they needed them the most; this causes them to be unable to trust God or anyone else.

Manipulated Youth. Young people who don't have a healthy sense of identity are much more prone to be involved in "at risk" behavior such as drug abuse, suicide, school dropouts, pregnancies, crime, gangs, runaways, satanism and other self-destructive life-styles.

They will do anything to gain acceptance and approval of the peer group. If the crowd says, "Let's do drugs...let's steal...let's drop out," or if the guy says, "Let's have sex," they always do whatever it takes to belong. They allow other people to make their choices and control their destiny. They follow the crowd going nowhere. They become moral wimps; they don't stand for anything except to go along, which increases their emotional pain and confuses identity.

Below the layers of fear lies the real person. Confronting that person in the mirror can be very scary, but not confronting that person can be disastrous.

Negative Perspective. Young people who view themselves negatively tend to see everything and everyone through a dirty window. They are extremely critical and pessimistic, always looking for the worst. You ask them, "How are you doing?" They say, "It could be worse." Don't worry it will be. This cynical attitude affects every relationship they have and everything they do. They will be very quick to tell you what you did wrong, or why you can't do something, and all the problems you'll face.

These are the classic under achievers. They don't trust anyone nor can they be trusted, and they are very unhappy with who they are. They are part of the problem rather than the solution. People with a negative perspective feel that nothing is ever quite right; there's a conspiracy and everybody is against them. Even if something appears to be perfect, if they can't find a flaw, they'll manufacture one.

God Basis for Identity

Our true identity is found by seeing ourselves as God sees us and in our personal commitment to and ongoing relationship with Jesus Christ. The more we know Him, the more we understand who we are. Our self-esteem is based on what God says about us in His Word and our experience of His unconditional love, acceptance and forgiveness.

Our worth and importance is gained by realizing God sent His Son to die for each one of us individually. You are not just another face in the sea of humanity that is lumped together. He knows your name, everything you feel and think; you are a very special person to Him.

Young people need to know that they are loved and accepted by God unconditionally and are free to be uniquely themselves. The sacrificial death of Jesus was to spare them personally from being rejected by God. We are made in the image of God, the identity of Jesus, His nature and inward character qualities. We are created to achieve, designed to do good works. This spiritual potential is based not on outward appearance, abilities, social heritage or the opinions of others but on God's power working in and through us.

Young people aren't reaching their potential because they see themselves as inadequate, incapable of achievement. They will reach their potential as they see God's plan for them. Fulfillment is understanding our true identity, and happiness is our relationship with Christ. In God's love, we are free from fear of rejection, failure, punishment and the future, free to become the person He wants us to be.

Three Important Feelings

There are three feelings that have particular importance in shaping our self-concept—belonging, worthiness and competence.[18]

As a teen approaches adulthood and the state of responsible and mature functioning in society, these three feelings are crucial to a healthy self-concept.

Belonging. Youth need to feel they belong, to feel they are wanted and accepted, secure and cared for, and enjoyed for who they are. There is an unspoken desperate cry among many youth across America; they are saying, "Can I be in your group? Please choose me!" The feeling of being on the outside looking in is devastating for young people. It is natural for teens to want to be "in" with the people they admire.

"The sense of belonging or feeling of being loved is vital to a healthy self-esteem. It's the sense of security a person feels when he or she is accepted by other people, a feeling of having a significant, meaningful relationship, with at least one other person. It's the knowledge that someone really cares for me. To belong is to be loved unconditionally, just as I am."[19]

Worthiness. Worthiness is feeling good or valuable. Youth's sense of worthiness is verified when they sense others' positive attitudes toward them. Worthiness is related not only to being right but doing right. When others criticize us and disapprove of us, we feel a loss of worthiness, making us defensive, depressed or angry.

In our culture, worthiness is based on appearance, performance and expectations, which creates feelings of low self-worth. True worthiness must be based solely on God's unconditional love, acceptance and forgiveness.

Competence. Competence "is a sense of adequacy, of courage, of initiative, of hopefulness, of ability to achieve and deal effectively with the everyday situations, relationships and problems." It is the positive sense that 'I can' which gives young people a feeling of being capable to confront and cope with life's complexities. "An immediate sense of competence that reflects the memories of accomplishments and failures of past experiences, the competence level is affected positively by successes, and negatively by failures." How youth deal with their pain, both past and present, is crucial to increasing their competence.[20]

Unshakable competence and self-confidence help young people overcome failure and turn pain into power. Being competent is a key to achieving their goals. Competence orients a person to circumstances, to time, to responsibility and to fulfillment in his or her role in society.

Fragmented Youth

The state of identity in the North American youth culture is fragmented and distorted. Young people find themselves in a strange land of mass media-constructed identities where image is more important than true identity.

Youth are further plunged into an identity vacuum by a high-tech culture in constant transition, with no value system, producing more feelings of inadequacy and insecurity.

The identity crisis among youth is characterized by a cultural paradox that has accelerated youth's emotional transition from youth to adulthood, yet kept them suspended in a perpetual state of adolescence.

This complex, fast-changing culture of the '90s will create an atmosphere where youth and adults will struggle with deep feelings of self-doubt, powerlessness and low self-worth.

The Cracked Mirror: The Identity Crisis

The only causes many youth of the '90s are committed to are constant personal gratification on the one hand and self-preservation on the other, producing the apathetic landscape. The other cause youth are committed to is being uncommitted.

Chronic boredom, moral confusion and fantasy are symptoms of a generation in spiritual crisis, searching for meaning.

Chapter 9

In Search of a Cause: The Loss of Significance

For what is a man profited if he gains the whole world, and loses his own soul? Or what will a man give in exchange for his soul? (Matt. 16:26 NKJ).

The American Success Cult

Never in history has the American culture been more success-conscious than today. We are inundated with books, tapes, manuals and seminars on how to be successful. A number of success gurus in our culture — writers, positive thinkers and top achievers in a variety of fields — tell us through word and example that the most important thing in life is to acquire the outward trappings of achievement, to move up the career ladder, accumulate a lot of wealth and realize your potential.

Our success-oriented culture has produced deep feelings of frustration, inadequacy, resentment and depression among today's teens. The pressure to achieve is enormous, and they are indoctrinated as children by family, the media, school and society to strive for the ultimate goal in life — success.

There's nothing wrong with wanting to be successful; we all do.

It is a basic human need. The problem is what we define as success and how we pursue it. Personal goals and career dreams become more important than relationships, so we sacrifice friends and family in our quest for success. We become preoccupied with ourselves, manipulating and exploiting others for self-fulfillment.

In our culture, if you're not achievement oriented or if you lack career ambition and an aggressive self-sufficient attitude, you are viewed as lazy, inferior and made to feel as if you're out of step and unmotivated. Many youth have frantically climbed the fast-track ladder to success only to find that the ladder was propped against the wrong wall.

The Success Illusion

Youth believe success will bring them happiness, fulfillment and meaning. It is always disillusioning to teens when the lives of television and movie stars, celebrities, musical performers and athletes are messed up and unhappy. Especially disheartening are the desperate adult lives of former child stars.

Dana Plato, Todd Bridges and Gary Coleman were the youthful stars of the television sitcom *Different Strokes*.[1] "Dana Plato, twenty-six, applied for a six-dollar-an-hour job picking up garbage and cleaning bathrooms. She was turned down. The next day she walked into a video store, armed with a pellet gun, and demanded money. Shortly afterward, Plato was arrested and charged with armed robbery. Two years earlier she had posed nude for *Playboy*, hoping to revive her foundering acting career."

Difficult Strokes

Gary Coleman, now twenty-three, the diminutive actor who was an '80s TV phenomenon, was born with an atrophied right kidney and lost the use of his other kidney at age five. Currently, Coleman has been surviving by using a portable self-dialysis machine since his second kidney transplant failed five years ago. He is suing his parents over their handling of his $18 million fortune. He hasn't spoken to them for over a year. Coleman has been unable to get any regular acting roles because he is no longer a marketable commodity in Hollywood.

Todd Bridges was acquitted of murder and manslaughter in August 1990 and has a police record that goes back to 1983. Bridges began snorting cocaine in 1982 and for the next several years was lost in a world of drugs. "In show business, the beginning is always filled with fantasy," says Todd. "You make a lot of money; you're taken care of; life is a breeze. But what happens is that reality catches up and hits you in the face."

"Fame is a drug," says Paul Peterson who played Jeff, the son on *The Donna Reed Show* in the '50s and '60s. He then used drugs for the next ten years. "When you're a teenager and told your career is over, that's devastating."

The pigtailed little girl who played Buffy, the wide-eyed moppet of CBS's *Family Affair* (1966-1971), never finished growing up. Anissa Jones committed suicide at eighteen; she took a massive overdose of cocaine, Quaaludes and barbiturates. Friends said she couldn't get her life together after show business.

Thirty-one-year-old Danny Bonaduce, who played in the hit series *The Partridge Family* during the '70s, was arrested on assault charges. He had already been arrested twice for cocaine possession.

Adam Rich, twenty-two, who played Nicholas on the popular *Eight Is Enough* family TV show, was arrested on suspicion of burglary. Before that, he had plead guilty to drunk-driving charges and had been treated for cocaine and substance abuse.

These young people are caught up in the Hollywood cycle of desperation, unable to get their lives together and deal with reality.

Actor River Phoenix was young, talented and full of promise. His death at twenty-three stunned friends and shocked everyone. How did the star who lit up the screen in *Stand By Me* and *Indiana Jones and the Last Crusade,* who received an Oscar nomination for *Running on Empty,* get to be L.A. Coroner's case number 93-10011, a lifeless body containing toxic levels of cocaine and heroin, as well as traces of marijuana and Valium?

River Phoenix became a part of the jet set, the live faster crowd. "However, his tragic drug overdose death has not slowed the Hollywood party scene one iota, demonstrating just how entrenched the drug culture is in America" says *People Magazine* (January 17, 1994).

Lauren Chapin, who played Cathy Anderson in the TV series *Father Knows Best,* describes a period in her life when she was desperately looking for happiness. She became a heroin addict, a high-priced prostitute, went to prison, was poverty stricken and spent time in a mental hospital. Lauren says, "I know all the signs of impending disaster — I had them all. I slept with many, many people trying to find love, to find self-worth; and the more people I slept with, the less self-worth I had."[2] Today Lauren is a dynamic Christian who travels all over America telling people about the real love, peace and happiness she found in Jesus Christ.

The lives of literally thousands of successful Hollywood superstars — Marilyn Monroe, Elvis Presley, Judy Garland, Howard Hughes, Jimi Hendrix — whose lives were devoured by the success monster, and the tragic lives of Hollywood jet-setters have been chronicled for years. Their lives have been ravaged and destroyed by multiple relationships, drug abuse, obsession, paranoia and suicide.

The mystique of success that permeates the American culture has intensified feelings of confusion and frustration among youth in their concept of success and happiness. It's assumed that when you reach the success peak, you'll be magically happy. Our success-oriented society has created an illusion of meaning and purpose. *Real happiness is not just in attaining or achieving; it can't be based just on performance or success.* When success becomes the means for achieving happiness, it signifies a fleeting pursuit of nothingness.

Success and significance can be two totally different entities. It is possible to have a successful and meaningful life; but success without purpose is a desperate and empty place to exist.

Teens Role Models Missing

Most teenagers do not look to *90210*, Pearl Jam, Michael Jackson, or even Mother Teresa for inspiration. Nor do they care whether pro-basketball player Charles Barkley wants to be their role model, says *USA Today.*[3]

In fact, more than half don't have any role model at all, says a startling recent Gallup survey. Fifty-one percent of nearly one thousand teens age thirteen to seventeen nationwide don't have anyone they admire and want to be like.[4]

The lack of role models reflects "the plight of lots of American youth today," says child-adolescent psychologist Henry Gault of Northbrook, Illinois. "They are frightened, disenchanted, having a hard time finding someone to idealize."[5]

This disturbing trend illustrates the disillusionment, disappointment and cynicism that currently pervades the youth culture. The lack of role models is troubling because young people without heroes take their cues from popular culture. This is particularly alarming considering the brutal and bizarre messages that are being sent by popular culture.

The mental health community states, "It is very important that young people have someone who gives them strength, courage and motivation." Without role models (heroes) the world becomes a pretty bleak place to live.[6]

Sense of Destiny

Youth today are hungry for a sense of destiny, to feel their life has meaning and significance, that they count and that they can really make a difference. However, in a materialistic success-oriented culture, a meaningful life is measured in accomplishments, performance, acquiring more money and things, and reaching career goals. We have created a false sense of significance by exalting superficial success. Society has failed to provide youth with meaningful roles and challenges. They are experiencing a loss of significance. Teens who don't have a real sense of direction or purpose become more fantasy oriented in everything they do.

Reasons Why Youth Feel Insignificant

In a comprehensive survey by *USA Today,* fifteen thousand people were polled, and the major concern that emerged was the "desire to take control of our lives."[7] Many youth feel their lives are out of control due to the societal changes; problems and pressures they face have increased rapidly and they lack security from the family.

In the same survey, *USA Today* went on to say, "We have a tremendous fear of being ordinary or not special, of living and dying unnoticed, with someone else setting the agenda of our life's vocation." The need to leave our mark on our culture and people's lives is crucial to youth' feelings of significance.

Youth in the '90s will desperately look for significance and meaning within this high-tech system, yet hopelessness and anger will increase for many youth. A mindless pleasure-seeking and senseless violence will reflect the vacuum of meaning. This dangerous trend has put the future of our youth and society in jeopardy.

Competition in Teenland

The television camera zooms in for a close-up of high school football players on the sidelines during a big game. Strutting defiantly before the camera with arrogant facial gestures, they flash the "Number 1" sign, as if to say, "How far below us you are." That scenario is a social statement about the emphasis we place on success and competition in America. It is the survival of the best and brightest and most promising.

In America, there's no place for defeat, especially if you're a teenager. As a result, many youth simply decide not to make the effort or participate at all. They choose to avoid reality when reality means not succeeding or not measuring up to the expectation levels of their peers, parents and society. They don't even try, because to do so is to risk failing.

The Exaltation of Sports

As a former all-conference college football player and high school football coach, I can honestly say that sports was a positive influence and a major part of my life. In fact, my whole world revolved around playing football. Playing high school football can be a tremendous and valuable experience, assisting in the development of character qualities: discipline, sacrifice, commitment, teamwork, loyalty and other admirable traits. However, there is an unhealthy obsession with sports in America.

The things in our lives that can be the most dangerous are not necessarily evil or bad of themselves; they can become destructive when we are obsessed by them.

I remember as a young boy watching my heroes of the gridiron, waiting and anticipating the moment I would play for the illustrious Woodlawn High School. Located in Shreveport, Louisiana, Woodlawn was a football factory during the '60s. When I arrived as a sophomore, Terry Bradshaw was the starting quarterback. He went on to lead the Pittsburgh Steelers to four Super Bowl championships and was inducted into the NFL's Hall of Fame. Following Terry at Woodlawn High School was Joe Ferguson, who played eighteen seasons in the NFL as an outstanding quarterback. There were scores of other all-star players and powerful teams that had established the "Woodlawn Legacy."

When you walked on the campus, you could feel it — a sense of destiny that you were part of something great. There was a certain mystique about playing football as a Woodlawn Knight: to wear the red and blue was what boys dreamed about and trained for, to get their chance to fulfill a magic destiny. Anyone who has played will tell you the experience ranks up there with a handful of other magical feelings you might be lucky enough to have in your life, like getting married or having your first child.

Now, here I was, finally a Woodlawn Knight, one of the many hopeful athletes that would carry on the glorious tradition. As I was putting on my football gear, I reflected on the last five years of my life spent in preparation for this moment. From the time I was eleven years old, I had worked out religiously in weight training and running; my goal was to excel, to perform, to compete, to win — all else was secondary and insignificant.

I remember the electric atmosphere at the Woodlawn games where eighteen thousand to twenty thousand screaming football fans were jammed into the stadium. Everybody — or so it seemed — your classmates, parents, friends and people who didn't even have kids playing were there to cheer for the Knights. It was as if the world stopped for a moment and you were on center stage. Nothing else in life mattered. Everything hinged on what would happen on the field.

One exciting week after another, and the world seemed only to consist of cheers, praise and glory — and it seemed it would never end. Life seemed to have no meaning outside football. After all, without it, who would you be? I remember the incredible camaraderie between teammates — the friendships, the commitments to each other and the cause. You knew what was expected. You were on a mission. There was blood, sweat and tears; but there was ecstasy, a feeling like no other. Saturday, after a big game, the feeling of being the conqueror; you won; you proved yourself; you're in total control and the world is at your beckon call. You are this invincible warrior, and nothing or no one can stop you.

Then suddenly it's all over. You sit in the locker room for the last time, not really wanting to take off your uniform. It's almost as if the uniform gives you identity, control and meaning. You know you'll never wear it again, and there's something scary about that.

You live in a fantasy world for maybe one or two years of your life. You see your name in lights, and people follow you just to be around you — and now it's over. The clock has struck midnight, and there's no turning back.

The Sports Illusion

Thousands of teen athletes get caught up in the intoxication of high school sports, where nothing in their lives will ever be so wonderful, so fulfilling as playing high school football or some other sport. For a little while, they are in demand, like a hot rock group. No matter what they do, it's a hit. Everything they do is right, and many will never find that feeling again.

The tremendous emphasis on sports in America has increased dramatically during the past thirty years, reaching dangerous heights of obsession among teens. Sports in our culture has been exalted to a new social status where we don't just play or watch, we worship the gods of the stadiums.

I'll never forget the disappointment following the football season my senior year. I had a successful season and career at Woodlawn, but I was very small by college standards at 5'7" and 155 pounds. The college scouts snubbed me completely; the word was I was just too small and too slow to play college football. There would be no scholarship. My world came crashing down as my dream seemed shattered. I kept hoping that someone would take a chance, but it never happened. I felt utterly lost; my sense of security, identity and significance was tied to my athletic success and performance.

I was more fortunate than most as I walked on as a try-out at Louisiana Tech University after graduating and earned a full football scholarship. I had a fulfilling college career. But thousands of teens get ground up by the system and have no idea what to do with their life after sports. Every year millions of American kids play their hearts out, dreaming of the opportunity to play college athletics, and maybe even have a shot at professional sports that never happens.

The unrealistic expectations created by society and the media and the near-impossible odds of getting a college scholarship magnify their disappointment. The Center for the Study of Sports in Society reported recently in an extensive survey of athletes' chances of getting a scholarship: Of the 1.5 million eligible high school athletes each year, only one in seventy-five will get a scholarship to play in college. And of the elite who receive scholarships in revenue sports, like football and basketball, fewer than 30 percent will graduate from college. Only one in twelve thousand makes it to the pros. The Center for the Study of Sports goes on to state that out of every 750,000 high school basketball players, only twenty-five will make it to the NBA.[8] The fantasy world created by competitive sports causes many youth to be unprepared for reality and life.

The average career length of the majority of pro-athletes is three to four years. That means when they reach the age of twenty-five to twenty-six years, their careers are over. Life is much tougher than one hundred yards.

Sadly many student athletes are not studious, and they are not prepared academically or emotionally for the real world or for a career. The short-lived success in sports blinds youth to their long-range responsibility and affects their future happiness as adults and parents.

Athletics lasts for such a short period of time. It ends for people. But while it lasts, it creates this make-believe world, where normal rules don't apply. We construct this false unrealistic atmosphere. When it's over, the harsh reality sets in; that's the cruel joke we play on youth. Everybody wants to experience that superlative moment, and being an athlete can give you that. It's Camelot for them, but there's even life after it.[9]

With the kind of glory and adulation these kids have received for a season of their lives, it's very difficult for them to understand and adjust to real life. High school sports has gotten youth "all dressed up with no place to go." In America, we applaud and cheer loudly, and forget quickly. In this competition-based culture, you're only as good as your last performance.

Steroids Epidemic

In this performance-based, sports-crazed culture we have lost perspective as high school athletics programs have reached excessive extremes.

A study just released by the Center for Study of Sports in Society found 36 percent of high school athletes surveyed knew someone who used steroids. "It's an epidemic," says Dr. William Taylor of American College of Sports Medicine. "We're still in the up phase, and it's going to get worse before it gets better."[10]

As another study by the inspector general's office said, four hundred thousand to five hundred thousand of all adolescents, grades seven through twelve, use or have used steroids. Many adolescents use anabolic steroids, not just for sports but also for appearance. Many experts say society places too much emphasis on winning. Coaches and parents might contribute indirectly or directly to an athlete's perception that he or she might not be fast enough or strong enough. Teens know anabolic steroids can make them bigger, stronger and faster. However, long-term steroid use is definitely dangerous.

Recent research indicates that steroid use has been a major factor in heart disease, a cancer-causing agent, degenerative bone, elevated blood pressure, liver cancer, prostate cancer, dangerous cholesterol levels, hormonal problems, joint problems, psychiatric problems, and other possible harmful effects. The use of steroids especially among teens is a "time bomb" that will explode.[10]

Charles Yesalis, professor of human development at Penn State and a noted expert on steroids, said, "Steroids assist the child in what some people refer to as one of the major religions in our society: sports."[12]

Roid rage is a term used to describe the uncontrollable, unpredictable, explosive, violent, angry aggression among steroid users. Incidences of rape and violent assaults have been attributed to steroid use.

Robert Atwell, president of the American Council on Education, states: "It's the nature of this highly competitive society of ours that loves winners and hates losers. High school and college athletics feed this insatiable appetite of Americans to win at all costs."[13]

The Lyle Alzado Tragedy

Recently, on the cover of *Sports Illustrated,* forty-two-year-old Lyle Alzado, former all-pro and fifteen-year NFL star admits to massive use of steroids and human growth hormones. He believes this caused his inoperable brain cancer. He is currently taking chemotherapy treatments, has lost his hair, and sixty pounds. Alzado says, "I'm sick and I'm scared." Fighting for his life, he is now just a shell of the once mighty football warrior that was in total control. Alzado says 80 percent of the athletes he knows use performance enhancing steroids. He says, "I'm sorry I lied. I'm sorry success meant so much to me. I would give my superbowl rings and career for a healthy life."

A sad postscript: Lyle Alzado, former NFL All-Pro, died of brain cancer at age forty-three, just over a year after his diagnosis. Alzado attributed his cancer to twenty years of extensive steroid use. He admitted he couldn't live without steroids. The disease (cancer) proved an unbeatable foe, reducing this massive gladiator, known for his bone-jarring violence on the gridiron to a whispering shadow of a man.

Spectator Mentality

Sports also feed the "spectator mentality" among youth and adults. Professor Jacques Ellul in *The Technological Bluff*, says that we are obsessed by a stream of endless diversions that make us more prone to addiction, inaction and apathy as a society. Sports in North America are a great diversion, a social trap for youth and the rest of society. They are diversions not just in the sense of amusement or pleasure, but in diverting us from thinking about real priorities, others' needs, our human condition and the need for involvement in our culture.[14]

Jacques Ellul states, "I would say quite plainly that the greatest threat to Western society today is not communism, or Americanism, or the economic crisis, or drugs, or alcohol, or resurgent racism, but our absorption in sports, games and other distracting amusements that cause a degradation, disengagement, escapism and the loss of meaning that come in through amusement distractions." Our preoccupation with sports and amusement is one of the most dangerous factors affecting the current youth culture and future society. *Youth become fascinated with various distracting amusements, constant entertainment and continual self-gratification; this produces mass mediocrity in our culture.*[15]

The electronic mass media has transformed sports into an

enormous spectacle and daily ritual for millions of Americans. As a result of shrewd, intense marketing efforts, sports have become a national obsession and major industry: the bottom line is money. The consumption of sporting events in contemporary culture is a way of life. Even if there's a major crisis, we must find a way to see our games.

Decade of Envy

We conditioned the generation of baby-boomer teens in the '60s to believe that, not only could they have it all, they deserved it all. The current generation of teens expects no less, and yet the unprecedented convergence of demographics and economic transition threatens their dreams. A job market that is over-saturated with college graduates, with no guarantees of a position and fierce competition in the workplace creates a hostile environment. The upheaval atmosphere of high-tech streamlining and corporate mergers has reduced job security and limited opportunities for teens and has created an uncertain and stagnant economy. *As the door closes on the era of having it all, we're ripe for a dangerous epidemic of envy in the '90s.*

The desires and expectations of youth have continued to be fueled by the lavish life-styles and fulfilling relationships they are shown by the media. Despite their need for secure relationships and financial security, the fulfillment of the American dream will be available to fewer teens during the '90s. These cultural conditions are a catalyst for envy:

- Too many teens expect and cannot find a well-paying job after graduating from high school.
- Too many teens who expected to attend college or professional schools will not be able to afford it.
- Too many teens who graduate from college expecting to get a good job will not have one. The term NIKE — No Income Kids with Education — currently describes half of the college graduates who must live at home because they can't get a job. Seventy-five percent of all eighteen- to twenty-five-year-olds live at home.
- Too many teens who expected to attain high career goals and an extravagant life-style (more common in less austere and

competitive times) will be disappointed.

- Too many teens expecting a fulfilling relationship will not find one.
- Too many teens exposed to affluence through the media live in low-income and poverty conditions.

These factors have created a perilous atmosphere in the '90s that could be supercharged with envy, desperation and anger.

Envy is not a gentle emotion; it's aggressive — "I want what you have, and I want to take it away from you; and if I can't do that, I'll spoil or destroy it!" Envious people live in a perpetual state of frustration and anger, always focusing on what others around them have, feeling cheated in comparison. Envy is unlike jealousy, which is based on love and focuses on possessing the loved object and removing the rival; envy originates in hate and can be all-consuming, even murderous, in intensity and actions.

Your Sneakers or Your Life

A recent *Sports Illustrated* cover entitled "Your Sneakers or Your Life," focused on the frightening trend in America's cities where kids are killing kids over sneakers and other sports apparel. In some cities, violence over sportswear is commonplace. In Chicago, about fifty incidents involving sports jackets and athletic shoes are reported each month.[16]

Youth are enticed by and engulfed in a flood of high-powered TV advertising techniques using well-known stars and fascinating images with catch-phrases that make obtaining the athletic shoes seem extraordinarily hip, cool and necessary. These shoes and other sportswear have become status symbols and reflect the attitude: I must have this to be somebody.

Sociology professor Mervin Daniel at Morgan State says, "These kids are driven by peer pressure and greed. What is advertised on TV and whatever your peers are doing, you do it too." *Society's values are out of sync; we've lost perspective of what really matters. The result is deadly.*[17]

For fifteen-year-old Michael Thomas, it definitely was deadly. A ninth grader at Meade Senior High School in Maryland, Thomas was found strangled on May 2, 1989. Charged with first-degree murder was James Martin, seventeen, a basketball buddy who allegedly took

Thomas' two-week-old Air Jordan basketball shoes and left Thomas' barefoot body in the woods near school.[18]

Youth view everything in life as a means to get a better car, more clothes, more things; they believe that happiness is another product to be purchased. They attempt to substitute more money and things for what is really meaningful. This results in the loss of significance.

This is what life in the fast lane is all about. Youth today are trapped in an emptiness that only possessions can fill. Youth view money as their greatest source of security, but they can never have enough. They have come to believe that money and things can solve every problem and fear. They pursue this illusion and intensify their problems and their fears of never having enough, always wanting more. This materialistic, monster-consumer culture increases anxiety, fantasy and depression among teens.

Cultural Threat

Just as envy can destroy individuals, it can be disastrous for a culture when it becomes the norm. Widespread envy destroys a sense of community and relationships. Energy is diverted into attack and defense rather than in a kind of joyous recognition that there is enough to go around—even if there's not enough, we will share what we've got. But envy in a culture of entitlement can encourage mediocrity, violence and obsession.

The Monster of Materialism

In a materialistic, consumer-oriented culture, we equate success with money and things.

The materialistic mind-set came to the forefront during the 50s. As the level of affluence rapidly increased, good parenting became synonymous with gratification. Concerned parents wanted to give their baby-boomer children all the advantages they never had. Material fulfillment and caring were linked in the public mind. With each successive decade, the possessing-of-things mentality has been nurtured, creating a materialistic monster among teens. For youth today success is measured by possessions or monetary wealth.

Money has become the "new sex." *Newsweek* describes Americans as having achieved a new dimension of consciousness called "transcendental acquisition"—the pursuit of just a little more.[19] Many youth are substituting things for a lack of relationships and real purpose in their lives. The dominant spirituality of this generation is consumerism. Consumerism goes a step further than materialism. Consumerism has created a things-oriented culture, where not only are things worshiped but people treat each other as things.[20] The materialistic mind-set produces a manipulative and exploitive atmosphere where youth use each other like products or services.

Economic uncertainties and a fast-changing atmosphere have created a high-anxiety culture. Anxiety causes people to get caught up in the money-and-things treadmill. Youth sense the most important thing in life is financial security, due to their parents' emphasis on having the good life, and the fear they may not achieve it. Baby-boomer parents have helped perpetuate the materialistic, consumer mind-set as the key to life.

Instant Fix

We live in a society where everything from relationships and services to success must take place as quickly as possible. The media feeds this instant attitude; for $9.99 or $19.95 you can purchase almost anything you want.

Character qualities like discipline, patience, sacrifice and commitment don't sell very well. We would rather not have them. Youth expect success and fulfillment to happen instantly, conveniently and as painlessly as possible; after all, that's the way they do it on TV and in the movies.

The success-motivation industry is thriving; they can sell you instant and immediate success. By purchasing a tape series, a book or by attending their seminars, you will experience success now. I received some of their material recently; in bold letters it read: *It doesn't take years to change your life; it only takes a few minutes.* These super-success tapes will wipe out irrational fears and problems in as little as ten minutes. *Gain lasting self-esteem instantly. Learn how to handle hard criticism in twenty minutes. Change lifelong habits in less than one hour. Relieve inner conflicts in three quarters of an hour or less.* Gain the trust, respect and success you deserve immediately for a ridiculously low price, of course.

The "microwave mentality" says success and significance are as near as the TV dinner. Just pop it in, and with less effort and strain, you can enjoy lasting fulfillment.

Comfort Zone

The comfort zone is the area of thoughts and actions within which we feel most comfortable. It's all the things we've done or thought often enough to feel comfortable doing. Anything we haven't done before, which stretches our limits or makes us uncomfortable, puts us outside the confines of the comfort zone. Fear of failure keeps us in the comfort zone. Young people who won't accept a challenge, who try to avoid painful reality are stuck in the comfort zone. Too many youth are under-challenged; we have expected too little from them. As a result, we're getting what we expected — a rising tide of mediocrity. The comfort zone becomes the dead zone.

When youth won't accept a challenge or take a risk, they are too comfortable. The comfort zone breeds apathy. Youth have been over-entertained by the media and feel powerless to change a very complex high-tech world; the result is apathy.

In the comfort zone, any choice, action or inaction can be justified to perfection, substituting comfort for significance. The comfort zone distorts reality and causes society to deceive itself, where comfort is substituted for significance.

The Missing Dimension

Boredom is rampant in the youth culture today, symptomatic of the loss of meaning in their lives. Teens have experienced so much, so fast, so young that they have become bored with life. The most important and critical dimension is the spiritual dimension, which is our capacity to know God and fulfill His purpose for our lives. Too many young people have never developed the spiritual facet of their being. This is the major cause for a lack of meaning and boredom.

The Illusion of Popularity

Although many trends have swept across America in the last three decades, the problem of popularity (and the alternative, loneliness) still ranks as a top teen concern. "Whatever else is achieved, everyone knows that being popular is the ultimate prize for the American teenager."[21] But popularity can mean both pleasure and pain.

The peer group has always been a powerful influence on the behavior, attitudes and sense of significance of teens. However, the effect of the peer group has gained impact due to the broken family and lack of positive parental role models. Parents are influencing their children and teens less than ever because they are not there for them. This situation increases the need for popularity.

The pursuit of the popularity dream can be a catch-22 for many teens. Even after they've achieved popularity status, they feel the constant pressure to maintain the image. Here are some comments from youth about popularity:

1. Being popular means wearing all the right clothes, having as many cute boyfriends or girlfriends that you can, saying all the right things and having a perfect body.
2. Popularity means having a lot of friends, and it doesn't have to be for the right reasons — most of the time it's not.
3. Popularity means projecting a certain image, even if it's not really you. It means being fake just to impress and be accepted.
4. Popularity is attracting a large and admiring circle of friends, based on impression as much as reality.

Millions of teens chase the elusive rainbow of popularity and many never seem to catch it; many of those who do realize it was an illusion of success. Popularity for many youth is a mirage. The harder they try to hold it, the farther it slips away.

The Apathy Epidemic

If there is one attitude that characterizes the youth culture today, it is apathy, which is defined as a lack of concern, or disinterest; without emotion; indifference; and a lack of action or will.

Recently, at a national conference for student leadership, outstanding youth from all across America were asked: What are the major problems facing U.S. teens today? For the second year in a row, alcohol and apathy were listed by student leaders as the two most serious problems confronting today's young people.[22]

Here are some factors that have produced an atmosphere of

apathy among youth:

1. *Media-Saturated Society*: Youth are continually inundated with an array of exciting hypnotic media images and sounds, which makes real life boring. Media "over-stimulation" produces a desire that can be fulfilled only by watching, which increases their apathy; they are programmed to watch rather than do.

The media desensitizes youth by constantly exposing them to human problems, suffering, misery, starvation, war, death, disasters and other tragedies. They experience a "media compassion" where youth are moved to do something immediately, but it only lasts until they switch channels. *They become more numb and indifferent to the pain and needs of others. This is becoming an increasingly jaded generation.*

2. *Complex High-Tech Society*: Young people feel overwhelmed by a fast-changing, unpredictable society that causes them to feel confused and out of control. Also, high-tech society has made young people feel they are unimportant and incapable of affecting real change, as our culture has not provided significant roles for youth in which they can contribute. The result is uninvolvement, disenchantment and disillusionment. *Youth are caught in a turbulent society constantly in transition, becoming increasingly complex, and they are confronted with unprecedented situations. Also the competitive crunch and the fear of failure is producing widespread apathy.*

3. *Unemotional Relationships*: In an excessively sensual culture, sex is projected to youth as the key to emotional fulfillment and is viewed as a symbol of maturity. Society has not only condoned but even encouraged sexual activity among teens as part of enlightened behavior and understanding.

As a result, today's teens are having more sex than ever before; over 80 percent of all teens have had sex by the time they are nineteen. We've created a kind of frenzied sexuality among youth where premarital sex is promoted as the magical answer to solve their problems and meet their needs. Youth are having more sex, but are unable to experience true intimacy; the effect is unemotional, indifferent relationships. Premarital sex doesn't mean more love; it means more pain. The void of intense emotions is a result of the fear of rejection and continual self-gratification. Youth use sex, trying to fulfill emotional intimacy; instead, it causes an emotional ripping and finally emotional detachment or apathy.

Josh McDowell says, "Often we think of hatred as being the opposite of love. In reality, it's not; the opposite of love is indifference or apathy. The greatest affront to another human being is to act as if he or she doesn't exist."[23]

This sex-oriented culture has set up two generations for apathetic relationships where there are no tears, no joy, no shock, no commitment, no intimacy—only casual indifference.

Over-stimulated by the mass media, overpowered by a high-tech society, jaded by surface relationship and devoid of real purpose, an epidemic of apathy has been created through meaningless activity and cultural drift.

"Future Shock is a time phenomenon, a product of the greatly accelerated rate of change in society. It arises from the super-imposition of a totally new culture on the old one. Now imagine an entire generation suddenly and prematurely transported into this radical new world."

Alvin Toffler
Future Shock

This frantic-rushing culture has produced the "time warrior": the driven individual who can't stop too long or he or she will have to confront the emptiness in their own lives.

Chapter 10

Time in Three Dimensions: Futuristic Expectations

Do not forget this one thing, that with the Lord one day is as a thousand years, and a thousand years as one day (2 Pet. 3:8 NKJ).

Time Perspectives

The concept of time travel has fascinated humans for years. The possibility of being transported back to the past or ahead to the future is a very alluring prospect fueled by two powerful obsessions that profoundly affect our attitudes, choices and life-styles in the present. One is the desire to go back and change our regrets of the past (failures, disappointments, guilt and pain). The other is the fear of the future, being paralyzed by boredom, uncertainty, anxiety and fear about future relationships, events and situations.

The desire to be able to change the past, or to know and control the future, is a major preoccupation and behavioral motivation for youth and adults.

Nothing influences how individuals think and cultures interact more than our perspective on time. The impact of time on youth and their perspective on the past, present and future profoundly affect every facet of their lives.

Current research indicates that our anxieties about time greatly determine and shape our personalities, our individual behavior, our sense of purpose and how we cope with problems and pressures. The lack of perspective on the past, present and future has produced widespread depression, addiction, neurotic fears and a narcissistic life-style in today's youth culture.

Contemporary society is governed by a detailed timetable that dominates and dictates everything we do. Never in history have we been more conscious of time, with watches and clocks to remind us of the schedules we must keep. All year round, we get up, work, go to school, eat, sleep, play, visit—living by what the clock tells us.

The hectic, accelerated pace of life has created a loss of perspective among youth regarding the dimensions of past, present and future, creating a "time distortion." The three time dimensions seemed to have lost their distinctiveness, running together or overlapping, causing a preoccupation with one facet of time while completely excluding another. Each dimension is inextricably interconnected; if we are out of balance in one dimension, it will create a distortion and an inability to effectively deal with the other dimensions. This "overlapping time process" allows past events to intrude on the present, present attitudes and choices to shape and determine the future, and future hopes, fears and uncertainties to invade the present.

The impact of one time dimension on another can have tremendous positive or negative implications on the attitudes, expectations and choices of young people. Their perspective on the past, present and future profoundly affects their behavior and their future happiness as individuals. Let's examine the three dimensions of time and their effect on the current youth culture in North America.

Time Past

The first dimension is time past, the time that was. It is yesterday, encompassing all of the events and experiences that have already occurred. Psychologists and sociologists study our past to understand our behavior in the present.

Sometimes it's a lot of fun to look back and remember the past;

we call it nostalgia, enjoying an experience or event that happened in the past. You think about someone or something that was special to you, or maybe you hear a song, and magically you are transported to yesterday.

However, there's a dark side to our past as we remember experiences, people and situations that were very painful. When we think about them, our mood changes; we become depressed, frustrated, disappointed or angry.

Regrets of the Past. We've all wanted to go back in time and change something that happened or didn't happen. The "if only" syndrome has affected us all: "If only I hadn't done that. . . . If only I knew then what I know now. . . If only I had said the right thing, it would be different. . . . If only I could do it over again."

Who hasn't regretted a poor decision, a thoughtless action or a missed opportunity? As teens and adults we have a tendency to live in the mire of our past. Agonizing over failures and regrets, we develop a "woulda, coulda, shoulda" mentality. If only we could rewind our lives like videotape and erase the garbage, editing out the painful regrets of the past. This preoccupation with the past can have a paralyzing effect on the present, manipulating and even devastating a teen's future.

Common Failures and Regrets. Several major research studies asked youth between the ages of fourteen and twenty-three to share the regrets or failures they would change if they could. Here are the most common responses:

1. Thinking one failure means total failure
2. Loving for the wrong reasons
3. Falling into the sex trap
4. Being overwhelmed by loneliness
5. Being content with surface relationships
6. Believing good looks and popularity mean happiness
7. Allowing other people to control choices and life-style
8. Not being closer to parents
9. Not reaching out to other kids who were hurting[1]

Many teens live in a constant state of turmoil from regrets and failures of the past, continually looking back over their shoulder, haunted by what was. The real danger is allowing the negative past to control the present. Living in yesterday robs teens of present opportunity and fulfillment. The highest achievers have failed twice as much as the average person. They understand that their failures are part of the journey to ultimate success.

Guilt. No feeling is more devastating than guilt. The pain, fear of punishment and alienation caused by guilt is an emotional grenade. We live in a guilt-ridden society where teens and parents alike are in the devastating grip of guilt.

Dr. Keith Olson says teenagers experience several kinds of guilt. "True guilt is a situation or condition of fact, but false or condemning guilt is based on a feeling of pain and rejection and not reality."[2] Irrational guilt or false guilt can be defined as guilt that is without sin or wrongdoing; therefore, there is no rational basis for the guilt.

Guilt from the past can hang over our lives like a dark cloud, keeping us from experiencing real freedom and joy of the present. We've all done things in the past that we'd like to forget. Many past-oriented teens are trapped in time past, unable to break the bondage and pain of what was, so preoccupied with past regrets, failures and guilt that their perspective of the present and the future is distorted.

False Guilt is the result of something we unintentionally said or did that hurt another person's feelings. Teenagers can feel this guilt with stabbing intensity. Sometimes this kind of guilt is increased by fears of being rejected for one's mistakes.[3]

The *guilt complex* is another form of irrational, false guilt affecting the youth culture. Guilt-prone teens feel guilty about everything, and they have a negative and self-condemning attitude. Guilt-oriented people feel that they really deserve to be punished and aren't worth anything, making statements such as "I'm just a no-good loser. . . . It's always my fault. . . . I never do anything right." The guilt complex combines false guilt with true guilt and is marked by an inability to distinguish between the two. Adults and teens alike experience this crippling guilt, not only from what they think they've done, but also for what they think they should have done. Past-oriented, guilt-ridden teens are extremely vulnerable to risky behavior such as drug abuse, teen pregnancy, violence, suicide, dropping out and other destructive actions.

Manipulating guilt arises from a deliberate attempt to control someone. Teenagers can be extremely manipulating when they want something or someone. The guilt pressure in relationships ("If you really love me—") can be immense. A peer group's controlling influence can cause teens to do just about anything to avoid being left out. Manipulating parents can create a cycle of guilt in an effort to control their teenagers.

Guilt and Conviction. Robert McGee, founder of Rapha, distinguishes between guilt and conviction, emphasizing the condemnation our sin deserves and the loving motivation prompted by God to deal with wrong actions and bring honor to Him.

> *Guilt* focuses on the state of being condemned, one's unworthiness as a person and the feeling you deserve to be punished. Guilt causes alienation from God, others, self-rejection and magnified feelings of depression, fear and shame. This further isolates youth from relationships or drives them to destructive relationships and life-styles that perpetuate their fears, guilt and pain.
>
> *Conviction* focuses on the destructive effects of and the root causes of guilt which occur when a person sins against God. Conviction is a function of God's Spirit to protect us from the potentially dangerous and destructive emotional and spiritual consequences of guilt. Its purpose is restoration and forgiveness of past events and situations which affect every relationship youth have.
>
> Conviction produces a fear of the destructiveness of the act itself. This behavior is destructive to me and others, and robs me of what God intends for me.[4]

Conviction can result from a life-style that is totally self-centered, where youth use people for their benefit or do something out of fear, hate or deception; the result is necessary convicting guilt.

Escape to the Past. When the present is stressful and disappointing and the future is uncertain, the past looks very appealing. The nostalgia illusion sees the past through rose-colored glasses, choosing only to remember the good times. The past represents that perfect problem-free time frame, which was never really as ideal as we remember it. We tend to block out any unpleasant memories of the past. The song "Yesterday" by the Beatles describes when "all my troubles seemed so far away. Now it looks as though they're here to stay, oh I believe in yesterday."

For many teens, the past was a wonderful and exciting time compared to the present. The past was when they were going steady with that special someone — now they're alone. The past was when they were living in their hometown — now they've moved and everything seems so different and strange. The past was when Mom and Dad were still together — now they're divorced, and they see only one parent regularly.

In reality, the past was a much happier time for some teens compared to the disillusionment of the present and the anxiety of the future. So, the past becomes the great escape, not only from the present but from reality. When the present is too painful and the future is too scary, teens become "frozen in time past."

Baby-Boomer Parents. The most recent research says baby boomers are the most disappointed and unhappy segment of the population. These boomer teens of the '60s and early '70s have found it very difficult to come down from the "wonder years" when the dream was alive. The '60s generation has had a very difficult time breaking away from the eternal youth mind-set of the past. The present has not met their expectations, so they get lost in yesterday.

> The baby-boomer generation is into nostalgia, a phenomenon one writer calls a "functional emotion" for baby boomers. Nostalgia, then, is a functional emotion which reinforces a sagging sense of identity and meaning that can help either a person or generation cope with difficult and disappointing times. In nostalgia, the baby boomers have found a haven from anxiety and depression and a means of reaffirming stable, secure identities and significance badly shaken during the passage from the adolescent years and the good old '60s days. For the baby boomers, it was not that the past was so wonderful, it is that the present is so troubling.[5]

Loss of Historical Time. We've discussed some of the negative influences the past can have on teens' lives. However, the positive and long-range impact of experiences from the past have helped shape our lives. Christopher Lasch describes our culture as one that has lost touch with its past:

> The cultural devaluation of the past has become one of the most important symptoms of the cultural crisis in North America. A denial of the past, superficially progressive and optimistic, proves on closer analysis to embody the despair of a society that cannot face the

> future. We are fast losing our sense of generational continuity, the sense of belonging to a succession of generations originating in the past and stretching into the future. It is this waning sense of historical time, in particular, the erosion of any strong concern for posterity, that distinguishes the spiritual crisis we face today.[6]

Nearly two thousand years ago, something happened that dramatically changed not only humanity's past but its present and future. Jesus Christ hung on a cross, suspended between heaven and hell, as He died and was raised for the sins of the human race. At that moment, the three dimensions of the time continuum converged at the cross and became forever united, affecting all three time dimensions simultaneously just as this historic event has changed human lives forever.

Time Present

Rushed Time. According to several major surveys, four out of five people say they are constantly pressed for time. The pace of life in North America is moving at warp speed, where everything is defined in terms of how fast and convenient you can do something. Our fascination with speed has created a culturally impatient society where we confine everything in our lives, including relationships, to short, convenient blocks of time.

Never has time present moved so quickly or had more impact for North American teenagers. Their world has not only sped up but is also much more complicated, more stressful and more dangerous than ever before. They sense life is moving too quickly. This causes them to feel overwhelmed and out of control.

Time present is rushing so fast it is merging with the future, causing youth to become "time disoriented." Accelerated time is drastically altering the way teens perceive reality and their perspective on the present. In today's driven atmosphere, young people tend to miss the present while anticipating the future. This is a restless generation that must constantly be on the move and doing something to be happy. If they stop for too long, they'll have to confront the loneliness and desperation in their lives.

Seizing the Moment. Life is a series of crucial moments, significant moments, moments of decision, moments of action. When youth are confronted with a specific situation, they sense that they have a unique opportunity, never to return again in just that way; but because of fear, insecurity or timidity, teens let the moment slip by. They do nothing; they miss their moment in present time.

Each time young people fail to take action, they become more jaded, desensitized and less likely to respond the next time a challenge arises. Many young people fail to comprehend the power and importance of the present moment.

There is a moment when you reach out to someone who desperately needs a friend. There is a moment when you decide either to take a stand for what you believe or continue to allow your friends to control your life. There is a moment in the midst of your pain when you decide to give in to it or rise above it. There is a moment when you look in the mirror and choose to be real or continue to wear a mask.

Present Choices. The present choices teens are making create a ripple effect that not only impacts the present but also shapes and determines their future happiness. The tremendous increase in choices and the acceleration of time has produced what Alvin Toffler refers to as "decisional over-stimulation." As our culture forces teens to make more difficult decisions in shorter periods of time, their feelings of confusion and stress are multiplied.

Very few young people understand the scope of pain and destruction they can bring into their lives by the cycle of choices made in the present. The kind of relationships teens have right now will be the kind they have when they are married. If they are insecure, manipulating and desperate in relationships today, these problems will only increase tomorrow.

Present Instant Gratification. Most teens are present oriented in their life-style choices and time perception. The dominant passion is to live for the moment, the immediate pleasure, the thrill and excitement. They are more concerned about present satisfaction than future happiness.

They are addicted to the present and believe "you only go around once in life, so you better grab it now because it may not be there later." Their future is uncertain, depressing and scary, so they live like there's no tomorrow. For too many teens, the present time is their only reality — what's here and now. What's immediate is real;

anything else is irrelevant. These youth sacrifice future happiness for the moment's pleasure.

Present-oriented teens don't want to think about the long-range consequences of their current life-style; they convince themselves that it will all somehow work out in the end.

Youth are engrossed in their present little world of MTV, sex parties, drugs, hanging out at the mall, cruisin' and drinking. The future seems so far off, so depressing, so unreal. They become obsessed with living for themselves and living for the moment, rather than for their predecessors or future generations.

Much of the youth culture has lost its perspective on the present time dimension. This causes them to lose perspective on the future, which can be devastating.

Priorities. After twenty-four hours, today becomes yesterday. The present is the only guaranteed time you have. The past is gone, never to return, and the future may never come.

Today, teens are constantly on the go with part-time jobs, sports, music lessons, concerts, malls, restaurants, school club meetings, dating and church. Their schedules are so frantic that they have appointment books to rival those of adults. A wide array of activities can cause them to lose track of their priorities.

A hectic and busyness-oriented society creates a heightened sense of urgency, the feeling that there isn't enough time to get things accomplished. As a culture we are busy, frantically pursuing a lot of things, but not the most important things. The urgent mind-set produces a "driven" attitude, which causes teens and adults alike to feel they must constantly keep racing and pushing to reach their goals. Parents substitute the urgent for the significant; the teenager wants more than anything to spend quality time with a father who doesn't have time because he's too busy being successful.

How many teens and parents would give anything to hear the words, "I love you," or "I'm sorry . . . please forgive me," or "I forgive you," and feel the caring hug of that person. But, so many other seemingly urgent things keep us from doing the things that matter the most.

The Disappointment Epidemic

Positive expectation has a dual nature: the belief that an event will occur and the desire for it to do so. It is the wish contained within every expectation that gives it life and incredible impact. Expectation is a powerful influence in our lives; it has the capacity to both enlarge and diminish our experience. It can inspire us to phenomenal feats beyond our comprehension, or it can drastically limit our lives to the commonplace, or even to a bleak, gloomy existence.

Expectations profoundly affect young people's attitudes, motivations and relationships, and also help to form their view of the world. Their perception of reality is based greatly on what they expect to see or experience. There are really two kinds of expectation — positive and negative — each reflecting how we envision what is to come. Positive expectation results in disappointment when it goes unmet; failed negative expectation brings relief and sometimes great joy.

Disappointment is based on a past expectation of an opportunity, event or experience we thought was going to be an exciting encounter but wasn't. It turned out to be a disaster, nothing like we thought it would be. Our expectations were crushed. Anticipation and expectation build excitement and raise our level of desire for a certain course of events. The higher our level of expectation, the deeper the disappointment.

Disappointment is a widespread phenomenon on the rise in the '90s among teens. Teens who thought everything would be great after high school were disappointed. Or someone they trusted and looked up to let them down.

Failing to belong to that certain peer group is extremely disappointing for teens. Wanting to date that certain someone who isn't interested in them at all can be very disappointing. Looking in the mirror can be very disappointing for teens who wish they could look like or be like someone other than themselves. The major disappointment for young people today is the lack of close family relationships or the divorce of their parents.

Disillusionment, depression and anger have created cynical attitudes. When what youth expect to experience and enjoy doesn't occur, their future expectations become negative and fearful.

Stages of Disappointment

Dr. David Brandt defines disappointment as the struggle involved in moving from the failure of a desired and expected outcome through the pain of loss to an acceptance of new circumstances.[7] He identifies the six stages of disappointment we go through as:

1. Expectation
2. Expectation Lost
3. Alarm
4. Resistance
5. Loss and Resignation
6. Acceptance

These stages of disappointment are very similar to the stages Elisabeth Kubler-Ross identifies for a dying person who is accepting impending death.[8]

Not all disappointments are equal; some are devastating, but others scarcely seem to affect us. It depends upon the level of emotional involvement in the expectation. The greater the investment, the more severe the disappointment.

Future Time

The time dimension that has always fascinated us and captivated our attention is the future — the time that is to come, what will be. It is tomorrow — that mystical, hopeful, fearful, unknown destination of the future.

Future Oriented. Never as a culture have we been more preoccupied with the future. Advanced technologies allow us to probe and project every aspect of life. The environmental issue is an example of a future projection that has become a major concern in North America and the world. The greenhouse effect and other environmental concerns are now focusing on the future, long-term consequences and possible prevention. Americans are mesmerized by the future and tantalized by the prospect of controlling it.[9]

Nobody has felt the impact of this future-oriented mentality more than the North American teen. The '90s will be a pivotal decade for the youth culture and the rest of American society. How youth perceive the future is critical in determining their attitudes, expectations, life-style choices and future happiness.

Reality 101. Ernest Fleishman, Scholastic Education Director, says, "The pessimism is surprising. Ordinarily, these are the years [in high school] when the future is supposed to be promising."[10] The figures are a warning sign; there is a lot of disillusionment, fear and negativism about the future.

In *USA Today* an article, entitled "Reality 101," painted a dismal job market picture for college graduates. Experts are saying they haven't seen the job market this bad for college graduates in more than thirty years.

The Synergy Effect. The present and the future are deeply intertwined as both affect and reflect each other. Present attitudes and actions definitely shape the future; and future expectations, fears or hopes create present reality. The paradox is that youth can prepare for the future by realizing that the future is an extension of one's present.

In this fast-changing, high-tech, uncertain culture, the deep desire among youth to take control of their lives and their future will emerge as a desperate need in the '90s.

Future Expectations. Young people's future expectations play a crucial role in their ability to cope with pressures and problems. Their desires build anticipation of the future. Negative expectations mirror their fears and the dreaded thought that their wishes will go unfulfilled. Expectations — positive or negative — have the power to limit or enhance our success because we tend to fulfill our expectations or the expectations of others.

Behavioral psychologist George Mead states that too much emphasis is placed on the past in analyzing what determines the nature of human personality. Psychology's focus on the past has caused us to ignore one of the most important determinants of personality: perception of the future. What people can become, according to Mead, is even more important than what they have been. People's hopes and dreams are highly significant to who they are now and who they will become.[11]

Pessimistic Outlook. The need for hope in the future powerfully affects teenagers. Recent research shows that a majority of today's youth view the future with anxiety and pessimism. A Gallup study revealed that 75 percent of today's youth see the teen years of their baby-boomer parents as being a happier, safer and more hopeful time for teenagers.[12]

"Kids no longer have a sense that things are getting better in the world," says Dr. David Elkind.[13] Today, the average teen's greatest fears are: losing their parents through divorce; being a victim of violent crime, such as homicide, robbery, assault or rape; not getting a job; not being successful; not having a happy marriage.

> What makes these negative views about the future so significant is the fact that, for most of us, 90 percent of our life motivations are based on the future: future job, future family, future home, future dreams, future expectations and fulfillment. We are motivated by our hopes and dreams for the future. When you have lost hope in the future, you have lost one of the greatest motivations for life in the present.[14]

Many youth today feel hopeless. They are preparing for nothing; as a result, they go for instant gratification. Temporary pleasure and excitement become the goals of teens who lose their motivation to realize their future.

The most extreme expression of distrust and a feeling of hopelessness concerning the future is represented by the frighteningly large group of teens who take their lives. Teen suicide has increased (300 percent) over the past thirty years, and is the third leading cause of death, as five thousand youth commit suicide yearly. The greater the level of underlying hopelessness, the more extreme the behavior or actions. This fatalistic outlook is rooted in deep insecurity and the feeling that life has no purpose or meaning.

Future Relationships. A major future concern among youth is the desire for meaningful relationships with family, peers and the opposite sex. However, in this fast-changing, transient society, life becomes more impersonal and uncertain. The duration of relationships is becoming shorter and shorter as we avoid long-term commitments in favor of short-term, self-serving relationships. Alvin Toffler says "we develop a disposable or throw-away mentality."[15]

The frenzied pace of life will interfere with our relationships; we will be unable to spend quality time with people on a consistent basis, and convenience will be substituted for sacrifice. Nearly two out of three marriages in America end in divorce, and the trend toward divorce is increasing. The U.S. Census Bureau recently stated that married couples make up the smallest percentage of the nation's households in two hundred years, reflecting two decades of skyrocketing divorce rates and delays in marriages. Young people are waiting longer to get married than ever before.[16]

The National Center for Health states that cohabitation is more prevalent today than ever. More unmarried couples are living together while establishing their careers and economic stability. "Half of all adults under the age of thirty will live with someone before they get married. Sixty percent of recently married couples indicate that they lived with their new spouse before getting married."[17] Cohabiting couples are 50 percent more likely to break up than married couples.

George Barna states, "By 2000, Americans will generally believe that a life spent with the same person (partner) is both unusual and unnecessary." During the '90s, getting married two or three times will become the norm until not getting married at all is the enlightened approach. "We will continue our current moral transition by accepting multiple sexual relationships with one person at a time — serial monogamy — to be the civilized and moral way to behave."[18]

The cultural attitude in America concerning marriage, sex and family is drastically affecting youth's concepts of relationships and commitment. The loneliness and isolation that is being mass-produced in this high-tech society will continue to increase as we approach the year 2000. Youth are losing their ability to communicate effectively and be sensitive to each other's needs. The need for quality relationships among youth will intensify as they desperately search for roots in a transient culture, someone to hold onto who won't leave.

Unemotional Relationships. This competitive, performance-oriented culture makes it difficult for young people to develop loving relationships.[19] "Reach out and use someone" will characterize future relationships. Youth's perception of love is severely distorted by the media and fragmented family situations, making real intimacy difficult to achieve.

The most sexually active generation of youth in history will continue to be more so during the '90s, as our cultural attitudes concerning premarital sex become increasingly permissive. This will produce an "emotionally detached" generation where youth will be incapable of deep commitment to anything except themselves. The frustration and disappointment they experienced in relationships that didn't measure up to their expectations will create an inability to trust anyone. Youth's perspectives on relationships and their value systems will be defined by a morally relativistic culture where we determine our own reality, and where noncommitment and self-seeking relationships abound. These noncommittal relationships will create a crowded emptiness in this emotionally exploited society.

Youth Subcultures. Within our larger American culture are subcultures, among them youth subcultures. These youth subcultures are systems of values, beliefs, behavior patterns, appearance characteristics and language that enable teenagers to form differentiated sectors in our society. These subcultures provide particular cultural views to all who are assimilated into their collective mind-sets. Morality, life-styles, attitudes toward the adult world and even attitudes toward God are established within them as social facts.

Youth subcultures are pervasive; few people escape their conditioning influences. Cultural forces — television, movies, music, media personalities as well as everyday peer relationships — conspire to establish the subculture's mind-set in teenagers everywhere. Any who don't accept the role definitions ascribed to them by subcultural systems are labeled "nerds" or "dorks" or "geeks" and usually ostracized. Across America young people are socialized into subcultures and are forced to conform to the life-styles those subcultures prescribe.[20]

Time Perceptions and Subcultures. One of the most subtle yet important ways that subcultures are established is through time perception. According to Harvard professor Edward Banfield, a given subculture prescribes its own particular sense of time for those who are socialized into it. Banfield claims that what is of crucial significance is how far into the future people are conditioned to imagine themselves. He says that some subcultures establish time perceptions that allow people to think far ahead and have images in their minds of what life will be like for them. Other subcultures condition people so that nothing is real to them except what is immediately present.[21]

Young people who are able to visualize their future potential and who have specific goals are future-oriented teens. They are willing to make present sacrifices and delay gratification to enjoy future rewards. Scott Peck defines "delaying gratification" as the process of scheduling the pain and pleasure of life in such a way as to enhance the pleasure by meeting and experiencing the pain first and getting it over with.[22] Delayed gratification focuses on long-range happiness rather than immediate gratification, which keeps teens from experiencing ultimate gratification. Future-oriented, achieving teens are full of ambition, are goal directed and have a specific plan of action for what they need to do in order to assure themselves a beautiful tomorrow.

When a subculture conditions youth to see the distant future as something very real and important, it prepares them to do whatever is necessary for future fulfillment. But when a subculture conditions young people to view the present moment — the here and now — as the only reality, it sets them up to be self-indulgent pleasure seekers who will sacrifice future happiness for the moment's gratification. The majority of teens are present-oriented in their life-style and attitudes. They live for the moment's gratification, the moment's relationship, the moment's thrill; they view the future as depressing and uncertain.

Transition to the Future. When the future arrives too soon, it creates a "time distortion." Teens are being rocketed into the future so fast that they actually lose their concept of the present. The future is rushing to intrude on the present at such a fast rate that most teens will be totally unprepared and unable to adapt, creating a future-shocked generation. Alvin Toffler says, in the future we will not be asked to adapt to a single new culture but to a blinding succession of temporary cultures. No previous generation has ever faced this situation.[23] The culture is also in a state of moral confusion; the result is mass anxiety and alienation from the future.

Future Anxiety. Anxiety pervades contemporary culture. Many experts say it's the number one psychological and sociological problem in America. Anxiety is defined as: 1) a state of being uneasy, apprehensive, or worried about what may happen; concern about a possible future event; 2) an intense state of this kind characterized by varying degrees of emotional disturbance; 3) an eager but often uneasy desire, such as "an anxiety to do well." Anxiety synonyms include distress, worry, being troubled, fearful, restless, uneasy, fretful. Anxiety affects not only the future; even in our present time, according to recent research, "one out of every six persons in America is seriously affected by anxiety and panic attacks. The fastest-growing segment is among children and teens."[24]

The rushing pace of life, combined with extreme change and less-secure relationships, multiplies the anxiety level among children and youth. Anxiety anticipates a future disaster: teens' anxieties — "I'm not going to get a job...This person I love is about to leave." Even if it's an inaccurate assessment of the situation, they believe it's going to happen. Dr. Archibald Hart says: "Anxiety picks up where fear leaves off and is mostly directed toward imagined or unrealized objects or conditions. Anxiety is more vague and more pervasive."[25]

Youth today feel an extreme sense of vulnerability, which feeds their anxiety. The threat of humiliation, rejection, abandonment or exposure of one's weaknesses can be emotionally paralyzing. Their lack of quality relationships, especially in the family setting, is a major cause of their vulnerability.

Dr. David Burns states that anxiety is also fueled by what he calls "emotional perfectionism," the belief that one must never be anxious, sad or angry about anything. This attitude keeps us from effectively confronting and dealing with our anxiety. The increasing anxiety epidemic among youth has caused an escapist mentality, which ultimately magnifies anxiety and distorts the future. Recently, I spoke at an educational conference, and a number of educators expressed concern over the growing use of Xanax, an anti-anxiety drug used among teens. *USA Today* stated that Xanax had become the U.S.A.'s third most commonly prescribed drug, up from sixth place a year ago.[26]

The New Cynicism. Social analysts cite the rise of cynicism in America in the late '60s to 1973, paralleling protests, riots, assassinations, the Vietnam War, Watergate and the subsequent resignation of President Richard Nixon. In 1975 came a television mega-hit, *Saturday Night Live,* which showcased the mocking, satirical and cynical mind-set that was fast becoming mainstream America.

The New Cynicism in the '90s views everything from politics to family, morality and relationships with an irreverent, ridiculing and disdainful attitude. Youth see life as one big con game where using, manipulating and exploiting is the American way. MTV's *Beavis and Butthead* reflects the cynicism and irreverance of a generation.

This generation doesn't trust anyone or anything anymore. They've been disappointed, used, betrayed and conned one-too-many times. Young people are cynical about relationships, parents, marriage, jobs, school, the future and their lives.

The New Cynicism seems to defy the traditional values of youth — idealism and optimism. Most youth today — 65 percent — view the world as a fake and empty place. They are always looking for the shaft, the rip-off or the trapdoor, because nobody or nothing is real anymore.

State of Youth—Future Tense. There are some dangerous trends emerging that will affect future generations of youth. The current plague of apathy that is rampant among youth could turn angry in the '90s. The current youth culture is like a dormant volcano; seething below the surface is a feeling that society and family's failure to meet youth's "felt" needs for personal fulfillment and happiness is producing an angry generation. This angry generation of youth could lash out in a rage of random senseless violence at the system they believe doesn't care about their pain. In a society that is becoming more impersonal and isolated, they feel disdain, cynicism and betrayal by the system. They don't have control of their lives, and feel irrelevant and insignificant. The youth volcano could erupt as we approach 2000.

The New Racism

Racism is based more on distorted perception than reality. Racism is founded on taught misconceptions and a basic ethnic distrust, irrational suspicions and unfounded fears. Racist attitudes toward others reflect our deep fears and insecurities. "Our attitudes toward others (races) may be the single most important indicator of the character of a people. Our feelings and perceptions about people profoundly affect our behavior as individuals and create the atmosphere of our culture." Since our most important behaviors, attitudes and innovations are an outgrowth of our feelings and perceptions about people, we gain deep insight into our culture by understanding those feelings.[27]

Research expert George Barna states, "As our research has suggested for several years, racial tension in America is on the rise. Americans (nine out of ten) agree that there is a lot of anger and hostility between ethnic and racial groups in America. We can virtually count on race riots ripping America apart in the next ten years unless radical steps are taken by key people in our nation to defuse the impending explosion."[28]

Subtle Racism

A major research study of current black and white attitudes shows: in the '90s there is a subtle, much more insidious and hypocritical racism that exists between blacks and whites. It is a change from the hard-core militant racism that existed in America's earlier years. Many blacks today still feel alienated, exploited and patronized by the system in white America. They feel there is a lot of racism below the surface that smiles and pretends to care but really doesn't. They feel that many whites project an image of concern and acceptance, but they are really unconcerned, insensitive and prejudiced.

Whites may feel they have done everything they can to help, but many blacks didn't take advantage of the opportunities America offers them. Many whites feel that every issue becomes a racial issue, and blacks try to blame every problem on them rather than accepting their responsibilities.

These attitudes of blacks and whites constitute a growing "new racism" in America. Racial tensions and frustration between blacks and whites are on the rise — as deep-seated feelings of hostility, resent, distrust and fear permeate our society and distort reality. *This could be a tremendous opportunity for black and white Christians to come together and demonstrate the love, power and reality of Jesus Christ.*

Young people's attitudes are a reflection and an extension of their parents' understanding and compassion, or prejudices, fears and hatred toward other races.

Economic uncertainties and high-tech transition will continue to cause the job market and career opportunities to shrink for many young people of all races as anger grows. There is currently competition and resentment building between races in the American culture who blame each other for their problems and frustrations. The pie is getting smaller, and we're fighting over who gets a piece of that pie. This could produce an explosive and dangerous situation during the '90s decade.

Pivotal Decade

If current trends continue unabated, an angry generation of youth could emerge during the next ten years, creating rampant anarchy. This potential crisis situation can serve as a unique opportunity and a catalyst for a resurgence of a revolutionary Christianity — there is potential for great gain or great loss.

George Barna says: "The '90s are a pivotal decade in the history of American Christianity. It is a time in which the church will either explode with new vision and aggressiveness or quietly fade into a colorless thread on the fabric of secular culture as irrelevant and insignificant."[29] What will we do? The challenge is there—the future is waiting.

Time in Three Dimensions: Futuristic Expectations

What does it matter if you gain the whole world, but lose your MTV?

"We built this city on rock and roll."

Jefferson Starship

Life has become a marketing event where everything is a commercial.

Chapter 11

We Will Rock You: The Voice of a Generation

Having their understanding darkened, being alienated from the life of God, because of the ignorance that is in them, because of the hardening of their heart; having lost all sensitivity, they have given themselves over to sensuality so as to indulge in every kind of impurity, with a continual lust for more (Eph. 4:18 NKJ; 4:19 NIV).

The Voice of a Generation

The union of television and rock music in the '50s with the coming of Dick Clark's *American Bandstand* created a national youth culture. Youth were no longer isolated from each other. The music-television media produced a sense of extended community among teens. For the first time, all over the country, youth were aware of what others were hearing, seeing and doing. There emerged a national youth consensus of attitudes, values, life-styles and interests. Before this time, teens weren't really conscious of any other youth outside their own local city or community.

Suddenly, a new youth consciousness burst on the scene, with television and rock music launching to the forefront the media-defined youth culture:

> The sheer pervasiveness and constancy of the electronic media, being everywhere all the time, the media have generated for young people shared understandings, concerns and feelings about the world in which they live. From news to sports, comedy, music and drama, the media create for youth emotional and intellectual portraits of themselves, the wider society, their place in it.[1]

Mass communication has become the great equalizer that puts youth in the same cultural area, regardless of their individual personalities or social backgrounds. Throughout the last three decades, youth have had media-shared experiences through teen films, rock music and rock videos, some of the most important cultural artifacts of each teen generation. Interpersonal and mass communication establish the tone and shape of the youth culture in North America.

The Rock Nation

The pulse, mood and shape of the youth culture in North America today and for the last thirty years has been defined and reflected by the rock music subculture. If you've watched a segment of MTV recently, you know that's a frightening statement.

The music seems to speak to the needs, fears, anger and despair of this rock generation when actually it only exploits them. Youth are locked in an intense emotional bonding with their music and rock stars.

Rock music has produced a superficial intimacy, hollow image identity and artificial, temporary meaning through watching, listening, purchasing of products and emulating rock life-styles.

It determines reality for many young people today who are unable to separate fantasy from reality.

This generation is a rock nation, where the "rock culture" is the "youth culture." "Come unto me, all who are bored, insecure and lonely," says the new video prophet, "and I will give you identity, intimacy and fun. My images are attractive and my sounds are catchy."[2]

The Rock Concert Experience

The atmosphere was electric; twenty thousand youth were jammed into a massive coliseum, waiting for their rock group to emerge on the platform. Standing in the midst of thousands of fanatical teens, I felt a tidal wave of expectancy — this feeling that something was about to happen that they couldn't miss. Suddenly, the band hits the stage, and tons of high-tech, state-of-the-art equipment, special lighting effects, and the rock stars' talent and charisma combine, exuding an almost supernatural mystique.

The chemistry is instantaneous as the young people merge with the group in a pulsating, rhythmic experience for the next two hours. A rock concert is an "ocean of emotion" as the fusion of youth and rock music explode. Hoards of young people stand, clap, stomp, dance, sing, scream, sway — totally captivated by their rock heroes.

All around me is a party set to music. A cloud of pot smoke settles over portions of the coliseum. The music is so loud you can literally feel it as it shakes the arena. Youth are engulfed by the sheer power of the music and the emotional rush of thousands of teens being together for a cause. Many young people are totally wasted as drugs and alcohol flow freely. Some girls and guys are making out, as others are passing out; the language is crude and obscene; the environment is one of complete unrestraint and immediate gratification. These youth seem to be suspended in time; nothing else really matters except the reckless abandon to their rock world.

The rock concert is more than an event, it is a major life experience for youth. It is also a microcosm of a teen's life — what they believe, feel, value and do.

The 60s Rock Generation

Rock music emerged in the 1950s and became a cultural phenomenon. The music instantly captured what youth felt, experienced and considered most important. *American Bandstand* was a touchstone for the youth culture as kids grew up watching, dancing and singing across America. Rock music became the embodiment of the youth experience.

In the 1960s, rock became a societal force as the catalyst for the counterculture movement. Rock music characterized, solidified and shaped the '60s generation as much as anything. The music consolidated the baby boomer's identity, bridging inner emotions with peers who felt the same way. After rock, they were an army. "It began with the music," Jeff Greenfield has written perceptively. "Nothing we see in counterculture — not the clothes, the hair, the sexuality, the drugs, the rejection of morality, the protests — none of it can be separated from the coming to power of rock music."[3]

The music *was* the message as an entire generation was identified, mesmerized and riveted by the music itself. From Elvis Presley and Little Richard to the Beatles, Jefferson Airplane, the Grateful Dead, Jimi Hendrix and Bob Dylan, rock was the driving force that powered and inspired the '60s generation.

The rock subculture has reflected and shaped the values, attitudes and life-styles of young people for the last thirty-five years. It is still the voice of North American youth today. While the baby boomers grow old listening to rock, it remains the barometer of youth culture.

Addiction to Rock Music

In *The Closing of the American Mind,* Professor Allan Bloom describes youth's obsession with rock music: "Today the majority of young people between the ages of ten and twenty live for music. It is their passion; nothing else excites them as it does; they cannot take seriously anything alien to music. When they are in school and with their families, they are longing to plug themselves back into their music. Nothing surrounding them — school, family, church — has anything to do with their musical world. Nothing is more singular about this generation than its addiction to rock music."[4]

The music has inundated every facet of young people's lives. In the home, there is the stereo; in the car, the radio and cassette player. MTV and other nonstop, twenty-four-hour music channels are designed especially for them. There are Walkmans so that anywhere they are, they needn't be kept from their music.

The Walkman is a major distraction for youth, diverting too much of their attention and time from people and purpose. The popularity of the Walkman headset further removes youth from the world around them, immersing them in their own private world of loud music and isolation. This decreases their meaningful interaction with peers and parents, and keeps them from seriously contemplating what is important and essential. Impaired hearing is incurred when youth listen to their Walkmans or stereos too loud and for too long.

The American Medical Association said, "If a teenager listens to rock music for ten thousand hours and watches just five thousand hours of television during the six years of junior high and high school, that averages out to nearly seven hours of rock music and television every day of the year."[5] Current studies say that 88 percent of American teens listen to rock music.

Interl', Inc., a marketing and church services company, said that "eighty to eighty-five percent of Christian teens listen to secular rock music, and that the three to five million churched teens are unaware of contemporary Christian music."[6] In this music-oriented youth culture, the rock phenomenon is a way of life, and teens must have their music fix.

The MTV-Youth Culture

MTV celebrated its ten-year anniversary on August 1, 1991 — honoring the day the rock wild child that revolutionized the music industry was born. This is the music channel with an attitude — rebellious, arrogant, impulsive and loud; MTV exploded across the youth landscape.

The MTV slogan boasts, "You'll never look at music the same way again." Slick, high-tech imaging at a frantic pace with the hottest sounds combine to give an avant-garde aura to the new music medium. The music television video vehicle has proved to be as pivotal as Woodstock, touching an emotional nerve among youth and growing into a pop-culture institution.

Today, MTV reaches into 55.4 million homes in the U.S.A. alone, and each year it grows by five million households, just in America. MTV's global reach is more than 194 million homes in forty countries, giving it an international as well as national impact. Roughly thirty-four million in the U.S. watch MTV weekly; the target age for viewers is twelve to thirty-four years.[7]

VH-1 (Video Hits 1) became a spin-off of the MTV channel, targeting the older kids, the baby-boomer generation (twenty-five to forty-nine years), who grew up listening to rock and watching television. Appealing to the tastes of the baby-boomers, the "My Generation" format features music clips from the '60s and '70s and classics of the '80s and '90s. The VH-1 channel is visually more tame than MTV and oriented more to pop music than the heavier rock music.

Instead of using just movies or recordings or television, MTV combined all three. MTV rapidly became the most dynamic of all teen media, integrating successful techniques from rock music, popular movies and live and recorded television programming. MTV is a fast-driven, nonstop, drama/music/dance/talk/variety show. It offers teens a channel designed just for them, and it's always there. As one MTV executive put it, "The key to MTV is that you can watch for awhile, walk away, go down to the store, come back and you haven't missed anything."[8]

MTV is the media monster that consumes the youth culture as the youth culture consumes it. "Sex and violence are the two elements that form the magnetic lures that power the rock-driven media machine. MTV is a generator of trends, life-styles and cultural change in the youth world. What makes this so scary is that MTV is the most thoroughly commercial and artificial attempt to create an entire subculture founded on personal, materialistic, self-gratifying consumption."[9]

MTV creates more needs and desires than it fulfills by targeting teens' emotional needs and fears through their favorite music and images. Their goal is to keep youth constantly watching and frantically buying more products in order to achieve happiness.

MTV tells youth that they can decide who they are and what life is all about, and the easiest way to do that is through consumption. "The video channel was high-powered, fun and unpredictable. It established no moral obligation, required no educational accomplishments and issued no parental rules or regulations."[10] MTV tells youth what they want to hear and accepts all who have the time and money to buy into the life-styles portrayed on the channel. "What makes MTV so powerful is not the flashy videos, but its hip attitude, its refusal to take anything—itself, its fans and the world — seriously, even as it appears to do just that."[11]

The only thing MTV is seriously committed to is making a profit, even at the moral and emotional expense of a generation.

Mood and Music

Extensive research studies conclusively show the powerful impact music has on our moods. *Mood* is defined as a particular state of mind or feeling. Music has the ability to create a mood or intensify an existing mood. Music definitely pushes youth's emotional buttons. Youth have very intense emotional feelings that run the gamut—happiness, depression, frustration, hostility, sensuality, boredom, excitement and a myriad of other fluctuating moods.

The major focus or content of rock music is the "communication of moods," specific or generalized states of emotion. A research study asked five hundred college students what gave them the most excitement or greatest thrills. Music ranked second to sexual activity. It was also found that music enhanced sexual satisfaction.[12]

Psychologist Abraham Maslow researched what he called "peak experiences" in human lives. He pointed out that of hundreds of cases studied, there were many different experiences which people singled out as their life's highlight. "Peak experiences" involving music ranked second on the list, surpassed only by sex. From such a statement, one can deduce the dynamics when sex and music are combined.[13]

In a study in several Midwestern bars where they played country-western music, they noticed when they played certain depressing, sad songs, the customers were prone to drink more and become more depressed. In a research experiment conducted by a group of restaurants, it was found that when they played faster, upbeat music, the people tended to eat faster and leave sooner than when they played slower, more tranquil music.[14]

When a teenager's world is falling apart, and he feels hurt and frustrated but cannot find the words to express himself, music communicates, diverts and appears to fill an emotional vacuum. Music creates or magnifies the emotional state of teens and is a way for them to express loneliness, anger, despair or uncertainty. Mood creation is dependent on two essential elements of rock music: rhythm and beat. Rhythm and beat are the twin forces that give rock its energy and power. Without them, rock is a car out of gas; it becomes irrelevant, ineffective and impotent. The music that moves youth has strong rhythmic feel and a certain "groove" that produces an emotional connection.

Rock music produces a "feelings reality" where teens would

rather feel than think. They become mood susceptible and become addicted to the "illusion of reality" in their choices and life-styles, depending on their mood. Youth confuse feelings or mood with reality; they can go together, but most of the time they don't. This causes more emotional pain.

The general mood rock music creates, promotes and encourages is uninhibited sexual, self-indulgent fantasies — the pervasive mood set in the music youth-oriented culture. The danger of this mood set is obvious as the power of a mood definitely affects youth's attitudes and behavior, and intensifies their needs and pain.

MTV and Mood

The emergence of Music Television Video in 1981 gave rock music greater impact and influence on youth by using a dynamic visual dimension. Musical image is a powerful factor in the creating of moods.

The essence of MTV is the mass production and manipulation of moods, emotions and desires of today's young people. MTV transports youth into a dimension where fantasy exceeds reality, where feelings exceed thought, where style is more important than substance. They want to make youth feel a certain way and respond, rather than cause them to think or contemplate.

The dispensing of high-energy, musical images twenty four hours a day promises to satisfy youth's desires and fulfill their dreams when, in reality, it only magnifies and frustrates them. MTV exerts enormous power in its ability to dictate the youth agenda: what they feel, what they talk about, what they do and what they deem relevant and significant in life.

MTV emotionally exploits young people by manipulating their emotions and creating appealing moods with provocative images and sizzling sounds that are devoid of moral values. "MTV gives young people what they want without clarifying what it is they get."[15]

MTV cares little about its emotional and moral impact on the youth culture and wider society:

> It's more concerned with generating and dispensing moods, emotions and desires that only they can fulfill. MTV and the youth culture are locked in an enormous feedback loop in which MTV responds quickly to the

> latest fads, trends and fashions trying to stay on top of what teens want, while never questioning the value or morality of those wants.[16]

The uniqueness of MTV's ability to manipulate youth is through the mass construction and marketing of moods and emotions that are totally separated from intellectual and moral substance. An MTV executive stated, "We're not dealing with plot and continuity; we're dealing with mood and emotion, which is an entirely new way to use that television set. They [young people] will accept almost everything over that screen."[17]

Music creates an emotional bonding and a nostalgic connection where we associate certain relationships, specific times, events, experiences and people with a particular song. Music imprints our minds and triggers memories and deep feelings about the past, present and future.

Combining images, moods, emotion and raw energy, MTV has created an irresistible force that is undeniably having an effect on the lives of young people.

The MTV Philosophy

Music videos have animated and set to music a tension basic to American youth culture: the feeling of instability and insecurity, which fuels the search to buy and belong.[18] MTV offers youth immediate emotional gratification, personal significance and identity they crave.

MTV executive chairman, Bob Pittman, characterizes the philosophy and mind-set of MTV's success and appeal in the following quotes:

"Our core audience is the television babies who grew up on TV and rock 'n' roll...The strongest appeal you can make is emotionally. If you can get their emotions going (make them) forget their logic, you've got 'em."[19]

"The MTV community is a remarkably shallow culture, based far more on fabricated, mass-mediated emotions and experiences than on tradition, logic and reason."[20]

"We're talking about dealing a mood to you. MTV is style, not substance."

"We rely on mood and emotion. MTV makes you feel a certain

way as opposed to you walking away with any particular knowledge."

"At MTV, we don't shoot for the fourteen-year-old, we own them."

"The only people who can understand the new way to use that television set are the people who grew up with it. . . . They will accept almost anything on that screen."[21]

MTV has created its own pop culture, continually dispensing innovative high-tech sounds and images, constantly selling "products," values, attitudes and philosophies in three-to-five-minute, fast-paced, moving segments, which is ideal for the MTV generation.

Valueless Music

The mood, morality and spiritual atmosphere of a society is a reflection of its music. Today's rock music not only mirrors our values, but also creates its own value system. Most of rock music promotes an anti-Christian morality and life-style. The danger is in a decadent culture; immorality becomes the socially accepted norm, not only rationalized, but applauded and honored. When entertainment determines our morality, we are on the brink of cultural collapse.

The rock philosophy is a relativistic attitude that says nothing is wrong or right, whatever you do is right; there is no truth, fantasy is reality. Another dimension is the hedonistic mind-set that says the pursuit of pleasure is priority; self-gratification and self-centeredness is where it's at. For me to feel good now is more important than anyone or anything in life.

The third rock philosophy is a nihilistic mentality; what you do doesn't matter; what you don't do doesn't matter; nothing in life really matters; everything is meaningless. This philosophy reflects the dark side of rock music that promotes death, despair and destruction. Life is really hopeless and futile, so we might as well live fast and dangerous. "All we are is dust in the wind."[22]

"Music tends to be a predictor of behavior and social values," explained an MTV executive. "You tell me the music that people like, and I'll tell you their views on moral and social issues from abortion to whether we should increase military spending, and what their sense of humor is like."[23]

Rock music's ability to create, manipulate and generate emotions and moods without any moral values has produced an immoral, valueless youth mind-set.

Root Causes

There has been much outstanding material written, and well-documented research done on rock personalities and the lyrics and content of their songs and life-styles. At a very obvious level, the lyrics, life-styles and beliefs of most rock musicians are blatantly anti-Biblical and anti-moral, powerfully impacting young peoples' lives.

We will examine the underlying reasons why rock music is so important to youth. There is no question as to its exalted place of prominence in young people's lives. As we focus on the root motivations, we can address the needs of young people and take the necessary steps to confront and solve the problem.

Rock Themes

We will examine the major themes that rock music promotes, which are: sex, rebellion, violence, fantasy, the occult, drugs and suicide.

The Sexual Theme. Rock music and sex fuse together in the perfect union; they feed off each other's power and attraction. The mystique and magnetism of rock music has always been its sexual dimension.

The most rampant element of MTV is the promotion of sex. The music and images are drenched with sexual content and a brazen sexual attitude that projects an emotional maturity and sophistication. MTV provides a constant blitz of sexually explicit lyrics, sexually intoxicating scenes with seductive girls and guys simulating sexual acts of all kinds—where fantasy exceeds experience. The sexual emphasis is pervasive; a research study indicated that over 80 percent of rock videos depicted sexual intimacy.

Society and rock music's promotion of teen sex as normal has effectively exploited young people's vital sexuality. Youth's enormous hormonal drives, combined with the need for affection, view these enticing, images with seductive rock lyrics; and this pushes the sexual panic button.

The arrival of MTV gave rock greater impact and influence on the sexual life-styles of youth with visual erotica. This new teen media phenomenon combined the powerful driving rock sound with mesmerizing, alluring images, intensifying the sexual effect and desires. Youth are now transported into a lustful world, complete with sex, and their superstars — Madonna, Paula Abdul, Michael Jackson, Prince, Jon Bon Jovi, Poison, Van Halen — strutting seductively, singing suggestive lyrics. The combination of sex, music sounds and images is hypnotic and addictive, increasing youth's sexual appetite.

MTV has created an erotic, over-stimulated atmosphere in the youth culture, which cannot be satisfied. An MTV slogan for youth is: "More sex in the '90s." We now have more teens (over 80 percent) at younger ages having more sex than ever in American history. Rock music has helped to create an emotional vacuum that sex will never fill. Rock helps produce sexual relationships that are manipulating, selfish, addictive and desperate.

MTV constantly promotes immediate self-gratification and promiscuous sex, as the keys to meaningful relationships, happiness and a way to be mature without any consequences. Rock music has been and is a major force in creating this current sensual atmosphere.

We've gone from "I'm Happy Just to Dance with You" and "I Wanna Hold Your Hand" to "I Want Your Sex," "I'm Too Sexy," "I Wanna Sex You Up" and "Unlawful Carnal Knowledge." Intimacy is delivered through the portrayal of sexual fantasies lived out on the screen.

Lonely and bored youths are seductively invited to lie down with make-believe lovers. Teen viewers are given images of sensuous partners who seem to care in a way that plays to their urges and sexual desires.[24]

The American Medical Association found in a research study that young teens who watched an hour of rock video daily were more likely to approve of premarital sex than youth who hadn't been exposed as consistently.[25]

Another danger in a sex-saturated, over-stimulated society is that it always creates more desires and frustrations than it fulfills or eliminates. "More sex" in the '90s for youth means more pain.

The Rebellion Theme

Rock has always symbolized youth's defiance against the system. Rock music was the vehicle for the social and moral rebellion of the counter-culture of the '60s. The '60s generation resisted, protested and challenged everything and everyone in its path and didn't trust anyone over thirty; the anthem for the revolution was rock.

Rock music promotes a rebellious attitude as MTV shows parents and other authority figures being unfair, cruel and oppressive or stupid, ridiculous and strange. The rock subculture projects a "them against us" mentality that says, "Hey, you've got the right to express your individuality." The rebellious anthem of MTV is, "I want my MTV," implying a "don't try and stop me" attitude. Rock music combined with the fragmented and insecure family environment breeds hostility and rebellion among teens.

MTV's "Headbanger's Ball" features heavy metal bands — like Guns 'N' Roses, Motley Crue, Metallica and White Snake — who promote a radical, rebellious attitude among teens that says, "You've got to fight for right to party" and "We take no prisoners."

The rock subculture is about a certain life-style and the rock value system that promotes rebellion. The way youth dress, wear their hair, how they talk, and their attitudes and modes of social and sexual behavior add a particular rock perspective on society and family. We, as a culture, have tolerated and even embraced the perversion and aberration advocated by rock music:

> What we fail to realize is that when we accept rock music's expressions of rebellion as normal, we only force youth to seek more extreme ways to express their rebellion. Rebellion is a necessary state through which all teens go, but our culture has robbed teens of the means to express their rebellion by absorbing abnormal expressions of opposition into the culture as legitimate forms of entertainment.[26]

The Fantasy Theme

Rock music creates a fantasy world that is based on the emotional needs and fears of youth. MTV, with state-of-the-art special effects, generates a fascinating fantasy life-style that has a spellbinding effect on what teens believe is reality. Constantly bombarding youth with nonstop music and images that promise to fulfill their desires and needs, MTV mass-manufactures fantasies as it reinforces youth's wishful thinking about themselves, which causes them to lose their ability to distinguish between fantasy and reality. Rock music creates fantasy relationships, identities and meaning, which increase teens' disappointment and pain. MTV effectively creates mood and emotion, which is more concerned with what youth feel than what they think, which feeds their fantasies.

One study found that music videos are punctuated by rapid shot changes, averaging twenty shots per minute. MTV combines high-tech electronics and high-concept visuals that keep the images changing rapidly and unpredictably, creating a hypnotic effect, appealing to the short attention spans of youth.[27]

This technologically sophisticated music media has conditioned youth to accept belief systems, behaviors and values that would have been rejected by earlier less-sophisticated, less-inundated generations.

Fantasy becomes an appealing substitute for youth when their world is more dangerous, more stressful and more uncertain than ever. MTV creates an illusion of intimacy by projecting exciting sexual relationships as the means to achieving real love, producing fantasy relationships.

Professor Allan Bloom says, "Rock music provides a premature ecstasy much like drug use. It encourages passions and provides models that have no relation to any life youth could possibly experience."[28] Youth's need for intimacy, identity and significance have made them more susceptible to fantasy. Through flashy music images, MTV fuels the fantasy mind-set. And where there is fantasy, there is emptiness.

The Violence Theme

Rock music inundates the youth culture with compelling and shocking violence. Exploding across the music television screen, rock videos display violence accompanied by the rhythmic driving sounds of their favorite heavy metal and rap groups: Motley Crue, Guns 'N' Roses, Ice-T, Ice Cube, Alice in Chains, Public Enemy, Skid Row and Omega Death. These groups promote murder, rape, torture and all kinds of extreme antisocial behavior and violence.

Some heavy metal groups use fake blood, raw meat, saws, chains, torture racks, knives, guns and other paraphernalia to shock their fans.

Sensual violence is glamorized and advocated as being avant-garde, the latest fashion statement or trendy life-style. Heavy metal songs and performances extol the virtues of torture, rape and murder of women. They usually portray women as sexual playthings and as victims — objects of pleasure, exploitation and abuse.

Two factors that are fueling widespread violence among youth are anger and the "desensitizing effect." Many young people are frustrated and angry at what's happening in their lives; they want to lash out at everyone and everything. Desensitization has fueled the violence explosion among teens; violence has been accepted as a normal and necessary way of life.

Lead singer Blackie Lawless said, "Nastiness is central to the W.A.S.P. performance; I don't mean vulgar nasty," he said, "I mean violent. We sound like a tin can ripped open with your hands. That kind of nasty. It doesn't leave a clean cut. The anger is what helps you relate to the kids." [29] When you have adolescents and you put in a healthy dose of hostility, you get a lethal combination. "I'm ticked off" is what makes rock 'n' roll what it is. Young people are ticked off; rock becomes the expression of those hostilities.

America's addiction to make-believe violence is like any other addiction; it takes more and more to accomplish less and less. Dr. Thomas Radecki, director of research for the National Coalition of Media Violence, says, "We see this subculture of hatred and violence becoming a fast-growing element of rock entertainment for the young." Researchers count eighteen acts of violence in each hour of video.[30]

The flood of violence through rock music videos and television has numbed viewers to real violence and its consequences. Music video violence is performed, not by villains, but by teenage idols. Too many youth believe violence is a way to solve problems, get results, have power, achieve their goals — and really be somebody. Rock music has helped to sanitize and disinfect violence; it's not only accepted, it's desirable; after all, this is the way they do it on MTV.

The Suicide Theme

Teen suicide is a national tragedy in America. There is a morbid preoccupation with suicide among too many young people today. Despite this, a large number of heavy metal groups sing about suicide as a way to deal with problems or beat the system.

Many heavy metal bands specialize in "death metal" or "black metal" songs, which express a grim fascination with death, destruction, hopelessness and suicide.

There's a widespread feeling of hopelessness and a sense of despair in much of the youth culture today. This "dark music" that promotes death and self-destruction can be a deadly combination when a confused and depressed teenager listens to a song advocating suicide as an answer to problems and pain.

Here are lyrics to the song, "Suicide's an Alternative/You'll be Sorry," by the band Suicidal Tendencies:

> Sick of people — no one real;
> Sick of you, you're too hip;
> Sick of life — it sucks. . .
> Sick of life — it sucks;
> Sick and tired, and no one cares;
> Sick of myself — don't wanna live;
> Sick of living — gonna die.

These lyrics portray an inevitable destructive attitude toward life, people and the future.

According to the National Educational Association, "many teenage suicides are linked to depression fueled by fatalistic music and lyrics."[31] "Dark music" can definitely help push a despondent teen over the edge. True, millions of youth listen to these songs and don't kill themselves, but there have been too many suicides by teens who were influenced by this suicide-obsessed music.

The captivating lyrics and images of black metal, encouraging suicide, death and destruction appeal to a desperate group of teens who are already at risk. What's scary is that the number of these desperate and depressed teens is increasing. When youth are experiencing so many problems and so much pain and they don't know how to stop it, suicide becomes a dangerous and tragic alternative.

Heavy metal rocker, Ozzy Osborne, sings "Suicide Solution":

"Where to hide? Suicide is the only way out. Don't you know what it's really all about?"[32] This "death metal" music feeds the philosophy that "life is cheap" and meaningless. Suicide appears to be the ultimate solution for youth, which, in reality, is the ultimate deception.

Smells Like Teen Spirit

Shocking, bizarre, avant-garde alternative rock emerged in 1992 as a new force on the rock scene. Alternative (grunge) rock groups like Soul Asylum, Red Hot Chili Peppers, Pearl Jam, Stone Temple Pilots and Nirvana are riding a ground swell of popularity that has touched a radical nerve in the youth culture.

The alternative rock nation exposes the hypocrisy and emptiness of the system, which does not acknowledge their pain. Their music and message capture and express the alienation and anger of this generation. These alternative antisocial groups confirm for Generation X what's cool and what sucks.

I Want To Die Nevermind

Once again, the rock world was shaken by the death of one of its gifted young artist, a tragedy that seems endemic to the pop music scene. Kurt Cobain who became the voice for Generation X as the lead singer for Nirvana, committed suicide at twenty-seven. His shotgun was found resting against him.

Nirvana, the multiplatinum Seattle grunge band, defined the sound of the '90s—tapping into the cynism, pain and alienation of this generation. The divorce, the violence, the drugs, the diminished opportunities for an entire generation, that is so successful to the sound and success of their music. Nirvana helped establish grunge rock as the sound and style of '90s disillusionment.

Nirvana emerged as a generational force with their enormously successful "Nevermind" album that sold nearly ten million copies worldwide. The song "Smells Like Teen Spirit" has become a virtual refrain, "Here we are now, entertain us."

Kurt Cobains bitter-edged-shocking-angry lyrics defined and captured the mind-set of a generation. Cobain spoke so openly on the subjects of drugs and depression and suicide that writers searching for easy obituary ironies didn't have to look very hard. Cobain himself even began joking about it: A song called "I hate myself and I want to die" was recorded but dropped from the last album. Tragically it becane a self-fulfilling prophecy for Cobain.

Kurt Cobain joined the ranks of other brilliant but troubled rock superstars: Presley, Morrison, Hendrix and Joplin all fatally overdosed on drugs, fame and despair.

The Satanic Theme

Today's youth have been exposed to so much, so young, that it takes a lot more to shock them. Rock music goes into a forbidden zone that violates every moral and social taboo — satanism. Satanic rock is the ultimate extreme that crosses over into the dark and foreboding world of evil. Young people get caught up in the fascination and the curiosity of the unknown and the power of darkness.

Heavy metal bands and performers — like Venom, Slayer, Metallica, Iron Maiden, Merciful Fate, Metal Church, Ozzy Osborne and others — promote and market Satan to young people. These groups use satanic symbols and other paraphernalia in their concerts and on their album covers to market evil for money. Selling satanism is both profitable and dangerous.

I've been present at several of these heavy metal, satanic-oriented concerts: Iron Maiden, Judas Priest and a few other groups. As I stood in the midst of thousands of youth gathered for this ritual, I felt a flood of demonic power and oppression. I watched, appalled and amazed, as these groups strutted in devilish defiance; they gave the satanic salute, held up satanic crosses and encouraged kids to get crazy for Satan.

Thousands of youth responded by making satanic gestures, holding up satanic crosses and displaying pentagrams; some were dressed in black robes.

These rock groups assure everyone that it's only a harmless game they use to entertain and a gimmick to attract youth and nobody should take it seriously. Cult expert Sandi Gallant of the San Francisco Police Department says, "No matter what heavy metal band leaders say, they are projecting an image to the kids that they are satanists. Teens want to emulate their stars."[33]

According to law enforcement officers and news reporters who have investigated satanic crimes, there is a common thread. The most consistent and constant factor they've found between youth and satanism is the music.

Reporter Tom Jarriel on ABC's *20/20* said:

> The satanic message is clear, both on the album covers and in the lyrics, which are reaching impressionable young minds. And the musical message comes across loud and clear at concerts and now through rock videos. The symbolism is there; the satanic pentagram, the upside-down cross, the blank eyes of the beast, the rebellion against Christianity and again and again, the obsession with death. According to most groups, it's all done in fun; but, according to police, it's having an effect on teens, a growing subculture that mixes heavy metal music with drugs and the occult.[34]

Why Teens Listen to Rock

Instant Gratification. Rock is the feel-good music that promotes immediate pleasure and nonstop fun, and encourages youth to live for the experience of the moment. Since most youth pursue a present-oriented life-style, this makes rock the perfect companion. Immersed in the self-indulgent, hedonistic, party-hearty *now* mentality of the rock world, young people want to do it and feel it now. Rock music doesn't want teens to think past the moment's gratification. Rock promises what it can never deliver — future happiness.

Feelings. Rock music enters the world of teens by identifying with what they feel and tapping into their enormous emotional needs. Their greatest fears and deepest needs, their hopes and dreams are put to words and music. One young person said, "Rock music says exactly what I feel but can't put into words." When parents, teachers, churches and others don't seem to care what teens feel, rock fills the void, touching an emotional nerve. Effectively exploiting teens' emotional susceptibility, rock music would rather teens feel than think.

Problems and Pressures. In this high-pressured, high-stressed, confusing world, young people look to rock music for an anchor, something they can always turn to, a friend they can depend on when their world is turned upside down. A teen said, "When I would have a problem or be really hurting, I would go to my room and turn on my music, and it always helped me deal with whatever."

In a recent survey in *USA Today,* teens were asked who they turned to when they had a problem. Their first choice was music; number two was their peers; and third was television. Mom was sixth, and Dad was their eighteenth choice.

Escape Reality. When reality is boring, disappointing, scary or too painful, young people choose to avoid it through their music. The fantasy world of rock becomes a refuge where life is not as complicated or threatening. Teens don't have to deal with pain, failures, responsibilities, guilt or anything else they don't want to. They just turn up the volume and get lost in a world that only demands they listen and enjoy. Escaping reality becomes a way of life for too many teens, which ultimately only increases their pain.

Peer Connection. Rock music is a major factor in youth's peer acceptance and friendships. Rock draws and bonds young people together; certain friends like the same groups and music. They want to listen to the same music and go to the same concerts with their friends. To not know the latest on the rock scene is to be totally out of it.

What youth wear, how they act and what group they belong to is greatly determined by the music they listen to. Rock creates its own social status where approval is based on music preference. The problem is, this produces conditional relationships: "If you want to belong to our group, you have to listen to our music, wear what we wear, do what we do." They become totally oblivious to anyone outside their group.

Need for Identity. Young people are searching for a sense of identity. Rock music is the mirror they look into to try and understand who they are. Rock speaks to their insecurities and feelings of inferiority, promising to remove them; it really only increases them. The music causes them to ask the questions: Who are my real friends? What's so important about school? Who am I in relation to my parents? How important am I? How do I belong?

Most youth struggle with low self-esteem and need something to affirm their worth as individuals. Music becomes a way for young people to assert their identity. Rock music creates youth subcultures, from metal-heads to rappers.

Teens wear T-shirts of their rock heroes, buy their albums and cassettes and have posters hanging in their rooms. They want to be just like their rock superstars, which is disturbing if not frightening. Not only are youth's individual identities shaped by music, their sense of generational identity is based on the music they listen to as well. The '60s generation was bonded together and identified by their music as much as anything.

To be is to consume; to consume is to be. MTV fuels the widespread feelings of insecurity and inferiority in the youth culture through creating the need to buy and belong.

Need for Intimacy. Rock music appears to make intimacy readily available for youth by projecting a media intimacy. The capacity that MTV has to create illusion in relationships is tremendous. Young people are already preoccupied with sex and looking frantically for real love in a significant relationship. MTV creates the apparently perfect relationship, and it only requires sex. Youth are emotionally and sexually vulnerable. Coupled with the hormonal explosion, sexual intimacy is more than inviting — it's necessary!

Rock music creates fantasy relationships based on sex that only intensify their pain and magnify their desperation for intimacy. Rock music also fills the relationship void left by the lack of family intimacy they long for from their parents. The music becomes the surrogate parent of far too many teens.

Venting Feelings. Rock music is a way for youth to express their feelings of frustration. "When I'm really ticked about something, I turn on music to shake the walls and kick the doors down by," said one teenager. Whenever young people feel hurt or angry about something, they get a psychological release through the music. The music they listen to sometimes depends on the mood they're in. If they're mad, they listen to music to rip your head off. However, music has the power to intensify our mood, so instead of alleviating their anger and frustration, it can increase it.

Music then becomes more than an outlet to express personal emotions, and can be a detonator for explosive violence or reckless actions, like premarital sex.

Sense of Significance. Many youth feel life only has meaning when they are plugged into their rock world; everything else fades into insignificance. However, the high-energy, intensely emotional bombardment of MTV entertainment has gone from shocking to boring. What is dangerous, exciting and shocking today is repetitive, dull and boring tomorrow. Youth become perpetually bored with life as they look to MTV to fill the vacuum for meaning and fulfillment. They suggest that buying the latest fashions and newest music cassette or CD will give them real significance. While promising to fulfill their need for a sense of purpose, in reality, they produce false meaning and a deeper frustration and boredom. As one writer for *Billboard* put it, "Unlike all other forms, video music clips exist to sell a product."[35]

Rock is a Cultural Force

Rock music is the cultural force that has continually defined and shaped the youth landscape, from the late '50s to the present. MTV's philosophy of exciting-feelings oriented entertainment conditions youth for more stimulation and non-stop fun—or it becomes boring very quickly. Rock superstar Bruce Springsteen muses, "57 channels and nothing on."

MTV is caught in the wild flux of its own creation. Built on careful, extensive research and high concept, the network is forever locked into the need for endless research, prognostication and reassessment. "As the ratings swing up and down as trends and fashions shift, as youth continue searching for identity, intimacy and meaning amid the desolation of modern society. This places youth on a whirlwind of change that spins over faster as conditioned consumers scream for more stuff." What was cutting edge a few months ago is now outdated and obsolete.

MTV will be plagued by the same social instability and cultural flux that it has found so profitable to exploit and promote. "MTV is the most thoroughly commercial and artificial attempt yet to create an entire subculture founded on personal consumption. More than a set of ideas and attitudes, consumption offers a dynamic and comprehensive life-style, where one is validated and verified by every act of purchasing."[2] So shop like you mean it! The relationship between youth and the entertainment mass media will decide the future of marketing and consumerism.

The conflict is over the hearts and minds of each new generation. In turning youth into greater consumers the entertainment media further erodes and undermines and redifines the social institutions (family—church—school) that have formed the personal and collective anchors for so many generations.

The major philosophy of MTV is to develop continual, committed consumers—where buying more things is the key to fulfillment and life is a nonstop advertisement. If MTV actually met the deepest emotional and social needs of youth, there would be little need for constant innovation or other competing social institutions like the family and the church.

In order to be understood as a cultural force, rock must be experienced as a sensation not as substance—as an emotional rush not reality. Rock is the mirror image of the youth culture. It reflects, defines and creates its own world of feelings, experience and reality.

In the '90s, instant gratification is too slow. We must have immediate, instant and continual gratification for a generation of excesses that denies, escapes and numbs its pain.

Once the language of disease and addiction could be applied to behavior rather than merely to biological disorders, almost any aspect of human life could be redefined in medical terms. A host of activities that had once seemed to be a matter of choice and barometers of character could now be transformed into pathologies.

Charles J Sykes
A Nation of Victims

Chapter 12

Driven to Be in Control: The Addicted Society

Who has woe? Who has sorrow?
Who has contentions? Who has complaints?
Who has wounds without cause? Who has redness
of eyes? Those who linger long at the wine, those
who go in search of mixed wine. Do not look on
the wine when it is red, when it sparkles in the cup,
when it swirls around smoothly; at the last it bites
like a serpent, and stings like a viper
(Prov. 23:29-32 NKJ).

The Addicted Society

During the '80s, we were confronted with a drug epidemic in America. We have become a drug-drenched culture. In the newspaper headlines across America and on the evening news, drugs became a regular feature story. *Time, Newsweek, 60 Minutes, Nightline, Geraldo, Oprah* and *Donahue* all addressed the disturbing and ominous drug trend. The land of the free and the home of the brave was becoming the land of bondage and the home of the addicted. Foreboding headlines like "The Drug Plague," "Drugs: The Enemy Within," "The Drugged Society," "The Chemical Generation" and "Death, Destruction and Drugs" heralded the drug disaster sweeping over America like a monstrous tidal wave.

President Ronald Reagan vowed to defeat this dreaded enemy, announcing the battle had begun with the anti-drug crusade. Nancy

Reagan got involved with her much-publicized "Just Say No" campaign against drugs aimed at the youth of the nation, with huge amounts of federal money designated for drug treatment and prevention. Massive drug education programs and "drug-free" schools and workplaces became a priority, mobilizing every segment of the American society in the fight on drugs. President Bush declared a "war on drugs" to stop the "scourge on the land," appointing William Bennett to the newly created "Drug Czar" position, which was specifically designed to plan strategies in the drug war. "The U.S. Government pumped $9.5 billion into drug-fighting efforts; yet cocaine, crack and other drugs continue to flood our nation's bloodstream. The drug problem is described as "the most serious internal crisis this country has faced since the Civil War."[1] All across the country, from rural and suburban areas to the inner cities, there is no place or family left untouched by the drug menace.

A Culture of Contradictions

Drugs refers to cocaine, crack, heroin, marijuana, PCP or angel dust, hallucinogens, methamphetamines, amphetamines and various other substances. The abuse of these drugs is still widespread and extremely dangerous. Cocaine and crack are still very popular and are the most addictive substances known to modern society; they are ravaging the lives of millions.

The number one drug of choice for youth in America is still alcohol (which is rarely if ever put in the same category as the hard core or dangerous drugs). Research indicates that 75 percent of all teens drink alcohol occasionally and over 50 percent drink it on a regular basis. The use of other drugs is steadily declining among youth.

The recent findings by the Institute of Social Research poll of seventeen thousand seniors in 1990 compared the percentage of high school students who occasionally used drugs in 1980. Marijuana use was 48 percent in 1980, 27 percent in 1990; cocaine use was 12 percent in 1980, 5 percent in 1990; crack statistics for 1980 are not available, but only 2 percent reported using crack in 1990. At 75 percent, in 1990 alcohol was used nearly three times as much as marijuana, twelve times as much as cocaine, and thirty five times as much as crack.[2]

Nearly all of the anti-drug efforts are focused at the hard core or "street drugs," while alcohol is treated as a misunderstood friend. Alcohol is part of the social structure in America. Alcohol use and the youth culture have always gone together as part of the "youth experience."

The handbook from the U.S. Department of Education, *What Works: Schools Without Drugs,* effectively addresses drug abuse and ignores alcohol. We've declared war on drugs but maintain a "drink responsibly" policy for alcohol. The media has helped create a "responsible irresponsibility" among youth where responsible drinking is normal and not drinking is abnormal.[3] Telling youth to drink responsibly is like putting an eight-year-old child in a car and saying, "Drive responsibly."

Alcohol is the socially accepted drug in America; we don't refer to it as a drug, and it is not considered dangerous. Most parents would much rather their young people consume alcohol than use the really dangerous drugs like cocaine or crack. In fact, parents often model drinking to their sons and daughters.

The alcohol industry in America is a billion-dollar business, and high school and college students are major consumers. The youth-oriented consumer market is bombarded with alcohol ads to establish a long-range, ongoing relationship with teens, appealing to the emotional vulnerability of youth by implying that consuming a certain beer or wine cooler can meet their needs.

The TV media shows youth, superstar personalities, movie and rock stars, and pro-athletes who do anti-drug commercials, telling young people using drugs is dangerous and destructive. These commercial spots are shocking, creative ads against cocaine, crack and other drug use.

Then the media turns around and encourages alcohol use with commercials that feature good-looking girls and guys, mood music and slick, high-tech electronics, creating an atmosphere of excitement, fun and emotional fulfillment. They show these beautiful young people who drink Coors, Bud, Miller, seemingly very happy and very successful, with lots of friends. The alcohol commercials imply to youth that good-looking people drink, cool people drink, people with dates and friends drink, people who want excitement drink, people going somewhere drink and people who are really happy drink.

These alcohol commercials don't show lonely, hurting or depressed people who drink. They don't show them throwing up, or as mangled dead bodies after an alcohol-related car accident. The top-rated television show of the 1990-91 season was *Cheers*, and for the past seven years, it had been one of the most popular TV shows. The setting is a cozy, friendly bar in Boston where the entire show revolves around the people in the bar. People sit around and drink — responsibly, of course — their problems are solved, they laugh, and you laugh and have lots of fun, and they rarely ever get drunk.

"By the time the average teen is eighteen years old, he or she has seen 100,000 TV beer commercials which are usually targeted for youth."[4] Former Federal Communications Commission head, Nicholas Johnson, stated that TV showed beer being used twenty-four times more than coffee and 120 times more than milk. Several studies reveal that children are beginning to drink earlier than ever before. A poll conducted by *Weekly Reader* found that TV and movies had a profound influence in making alcohol seem appealing to fourth through sixth graders.[5]

According to the Prevention Research Center in California, there is an average of ten to eleven "drinking acts" defined as "ingestion of alcohol or preparation to drink" per hour of prime time television; a viewer may witness about twenty drinking scenes per evening of TV viewing.[6]

Marketing Alcohol

Here are the major goals of alcohol advertising and marketing strategies of the liquor industry:

1. "Increase the number of occasions on which current drinkers consume alcohol. The goal is to raise the number of times during the day when people drink, the number of days when they drink, and the number of occasions on which drinking is the thing to do."[7]

Michelob beer's ad campaign began a decade ago with a catchy slogan: "Weekends are made for Michelob." Soon, the ad evolved into "Put a little weekend in your week." Then the sales pitch became, "The night was made for Michelob." Michelob moved within a decade from advocating drinking as a way to unwind on the weekend to promoting drinking as a habitual nightly activity. Michelob's campaign represents one of the many alcohol industry efforts to stimulate consumption.[8]

2. Increase the percentage of those who drink—in other words, turn the 91 percent of high school students who have experimented with alcohol into regular users.[9]

3. Position alcoholic beverages to compete with soft drinks as "thirst quenchers" and refreshment beverages. Evidence of this strategy includes the sponsoring of major athletic events, concerts and other social events while developing and marketing wine coolers.[10]

The Scope of the Alcohol Problem

The devastation that alcohol has caused in America is staggering. According to the National Council on Alcoholism, alcohol is a problem for fifty-six million families, costing an annual $116 billion. The American Hospital Association reports that half of hospital admissions are alcohol-related.[11]

For the eighteen million Americans with a serious drinking problem, life is a runaway roller coaster that inevitably leads to disaster. The amount of pain and misery that alcohol has wrought and is producing each year is incomprehensible. Alcoholism claims the lives of tens of thousands, destroys millions of families and sets in motion a cycle of destruction for young people.

The magnitude of the problem has been overshadowed in recent years by the national preoccupation with AIDS and the widespread use of drugs such as cocaine, heroin, marijuana and crack. "Take the deaths from every other abused drug," says Lorm Archer, deputy director of the National Institute on Alcohol Abuse and Alcoholism in Washington, "add them together and they still don't equal the deaths or the cost to society of alcohol alone."[12]

The alcohol toll is frightening. The National Institute on Alcohol Abuse and Alcoholism cites the following statistics:

- Over 100,000 people die each year from the effects of alcohol.
- Every sixty seconds, a person is injured in an alcohol-related accident.
- Every twenty-two minutes, someone is killed in an alcohol-related accident.

- Each year, twenty-four thousand people are killed in alcohol-related tragedies.

The crime level in America is drug-driven; the rise in crime and violence is directly attributed to the trafficking and abuse of drugs and alcohol. Law enforcement officials say 70 to 80 percent of the crimes committed nationwide stem directly or indirectly from drugs.

- A Justice Department survey estimates that over one third of the nation's 540,000 state prison inmates drank heavily before committing rapes, burglaries and assaults.
- About two in every five Americans will be involved in an alcohol-related accident in their lifetimes.[13]
- Drunk drivers were responsible for half of the driving fatalities in the U.S. in 1990.
- Alcohol was a factor in up to 70 percent of the four thousand drowning deaths and in 40 percent of the thirty thousand suicides.
- As many as 45 percent of the country's more than 280,000 homeless are alcoholics.
- Up to 83 percent of all fire-related deaths are considered to be alcohol-related, and 50 percent of all home accidents are caused by problem drinkers.
- Cirrhosis of the liver kills at least fourteen thousand alcoholics a year.[14]

Alcohol s Effect on Youth

Young people are drinking earlier than ever before. "Their first drinking experience today usually occurs at age twelve, whereas twenty years ago making the decision to drink didn't occur until sixteen to eighteen years," says Lee Dogloff, Executive Director of the American Council for Drug Education.[15]

The National Council on Alcoholism cites the following facts:

- Since 1966, the number of high school students who are intoxicated at least once a month has more than doubled.
- By the ninth grade, 56 percent have tried alcohol. By their senior year, 91 percent of all teens have experimented with alcohol.
- Alcohol-related car accidents are the number one cause of death for youth; over eight thousand teens and young adults

aged fifteen to twenty-four are killed yearly.

- Forty percent of sixth graders have tasted wine coolers.
- Over one third of high school students say that most of their friends get drunk several times a month.
- Seventy percent of teens between the ages of thirteen and eighteen drink some form of alcoholic beverage occasionally, and 50 percent regularly.
- There are more than four million teenage alcoholics in America.[16]

These mind-boggling statistics can't adequately measure or describe the incredible amount of pain and devastation experienced by millions of youth. The destructive effect of alcohol is vast, and young people are especially vulnerable since drinking is very much a part of the youth culture.

Alcohol-Related Teen Problems

A recent national research report was entitled "Youth and Alcohol: Dangerous and Deadly Consequences." It revealed that youth who drink alcohol regularly were more prone to be sexually active, to be involved in crime, violence, suicide and have bad grades; these are overlooked after-effects of the teenage drinking problem. "Alcohol is not consumed in a void; there are consequences," says Surgeon General Antonia Novello.[17]

- *Sexual Assault.* Fifty-five percent of perpetrators and 53 percent of victims said they were under the influence during the assault. In a high school survey, 42 percent of boys and 20 percent of girls said it was okay to force sex if a girl was drunk.
- *Suicide.* Seventy percent of youth attempting suicide are frequent drug and/or alcohol users.
- *Grades.* Among 1991 high school seniors, twice as many binge drinkers (five or more drinks in one sitting) had grades of "C" or lower.

Another current report says one fourth of U.S. teens are at serious health risk from alcohol and drugs, sexually transmitted diseases, poor nutrition, depression and violence.[18]

Alcohol consumption is a devastating and destructive life-style that is affecting more and younger teens than ever. In reality, young people aren't consuming alcohol — it's consuming them.

The Addicted Society

The number of Americans addicted to something has been increasing yearly since the '60s. Some fourteen to sixteen million addicted individuals now attend self-help groups that have sprung up all over the country, and these numbers are expected to double in the next three years.

The addictive society operates according to specific false beliefs: "I should be perfect," "The world should be without limits," "I should always get what I want" and "Life should be without pain and require no effort." This mentality has created mass delusion in the youth culture and contemporary society. Since these are all unattainable and unrealistic, the addict also comes to believe that he or she never measures up: "I am not enough," "I am unable to have an impact on my world." Externals such as people, alcohol, drugs, acquiring things and being successful then "make up for" the lack of personal power and control. These are the root motivations for our actions or addictive life-styles, even though we are usually not conscious of these underlying causes.

Twenty years ago the word *addiction* was used only to describe the alcohol or drug problem of an individual. Now, we have an entire culture addicted to such things as food, relationships, gambling, work, sex, exercise, substance abuse, appearance, shopping, success, consumption and a wide array of other addictions.

The atmosphere in today's culture is a generator for addiction. These needs and traits characterize contemporary culture and this generation: an emphasis on image, which is more important than who you really are; craving for power and control; denial of reality; dishonesty; lack of self-control; preoccupation with self; materialism; emotional insecurity and spiritual emptiness.

Popular culture and societal trends have produced conditions where alcohol use thrives. Growing numbers of youth succumb to this and other addictive trends. The addicted individual lives in a fantasy world where illusion becomes reality. The relentless pursuit of perfection, power, performance and possession of people and things fuels addiction among young people.

Compulsiveness Is Chic

The search for pleasure, achievement, fulfillment and happiness has produced a driven, compulsive society. Mental health experts say that "drivenness or compulsiveness is the epidemic of the '90s." They define *drivenness* this way: *Drivenness* is an insatiable drive to do more and be more. It's a drive that may be masked by admirable and positive motives but in reality originates in deep, perhaps even unconscious, feelings of inadequacy and shame. Drivenness, compulsion, applauded addictions — these terms describe the performance and perfection pressures that characterize this emotional health epidemic of the 1990s.[19]

Many young people are caught up in this "drivenness" cycle, feeling increasingly inadequate, out of control and driven to be in control. In America, we applaud power, perfection and performance, which is producing a compulsive-addicted life-style for many teens today.

The "shopping mall" phenomenon has become a major part of the youth culture. "Malling" is a way of life for teens where they go to hang out with their friends and spend money. "To escape the ordinary," go to the mall. Many teens feel they must go to the mall to experience real meaning, identity and fulfillment. The mall scene feeds the need to project a certain image; after all, image is everything.

When they're feeling depressed, restless or lonely, they go to the mall and buy something, anything to be somebody.

The compulsive-addicted life-style among teens focuses on their fears and meeting their needs. The result is devastating; not only do their needs go unmet, but their fears have now multiplied and intensified.

The teenage girl craves an intimate relationship. Sex appears to fulfill her need, but this only creates a destructive and addictive sexual cycle where sex becomes the dominant element buying real love. Now she must have sex, but she needs intimacy and becomes driven and more desperate.

The projection of the all-important image creates deep feelings of inadequacy, insecurity, a false sense of identity among youth and a tendency to abuse alcohol and other drugs. This fast-paced, high-performance, competitive culture advocates compulsiveness as a positive quality in today's world; society actually feeds this drivenness.

The Quick-Fix Mentality

The quick-fix mentality throughout the youth culture and society is an obsession with power, control and immediate gratification. It is a mind-set that drives youth and adults to habitually opt for the easiest, fastest, short-term fix to a problem, even when it causes more problems than it fixes, and sacrifices future happiness. Believing that alcohol and drugs are the quick-fix solution to their problems creates an illusion of reality.

Why Teens Use Alcohol and Drugs

The abuse of alcohol and drugs among youth is only symptomatic of deeper unresolved problems or unmet emotional needs. According to young people, these are the root motivations for alcohol and drug use:

Peer Group Acceptance. The need for friends' approval and a sense of belonging is a powerful motivation for youth to drink. They fear being left out; being ignored or rejected is just too painful. If drinking means avoiding these things, it's no contest. Youth tend to live according to the pressures and expectations of others, even when they are negative and destructive.

Immediate Instant Gratification. Young people live with a sense of immediacy, the need to experience pleasure, the rush, thrill, high, excitement, pleasure, fun. "Now" is essential for teens' existence. Immediate gratification is based on the premise that "I should always get what I want when I want it." In this fast-paced society, even immediate gratification is too slow. Drinking is the perfect catalyst for a radical experience, getting totally wasted, hammered, destroyed—because it feels good. Drinking actually provides artificial excitement and fun and causes youth to become immune to genuine pleasure and ultimate gratification.

To Escape Reality. When reality becomes too painful and depressing, youth choose not to deal with it. Alcohol becomes their escape from loneliness, stress, fears and problems with school, home and relationships. Alcohol has a numbing effect that is temporarily the magical solution. However, not confronting or dealing with pain actually intensifies it. Alcohol creates an illusion where youth can believe that life should be without pain and require no effort. Young people's efforts to confront their pain and problems and to know reality is crucial in determining their happiness and success as individuals.

The Need for Power and Control. Youth's feelings of invincibility and immortality coupled with an attitude that "It'll never happen to me" increases drug and alcohol use. In an increasingly complex high-tech society, with less family security and fewer dependable relationships and more stress from school, youth feel they are losing control of their lives. Drinking or doing drugs gives them a false sense of power; they feel they are in control, when actually they have less control and power than ever. Self-control is the real power.

Avoiding Boredom. Youth have never been more over-exposed and over-stimulated; boredom feeds their curiosity for a new, different and fun experience; they want to see what drinking or doing drugs is like. Alcohol consumption helps them escape their ordinary, boring existence for a little while. Alcohol use is a way of achieving unattainable goals; it gives teens a false sense of significance. Alcohol actually perpetuates their boredom.

Unmet Emotional Needs. Young people crave attention, affection and security; their need for intimacy and identity can motivate them to use alcohol. The fear of being inadequate, inferior and their feelings of insecurity cause youth to want to project an image they think others want to see. "To look more mature, to impress, to have status, to be somebody, you drink." Alcohol helps them create a "false image" which youth will go to great lengths to maintain. The need to "be cool" is a must in the youth culture, and at all costs alcohol and being cool go together.

The critical need for intimate relationships, especially with the opposite sex, is an overpowering emotional need among teens. Many teens feel lonely, insecure and isolated; their need for that certain someone in their life is critical. However, their fear of rejection or the fear of commitment keeps them from intimate relationships. Instead, they substitute alcohol for intimacy. This temporarily fulfills their need for connectedness without being vulnerable to rejection and without the demands and efforts of commitments.

Also, alcohol can cause youth to make decisions based upon deceptive feelings and real fears which produce fantasy. Drinking particularly affects teen girls who are much more vulnerable and susceptible to sexual involvement as inhibitions are swept away along with sound judgment. When youth drink, sexual activity increases — and so does the pain.

Just as drinking and driving can give them a false sense of confidence, alcohol makes them feel that their reflexes and reactions are faster and their ability to make choices is enhanced, when in reality just the opposite is true. Deceptive feelings and a false sense of control can be a lethal combination. Alcohol creates an illusion of reality and a false sense of power. Too many teens are "just saying yes" to alcohol use and too many are drinking, driving — and dying.

Driven to Be in Control: The Addicted Society

"No generation in American history has ever been terrified by its own offspring — that is, until now."

Paul Harvey

America has become a "high-tech Dodge City," with a lawless, violent and defiant generation that has no conscience.

Chapter 13

The Killing Fields: The Violence-Drenched Culture

For their feet run to evil, and they make haste to shed blood (Prov. 1:16 NKJ).

The Violence-Drenched Culture

Like an uncontrollable, horrible slime, violence oozes from every pore of American society.

For the second year in a row, America set a new record for murders, breaking the all-time previous high set in 1990, when we had 23,440 murders. In 1991, at least 26,250 murders were committed in the U.S. — a record the Senate Judiciary Committee expects to be broken for many years to come. The nation's murder rate has grown 30 percent since 1985.[1]

"A year which saw the rest of the world become safer . . . saw this nation become less safe for its own citizens," said Senator Joseph Biden, committee chairman. Among the findings:

- The average U.S. citizen is twice as likely to be a murder victim in the 1990s than three decades ago, even with a rising population.[2]

- The 1993 murder count is almost three times greater than the total number slain in Canada, France, Germany, England and Japan.[3]
- The rising murder toll was not confined to any single region of the nation, nor was it peculiar to any social or economic class. Rampant murder is touching every segment of American culture from rural and suburban areas to inner cities.[4]

A *USA Today* survey shows at least thirty-five large and medium U.S. cities tied or set murder records in 1993; at least another twelve cities posted their second-highest marks.

Experts believe the 1990s will continue to see record violent and murderous acts increase due to several factors. The committee cited three major causes for the increase:

1. A high number of seventeen- to twenty-four-year-olds; that group historically is the most violent and most likely to be victimized.

2. The drug trade, where drug dealers, hard-core addicts and youth gangs are fighting for turf as never before.

3. The ever-increasing glut of more weapons and more sophisticated deadly weapons, combined with the breakdown of the family and a general societal attitude that violence is a problem solver and life is cheap.[5]

During a typical week in America, deaths by guns total 464. More Americans die of gunshot wounds every two years than all those who have died from AIDS. Guns take more American lives in two years than did the entire Vietnam War.[6]

If we don't stop the growing tide of violence, the body count for the '90s decade could reach over 250,000. "One of the big differences in our society is the ready access to weapons, sort of a 'Wild West' mentality that has lingered on for centuries," says Hubert Williams, president of the Police Foundation. There are nearly two hundred million guns in the hands of the general public, almost one for every man, woman and child in America.[7]

The tentacles of violence are reaching everywhere into every level of society. We have created a frightening culture of violence. Each year, about one out of every thirteen teens experiences a violent crime. Approximately three million violent crimes are attempted or carried out on young people. Every twenty minutes a young person dies in an accident. In addition to a murder every twenty-four minutes, there's a rape every six minutes, a robbery every minute, a burglary every ten seconds, and a car theft every twenty-two seconds.[8] The U.S. has twenty times the number of rapes reported in Japan, England and Spain.

"Forty million Americans were victims of serious crimes in 1990, including those 23,200 who were murdered. There are more violent criminals, armed with more potent weaponry, showing more contempt for the police than at any time in American history." Cops today are outmanned, outgunned and under fire, feeling trapped between rising crime rates and angry citizens wanting immediate solutions to overwhelming problems.[9]

Our violence-saturated culture has produced a paradox where, on the one hand, killings, rapes, robberies and random violence have become so commonplace that Americans' sense of horror and outrage has been numbed; our culture is conditioned to death and destruction. On the other side of the coin, there is a foreboding cloud of fear over our lives, we wonder if something terrible might happen to us or someone we love.

Juvenile Armageddon

Crime has become the number one concern of the American public and the dominant issue on the political scene. People in the U.S. are fearful and feeling personally threatened by what they consider a complete collapse of the fabric of society.

> "In the next decade, the nation's most violent population, teens fifteen to nineteen years, will explode by 23 percent. In a culture that regards killing as cool and hatred as hip, we're facing a 'Juvenile Armageddon,'" says criminologist Jack Levin of Northwestern University.[10]

A recent FBI report stated that the number of teens under eighteen arrested for homicides soared more than 138 percent since 1983. Gunshots now cause one of every four deaths among American teenagers, according to the National Center for Health Statistics. Guns killed nearly 4,300 teenagers in 1990 and 5,100 in 1992, up from 2,500 deaths in 1985, the most recent year for which figures are available.[11]

For many teens, with their warped sense of morality and craving for thrills, gunplay has become a deadly sport. There is a frightening subculture of violence, where having power means using a gun. Too many weapons and too much insanity equals death and destruction for this generation.

Mainstream Violence

A frightening "gun culture" has so pervaded the nation's schools that more than one third of teenagers say they probably will die at young ages because of guns, states a recent national survey.[12]

The National Center for Juvenile Justice reveals the murder rate for the last five years for adolescents under eighteen has skyrocketed by 85 percent. One law enforcement official said, "Life means nothing to these kids today." The number of fourteen- to seventeen-year-olds arrested for crimes of violence rose a mind-boggling 3000 percent between 1955 and 1993.

The American Psychological Association 1993 report concluded:

> Forty years of research indicates that viewing television violence may lead to aggressive attitudes, values and behavior, particularly in children and teens. . . . There are indeed measurable harmful effects of media mayhem on both younger and older viewers.[13]

The child abuse epidemic, the rapid increase in poverty among children and teens, combined with the saturation of guns have created a culture of violence, which law enforcement experts say will continue to get worse in the '90s.

The Violent State of America s Children

Violence is killing thousands of children every year in our spiritually sick nation, according to the Children's Defense Fund. "Murder is now the third leading cause of death among children age five to fourteen," says Marian Edelman. "This is an emergency," she says. "We are witnessing the collapse of the social and moral foundations of American society."

- A U.S. child dies of a gunshot wound every two hours.
- A U.S. child is fifteen times as likely to be killed by a gun as one in Northern Ireland, where sectarian fighting rages.

- Nearly fifty thousand children were killed by guns from 1979 to 1991, almost the number of Americans killed in Vietnam.

The Fund also says more than 2.9 million children were reported abused or neglected in 1992, nearly triple the number in 1980.[14]

The American Justice System in Chaos

The American criminal justice system, for both adults and juveniles, is in total chaos and is overwhelmed by more violent criminals than it can begin to deal with.

National figures reveal a frightening and astonishing fact: The time prisoners spend behind bars has been steadily declining. Violent offenders will serve, on average, less than four years. The mean time served by murderers released in 1991 was only seven-and-a-half years.

Parole horror stories have become the norm. One federal study that tracked 109,000 former prisoners found that 63 percent of them were rearrested for serious crimes, including 2,300 homicides, 3,900 forcible sex crimes, 17,000 robberies and 23,000 assaults. Today, we have well over half a million violent convicts who are out on parole.[15]

Kids Who Kill

The youth culture in America has become the "killing field." More teens have guns than ever before, and more teens are dying. "Every 100 hours, more youths die on the streets in the U.S. than were killed in the Persian Gulf War."[16] The deadliest, most violent group in America are male youths age fifteen to twenty-four; they are increasing in number and are dressed to kill.

Surprising numbers of children and adolescents are victims of assault from fights, rape and abuse, the first major study of its kind suggests. "These events are much more common than anyone realized," says Dr. Bernard Guyner of Johns Hopkins University. Overall, one in 130 youths was treated for an intentional injury. Each year, over three million children and teens are attacked or assaulted at school.[17]

Teenagers are more than twice as likely as adults to be victims of rape, robbery and assault, according to a government report. The study concludes that victims of violent teen crime usually know their assailant and that more than 60 percent of the violent teen crimes are committed by offenders who are under eighteen years old.[18]

Homicide is the leading cause of death for black males, age fifteen to twenty-four. The number of black teen gun killers has increased by 555 percent since 1984. For young black males, age fifteen to nineteen, the murder rate was more than nine times greater than for their white male teen counterparts. Gunfire is the number one cause of death for black males, age fifteen to nineteen. Inner city emergency rooms treat three times as many gunshot wounds as six years ago. National health officials say exploding violence among the nation's youth has made homicide the second leading killer of people age fifteen to twenty-four.[19]

Homicide deaths have recently surpassed the tragically high suicide rate, making it the third cause of death among youth; accidents are number one.

Most experts are projecting that the 1990s will be the nation's most violent decade in history. There is rage out there. "You have the drug epidemic, the proliferation of guns, gangs terrorizing entire communities that live in utter poverty and hopelessness. These days the odds are much better that you'll be murdered than win a lottery."[20]

More frequently than ever, people are ending up on a morgue slab for no reason at all, other than being in the wrong place at the wrong time. Scores of people were killed this past year for taking a parking place, looking at someone's date, pulling in front of someone in traffic, having expensive sneakers or playing the radio too loudly.

Males account for 89 percent of all violent crime committed in America.[21] They have become a new lost generation, fueled by the violence of drug activity, armed through quick and easy access to high-powered guns, angered by an economy that provides little hope for the future and guided by an entertainment media that glorifies murder. The number of murders committed by juveniles likely will quadruple by the end of the decade, partially because of child abuse, drug abuse, fatherless families and poverty, according to an American psychological association study.[22]

Youth aren't settling their arguments with fists; now, they use guns. There's a new breed of youth out there that is stone-hearted, cold-blooded; they'll kill you for the thrill or just because it's convenient.

America Home of the Most Violent

In a comprehensive study entitled "The Day America Told the Truth," it was revealed that the official crime statistics in the U.S. are off by more than 600 percent. The recorded statistics are greatly misleading and sorely underestimate the actual crime in this country that is staggering. Sixty percent of all Americans have been the victims of a major crime. Fifty-eight percent of those people have been victimized twice or more. Americans live in continual fear of unpredictable violence and crime.[23]

Crime statistics are calculated on a yearly basis, meaning that the official statistics only report the chances of an individual American being victimized in one year.

James Patterson and the research team for *The Day America Told the Truth* relate these facts:

> We decided to take a different approach, asking Americans if they had ever been the victims of crime. Fully, 60 percent or 600 in every 1,000 adult Americans have been the victim of at least one crime. The figure is shockingly six times higher than the single year official estimates. We further found that 350 in every 1,000 Americans have been the victims of at least two crimes, 3.5 times the single year estimates.[24]

Young men, age fifteen to twenty-four years, do most of our killing and dying in America. The official worldwide crime statistics show the homicide rate among young American males is twenty times that of Western Europe and forty times that of Japan.

Our fears are grounded in the facts of our daily lives, the real crime statistics that come from our own experience. We live in the most violent country in the world.[25]

Media Violence

The media-created, mass production of graphic violence in our society has brought the level of stimulation so high that it takes more and more brutal, vicious images to excite us.

By the age of eighteen, the average American child will have seen two hundred thousand violent acts on television, including forty thousand murders, according to Thomas Radecki, research director for the National Coalition on Violence.[26] We have two generations who have grown up with television and movies and are desensitized to violence, and another generation who are now children becoming conditioned to a violent mentality.

In the last forty years, over 235 studies on the effects of television violence on individual behavior have been done. The scientific evidence has been analyzed and discussed in over 2,500 articles, books and reports. The consensus of sociologists and psychologists and other experts in the media field have concluded: A large majority of studies show that viewing television and film violence does not help children and teens get rid of anti-social, violent inclinations. Quite the contrary, it leads to increases in aggressive and anti-social behavior, and this is true for all ages.[27] The study goes on to confirm the relationship between viewing violence and real violence.

Mean World Mentality

Television creates a distorted view of reality. Constant exposure to violence develops what Dr. George Gerbner calls "mean world syndrome." Children and teens watching prime time TV are more prone to feelings of hostility and seeing the world as dangerous. In this mean, dangerous world, it's do-it-to-them-before-they-do-it-to-you survival, because most people cannot be trusted and are just looking out for themselves.[28]

In a research study, TV crime was more than one hundred times more likely to involve murder than real-life crime. TV crime is twelve times more likely to involve violence than real-life crime does. The study also showed that while violent crime represents only 15 percent of real-life crime, 88 percent of TV crime is violent.[29]

Television has produced a mean world mind-set where violence is normal and necessary. This encourages some people to commit acts of violence.

In 1950, when TV was in its infancy, in the entire U.S. only 170 persons under the age of fifteen were arrested for serious crimes such as murder, rape, robbery and aggravated assault. By 1979, the rate of serious crime committed by teens and children under fifteen had increased 11,000 percent.[30]

We have produced an "instant violence gratification." If a guy needs some money, he robs a bank, or maybe makes a drug deal. When a male teen is angry at somebody, killing is no longer unthinkable; it's natural. When a girlfriend breaks up a relationship, killing her is the answer. Forty years ago, these actions would have been unthinkable, yet today they occur with frightening regularity. After all, that's the way they do it on television.

Movie Madness

Exploding across the cinema screen is graphic violence and gore on a scale previously unimaginable. Featuring nonstop violence and destruction, movie mayhem offers *Robo Cop, Die Hard, Predator, Total Recall* and *Terminator*, the latter establishing Arnold Schwarzenegger as a mega-star; they broke box-office records and are enjoying phenomenal success, as high-tech violence is taken to new levels.

The attraction of the films is the raw violent action — "kick down the doors," "rip off your face," "blow you away," "take no prisoners" — as movie superstars shoot, smash, crush, blast, shatter and destroy all those in their path.

The special effects are mesmerizing as state-of-the-art technology transforms movie violence to a new dimension that is louder, more vivid and more realistic than ever before. The combined body count for those violent action films runs into the hundreds, and we still want more. "On the escalation of violence, no sooner has some movie established itself as the new standard, the pressure mounts in Hollywood to outdo it," says Todd Gitlin, professor of sociology at University of California, Berkeley. "Serious aggression never occurs unless there is a convergence of large numbers of causes, but one of the very important factors is exposure to media violence. If we don't do something, we are contributing to a society that will be more and more violent."[31]

L. Rowell Huesmann, psychologist at the University of Illinois, studied one set of children for twenty years. He states, "We believe that heavy exposure to televised and film violence is one of the causes of aggressive behavior, crime and violence in society today."[32]

Youth are so inundated with fascinating violent media images, it's impossible to resist growing numb. Youth, and adults as well, risk becoming insensitive to the horror of suffering and the pain of others.

The Slasher Phenomenon

The emergence of the slasher horror films in the mid-'70s introduced an unprecedented aspect of violence. Before the '70s, horror films were spooky and scary, but not grotesque. Things changed with three blockbuster "slasher" film series that combined horror with a vicious violence and were huge hits in the youth culture and major box office successes generating numerous sequels. *Friday the 13th,* featuring Jason, *Nightmare on Elm Street,* starring Freddy, and *Halloween* are movies that brought new meaning to the word *horror.* Another popular slasher movie that plunges to new depths of gore is *Texas Chain Saw Massacre;* it showed people being skinned, burned alive, dismembered and cannibalized.

Freddy and Jason are killing machines as they slaughter, torture and mutilate teens, but they can't be killed, which adds to the terror. All types of cutting weapons of destruction are used — knives, axes and chain saws. Many experts say this fascination with slasher/horror films is an important barometer of America's cultural mood. If that is true, then the mood in popular culture is cool, calm and brutal.

The popularity of the horror film is indeed startling. In 1947, horror films represented 4 percent of the world's annual releases; by 1967, the number had grown to 7.6 percent; and by 1987, one out of every six films made in America could be classified as a horror film.[33] We have become a culture fascinated and preoccupied with horror. "While theater viewership of uncut and graphic horror has increased approximately fifteen-fold since 1979, total viewership of horror, including home video viewership, has increased 300 percent."[34]

These slasher films combine state-of-the-art murder techniques with violence, transporting teens into a new realm of horror. The question in the slasher films is not who will get killed next, but how will it be done, as every conceivable method of killing and mutilation is used.

Those experts who have researched the desensitizing effects of regularly watching slasher films agree that the material negatively affects high school- and college-age males: it reduces their sympathy and understanding for real-life rape victims; it increases their willingness to coerce women sexually; it increases their level of anger and disinhibits them from expressing that anger toward women.[35]

These high school- and college-age males, after a week of constant exposure to slasher films, changed in their evaluation of how violent, degrading and offensive scenes were. Material that the youth had previously found anxiety-provoking and depressing became less so. A major element of the slasher films is the sensual appeal; extremely violent scenes are often followed by relaxing music or mildly erotic love scenes. Many of the films are set in nice "normal" suburban environments. Slasher films mix savage violence with sexual exploitation and brutalization of mostly teen girls and young women. The very manner in which sexual scenes are shot causes rape to look like an activity that is energizing. "In all of pop culture (as in most of society), women are the victims of choice."[36]

A recent survey of 1,700 students in the sixth to ninth grades revealed that 65 percent of the boys and 57 percent of the girls said it was acceptable for a man to force a woman to have sex if they had been dating for more than six months, and 51 percent of the boys and 41 percent of the girls said a man had a right to force a woman to kiss him if he had spent ten to fifteen dollars on her.[37]

A study reported in the Journal of Personality and Social Psychology informs us that "teenage boys who can watch horror movies, like the *Friday the 13th* series, without showing signs of distress are seen by their dates as more attractive because of their bravado." Slasher films are rented at video stores mostly by teenage boys, frequently to watch with their dates. It is the "masculine mystique" — toughness, fearlessness, emotional detachment, insensitivity — that these young men are demonstrating to their dates, not their sense of humor. It seems that many of the young men who show off their "masculinity" to their dates by remaining cool at slasher films may simply have become desensitized to the grotesque, extreme violence through long-term exposure.[38]

Many young people view slasher films as being in vogue. To see them is to be "in"; it's making a social statement. Millions of American teenagers, but also younger children, have been watching slasher films in movie theaters and on VCRs over the last fifteen years or so.

The National Coalition on Television and Film Violence states, "It is now a standard part of American culture to view numerous extremely graphic and brutal horror films before the age of twelve." The article goes on to point out that "the current generation of youth and children are being raised on the most sadistic material ever conceived by humans."[39]

Journey into Madness

Item: Bossier City, La.—Two high-school football players, Bryan Widenhouse, seventeen, and DeWayne Mosley, seventeen, described as sharp, good kids, gifted, and model student-athletes, committed a calculated murder of former best friend and football teammate Dramonte Smith, seventeen.[40]

Dramonte Smith was wired by police with a listening device to help break a prolific theft ring that involved Smith, Mosley and Widenhouse. Mosley and Widenhouse, who were popular students from upper-middle-class families, repeatedly fired a pistol and rifle into Smith's body. Both boys have admitted to the slaying.

Dr. Anna Singdahlsen says, "One thing that I think is involved is that those kids have had everything they've always wanted. They've never developed a conscience. They get to the point where they think, 'Well, if I want it, I'll take it.' They know what the rules are, but they believe they're above the rules, they're special, they're privileged. Then it becomes a small step from taking others' possessions to taking a life."[41]

Item: Dedham, Mass.—Rod Matthews, fifteen, beat to death classmate Shawn Quillette, fifteen, with a baseball bat to find out what it was like to kill someone. Matthews plotted the killing as he lured Shawn into the woods with the promise of fireworks, then cold-bloodedly bludgeoned him to death and took other youth to see the bloodied dead body of his classmate. "Suspects are getting younger and more vicious," says Sgt. Ken Vachris of Houston Police Dept. "The change I have seen is young kids — the value they place on life is nothing. Most of the time, you see no emotion or remorse about killing someone," says Sgt. Doug Bacon. "Taking a life affects them about as much as eating a Big Mac; it's no big deal."[42]

Item: Fountain, Col.—Last Saturday night, this normally quiet community of eleven thousand was struck by the most shocking crime in its history. Police say five of Fountain's teenage boys, all liked, well known and popular, one a football player, beat to death a soldier, Layne Schmidtke, twenty-four, from Fort Carson, on a downtown street in nearby Colorado Springs, while a crowd of thirty other teens looked on. "There really isn't a motive," says Colorado Springs Police Lt. Rich Resling. He sees a trend: "It's a social phenomenon. I think teenagers are more violence prone."[43]

Item:—Los Angeles is the base of operations for much of the gang violence spreading across the U.S. The grim statistics: Two people will be killed and sixteen injured there today, and the worst of the violence and mayhem is among teens and children. Some are slain for vengeance; others are young innocents caught in the deadly crossfire of random violence and the madness of gang wars.[44]

Kids kill today on impulse, by cold-blooded, premeditated plans, for apparently no reason at all and for the emotional thrill of killing.

The Gang Explosion

In the last ten years in America, gang membership has increased six-fold, going from twenty-five thousand members to over two thousand gangs with 280,000 members nationwide and growing daily.

Assistant Attorney General Tommy Gurule, who is conducting a national field study on gang violence with the U.S. Justice Department, says these gangs are different from gangs of the '60s and '70s because they fight over drug markets instead of neighborhood turf.[45]

The gangs of today are also armed to the teeth with sophisticated semiautomatic assault weapons that would rival a military combat troop. The favorite street weapons used by gangs are shotguns, handguns, Uzis, AK-47s and AR-15s. These are used to blast away at any threat to their drug profits from police and rival gangs, or just to kill for the thrill.

Los Angeles is the gang capital of America as more than 100,000 gang members have created their own violent subculture, now a growing epidemic across our nation. America is becoming a "Gang Nation." Since 1984, when the arrival of crack cocaine touched off a gang explosion, a new style of youth gang and gang violence throughout America has been born. Gangs have spread like a plague upon the land during the last five years as brutal violence, crime and death have followed.

Drugs and quick money drive this fantastic growth rate among gangs. They create their own economy, which is fueled by drugs and violence. Crack cocaine emerged as lucrative, highly addictive and easy to deal. "It did for gangs what the Barbie doll did for Mattel," says Steve Valdiva, Executive Director of Youth Gang Services Project in Los Angeles.[46]

The Gang Nation

Suddenly the lead stories on the local and national newscasts were about the latest gang-related shootings. Terms like "pay-back killing" and "drive-by shooting" became well-known in the public's vocabulary. Drive-bys are not just gang related; it's now become a style of committing murder in America. "It's destroyed all youth," says Wes McBride, Sergeant for Operation Safe Streets in Los Angeles. "They're not afraid of us. They've lost all feeling for human life. . . . We're seeing more of that," says L.A. Police Commander William Booth.[47]

Gang violence and homicides have drastically increased in scores of cities across the U.S. Hundreds of innocent people — adults, teens and children — have become victims of gang violence. In parts of America, violence and killing is so commonplace, it doesn't faze teens anymore. In D.C., Miami and L.A., local youth were asked about the recent shooting deaths of other youth; their comments were, "It's just the neighborhood. . . . It's no big deal. . . . That's just the way it is." The death of young people in too many areas of the country is becoming frighteningly normal.

The Gang Subculture

Gangs have their own culture, their own rules, their own perception of reality, their own language, their own unique identities. They're obsessed with the symbols and colors and power that identify their gang and give them identity.

Types of Gangs. Los Angeles is a city of gangs. There are black gangs, Hispanic gangs, white gangs, Asian gangs, immigrant gangs and hybrid gangs. The largest and most predominant gangs are the black gangs. The Crips and Bloods have gained national notoriety with gangs across America. There are hundreds of Crip and Blood sets (a set is an particular gang clique) — Playboy Gangster Crips and Rollin' '60s Crips, or Bounty Hunters Bloods and Outlaw Twenties Bloods — out of L.A.

Getting in. Every gang has its rituals for the "jumping in" process; usually it's a fistfight. A recruit has made the grade if he's still standing after a ten-minute bout with as many as ten gang members. Other gauntlet-like tests may also be required.

Names. After joining a gang, a member gets a new name. It's often a literal description of a member's personality or appearance: "One-shot" has a reputation for sharp shooting. Other names: Baby Sin, Sidewinder, 6-Roc, Boss Hog, etc.

Clothes. Gang members follow strict dress codes. Hispanic gangs painstakingly iron khaki pants with a sharp crease down each leg. Their white cotton T-shirts are heavily starched and worn under plaid flannel shirts buttoned only at the collar. Headgear: bandannas or black hair nets.

Black gang members wear the same khaki pants or Levi jeans but so low their boxers show. Their plaid flannel shirts are unbuttoned. Baseball caps are worn backwards because the brim gets in the way when firing a gun. Bandannas in gang colors (red or blue) are worn. Bloods and Crips gang members never go anywhere without a bandanna which is either worn on the head or hanging out of their pants pocket. Other gang paraphernalia: corduroy bedroom slippers from Montgomery Ward or expensive ninety-dollar leather athletic shoes, like NIKE's Air Jordan, Reeboks, British Knights, L.A. Gear and others.

Major league baseball caps, major college and NFL jackets and hats are popular with gangs; the Los Angeles Raiders' hats and jackets are favorites, along with a thick or rope gold chain.[48]

Gang Slang

Language: Gang members have their own unique language.

Gang hand signs—Gang members identify themselves by signing with their hands in gestures similar to the deaf. For example, the index and little finger extended with second and third fingers folded in is the sign of a Blood from the "Brim" set.

Throwing or flashing—Hand positions that have specific meanings or certain significance to gang members.

Cluck heads—crack addicts.

High roller—big dealer.

Bailer—the Bloods' term for big dealer.

Home boys (Homies)—fellow members of the gang that is their family; they are totally committed to each other. Crips also use "Cuz."

Original gangster—a respectful, admired term referring to a veteran gang member that has earned his gang stripes.

Gang-bangin'—being in a gang.

Flaggin'—waving red or blue bandannas or proclaiming gang affiliation on enemy turf.

187—a spray-painted "187" in red graffiti is an executioner's signature or death threat. One-eighty-seven is the police code for murder.

Slippin'—being careless; not watching your back.

Boo-yah—expression for killing. Someone is "boo-yah"—the sound from a sawed-off shotgun.

Jointed up—initiated by being beaten by other gang members.

Busting fresh—dressing to the max or at the height of fashion.

Smoke 'em—kill them.

Trip—getting out of line or making mistakes.

Tiny gangsters—younger gang members age nine to twelve years.

Put in work—getting busy to rob, shoot, kill; any activity that is dangerous.

Hoods—a term gangs use for neighborhoods, gang turf or affiliation.

Bangin' and slangin'—hanging out, gang-banging; and selling dope.[49]

Why Youth Join Gangs

The need for identity. Gang members have a sense of importance, respect and self-worth, even though it's a false sense of identity, a feeling that "I am somebody." The tough, fearless macho image fills an identity vacuum for black youth. They get a gang name and a new identity. Gang members who have been shot or stabbed several times are admired and worshiped as heroes. Crips and Bloods are telling nine- and ten-year-old children, "We're somebody; you can be somebody too — join our gang.

"The most potent feelings of self-worth for a gang member come from murder."[50]

Need for family. Most gang members come from a broken, abusive or nonexistent family where there is no father or positive male role model; many don't have fathers or mothers for stable, healthy, parental roles. Many black youth are raised by mothers, grandmas or aunts. The gang is appealing to black youth because it's about being committed to other people and creates a feeling of unity. The gang becomes their whole world. Gang members would do anything for their "home boys." The gang gives them a sense of belonging, togetherness, security and masculinity.

Studies of delinquent boys have convinced many sociologists that boys raised by mothers alone are particularly prone to violence because of their susceptibility to "hypermasculinity, or extreme masculine behavior to prove their manhood."[51]

Desire for fast, easy money. Most gang members come from low-income to poverty-level situations and have dropped out of school and joined a gang, trying to escape the poverty cycle. Black youth see the gold chains, jewelry, cars, clothes, etc., that gang members have from dealing drugs; money becomes a powerful recruiting tool. A materialistic, consumer-oriented society continually exposes them to media images of the fabulously rich and lavish life-styles which intensifies their desire for money and things. They want a lot of money now. The only way to do it is illegally. Gang activity provides immediate money in large quantities; this attracts black youth. Once they've had the "green $ experience," having lots of money and things, they are addicted to this affluent life-style — and there's no going back.

Alienated from society. Black youth, especially males, feel alienated from mainstream culture. They feel ripped off, exploited and ignored by the system; the gang gives them a way of venting their anger and frustration. Black youth create their own system and gang subculture that is in total opposition and defiance to a system they distrust and see as hypocritical and uncaring. Gangs say, "In your face!"

The rap music phenomenon that burst on the scene in the late '80s became the voice for many black youth in America, expressing their feelings and frustrations with the hypocrisy; however, too much of "rap music" contains sexually explicit, obscene, violent lyrics and promotes antisocial violent behavior as well as the brutalization and subjugation of women. Flavor Flav has been widely criticized for glamorizing gang violence.

"Gangsta rap" reflects and describes the street mentality and gang life-style of black youth in the U.S. Rappers like Flavor Flav of Public Enemy, Ice Cube, Ice-T, Snoop Doggy Dog and others voice their resentment of mainstream America and portray inner-city warfare and violence.

Ice Cube starred in an inner-city movie about the violent effect the gangs' life-style has on families, friends and black youth's future. Ice Cube's *Kill at Will* album deals with the impact of violence. *Amerikkk's Most Wanted* established him as the angriest, if not the best, voice for inner-city youth.

The desire for power and control. Many black male youth feel manipulated, exploited and rendered powerless by the system. The gang represents being part of something with power and being in control of their lives and others. Being in a gang means drugs, money, colors, turf executions — which means power. One of the greatest fears of gang members is that their enemy gang is more together, more organized, more powerful than theirs. In reality, gang power creates a false sense of power and an illusion of control that only lasts until you slip up or forget to watch your back; continually looking over your shoulder creates a feeling that mocks power. Gang members are constantly thinking about getting murdered or captured.[52]

The attraction of danger and excitement. To escape the drudgery, boredom and monotony of the daily grind, they look to gang life, which symbolizes an exciting, thrilling, on-the-edge experience. They enter to find the gang-bangin' world of drugs, violence, money and assassinations, where kids hum the latest movie theme music to themselves while killing people.

G-Roc, a Crip gang member, describes the gang-bangin' scene as "a mission, like drivin' through an enemy 'hood, bein' in danger o' yo' life. We gonna show how gang-bangin' really is. Like kill, buddy! Get yo' artillery weapons up! It's gang-bangin'. Whatever you wanna do, it's on. Gang-bangin' is on."[53]

Factors that Contribute to Antisocial Violent Behavior

No Father or Inadequate Fathering. The best available data suggests that high levels of violent behavior are frequently linked to a boy's having had no father or negative fathering.

Sociological studies of juvenile delinquent boys indicate that a high percentage of them come from families in which either there is no father in the household or the father is on hand but is abusive or violent. Cross-cultural studies suggest that violent behavior is often characteristic of male adolescents and adults whose fathers were absent or played a small role in their life. For boys without fathers, the mass media and their own peer group tend to be the main sources of their concept of what it is to be a man.

The tendency toward violence has been aggravated in the last twenty years by the enormous increase in the number of teen pregnancies out of wedlock, particularly black teenage girls having babies. "Our inner cities are now filled with millions of fatherless boys who are extremely susceptible to 'hypermasculinity,' where violence becomes the outlet to achieve dominant power and manhood."[54]

Inability to Empathize. The qualities of the "masculine mystique," toughness, fearlessness, emotional detachment and insensitivity are diametrically opposed to the ability to be empathetic. American culture conditions young males from early on to repress feelings of attachment, dependence, vulnerability, caring, transparency and intense love and hate.

In a twenty-six-year, longitudinal study of empathy, researchers found that the single factor most highly linked to empathic concern was the level of involvement by the father during child care. Increasing male violence among youth ages fifteen to twenty-four is linked to being "devoid of empathy," unable to be compassionate, sympathize or care about other people's feelings and pain. This emotional jadedness (detachment) causes males to be more prone to commit violent acts.[55]

This lack of empathy has produced a cold-bloodedness in the youth culture where youth are ready to shoot first and not ask questions, where someone's death is about as significant as eating pizza with friends.

Sense of Entitlement. Young people don't want a job, they want a position. They don't have any idea how they're going to get this prestige and power; they just expect it — now! The entitlement mentality breeds greed and envy that produce floating bitterness and antisocial violent behavior. Teens with this attitude do not want to accept responsibility for their actions; they always shift the blame to something or someone else. Even violent behavior is rationalized and justified as understandable behavior. Also, because many teens believe their crime will go unpunished, they become more arrogant and violent.

Mass Media and Moral Desolation. The electronic mass media on the one hand has desensitized youth to violence by bombarding them with violent, antisocial images. Not only is violence normalized, but it is portrayed as a desirable quality, especially for male youth where dominance, control and power through violence prove their manhood.

Combine the media effect with a bankrupt moral value system, where right and wrong and good and evil become the same thing, then violence and killing are rationalized and justified.

High-Tech Dodge City

The gang scene in America reflects the alienation and random vengeance of a generation of angry youth: cold-hearted "lost boys" decked out in bandannas and baseball caps, carrying deadly automatic weapons, cradling shotguns and heavy caliber pistols as they flash the gang hand signs.

They exude a fierce, emotionally detached presence; when you look into their eyes, you get swallowed up by the calloused emptiness. They look like modern-day outlaws lost in time and ever ready for battle and death. America has become a "high-tech Dodge City." There are more sophisticated bad guys, carrying more lethal weapons, producing a generation of efficient, cold-blooded killing machines with an insatiable appetite for violence and death.

The atmosphere is deadly and dangerous, where "live fast, die young, and leave a good-looking corpse" is more than a motto; it's a life-style.

Violence in America has reached frightening dimensions. What's really scary is the level of tolerance that is developing. We are beginning to accept violence as a normal occurrence, a fact of our time and our life-style. Once you accept something as normal, it continues to grow.

"If we don't make a dramatic change in our value system, in our cultural approach, in our return to individual accountability, the future will be in peril." G-Roc, L.A. Crip gang member, says, "It don't matter what you say about gang-bangin', you know, don't matter if anybody understands it or not. We just bringin' home the hate. 'Cause everybody one-eight-seven (police code for murder). That's the kind of world we live in."[56]

In thirty years in America, we've gone from *Father Knows Best* to Father, where are you?

Chapter 14

Aliens Are in My House: The Lost Family

There is a generation that curses its father, and does not bless its mother (Prov. 30:11 NKJ).

Ozzie and Harriet, Where Are You?

In the early '50s, there was a euphoric optimism following World War II, a general prosperity and a sense of opportunity that engulfed the American culture. The traditional American family was very much intact and thriving as the baby boom hit full force. Motherhood became a major industry as eleven thousand babies were born in America each day, totaling four million a year.[1] Suddenly, it was very trendy to have children and devote all attention to the family and raising kids. From birth through the teen years, baby boomers were the focus of an entire society, with indulgent parents, ultra-high expectations and non-stop gratification. No other generation had been the object of so much parental concern and attention, and none had been its equal in terms of privilege and advantage while growing up.

To make sure parents did everything necessary to help their kids grow up fulfilled emotionally, Dr. Spock's book on child care became the best-selling new title ever published. These Spock children were the center of attention, and no sacrifice was too great. Throughout their teen years, the baby boomers were accommodated to make sure they got every benefit available.

The massive size of the boomer generation gave them tremendous power in society and, unconsciously, a false sense of power and influence. Good parenting became synonymous with gratification and the elimination of frustration and disappointment. Concerned parents wanted to give their children all the advantages they never had. These social forces and the catered-to mentality created an atmosphere of immediate, constant gratification; this became a status symbol and identification for parents who were considered good, caring and loving.

Media Unreality

As children, boomers were raised on *The Donna Reed Show, Father Knows Best, Leave It To Beaver* and *The Adventures of Ozzie and Harriet.* These "always happy" TV images of the family helped set up a generation for ultimate disappointment and illusions of reality.

The ideal world that was portrayed by television, especially in the family setting, created a "glass house effect" concerning marriage and family life. This glass house TV world was a place where unhappiness, problems and disappointment were not allowed, at least not for very long. Boomers grew up on Walt Disney productions, where manufactured fairy tale endings were a part of life.

The media helped produce the "perfect family" mentality where the home was safe, secure and loving, parents always had the answers and there was always a happy ending. The boomer generation (now parents) grew up believing good relationships would simply happen "if you wish upon a star!" These were the "wonder years" where magically, somehow everything would be okay; we believed this even as adults.

The traditional American family in the '50s and early '60s was in. Fathers worked; most mothers stayed home; divorce was shocking and rare; step-families and single-parent families were an oddity; day-care centers were almost nonexistent; adultery and living together were scandalous, even in Hollywood.

In the movie *The Parent Trap* in the early '60s, Hayley Mills doubled as twin sisters separated by a seldom-occurring divorce. The movie revolves around the two teen sisters plotting and scheming to get Mom and Dad back together so they can be a family again. By the end of the movie, the parents are reunited, remarry and they all live happily ever after.

However, below the surface in a lot of seemingly ideal families of the '50s and '60s were many negative, addictive and harmful relationships. The television facade began to unravel with problems, abuse and pain in the real homes and lives of many boomers, but they couldn't turn the channel. Many boomer kids who had abusive family experiences still thought it was normal, since nobody at that time ever mentioned child abuse, at least not publicly. The boomer generation would cling to the happy dreams and hopes projected by the media images that defined the family and marriage, and vowed that they would be different when they had families of their own.

The baby boomers grew up with this message: There are no limits on tomorrow; anything is possible. The mass media, combined with doting parents, helped create a false sense of self-importance, entitlement and self-centeredness that has interfered with meaningful family relationships. The electronic mass media has helped shape and determine the expectations, attitudes and choices of the baby boomers concerning marriage and the family. Ozzie and Harriet, where are you?

The Fragmenting Family

This is a period of historic change in American family life; the traditional family of the '50s doesn't exist anymore. The upheaval is evident everywhere in our culture. As children have babies, teens and college-age youth refuse to grow up and leave home; others run away from home, and some join youth gangs. Affluent yuppies prize their BMWs more than children; women abort their babies in favor of careers; rich and poor young people display at-risk behavior; people casually move in with each other, and out again. "The traditional family unit — the working father and a mother who stays home to care for the two children — has been replaced by a different kind of household. In 1960, this stereotypical family type represented 60 percent of all households; today, it reflects just 7 percent of our households."[2]

Today's fragmented family consists of multiple relationships including single parents, step-families, couples living together and homosexual couples. "The average American family in 1991 consists of a married couple with one child, in which both parents are employed. At least one of the parents has been divorced or will be divorced. Parents are having fewer children and having them later in life."[3]

The divorce rate has tripled (300 percent) since 1960, and today 53 percent of all first marriages will end in divorce. Six out of ten second marriages will end in divorce within ten years. Since 1972, there have been over one million divorces each year. Forty percent of all children born in the past decade will probably live in a step-family before they are eighteen. "Increasing proportions of households are 'blended' families' homes in which the children from two or more marriages are combined as a result of remarriages. There is a growing trend toward partners having children without being married."[4]

Departing from the Norm Is Normal

In 1992, about one out of every fifteen children will be born out of wedlock. Presently, one out of every four households consists of a single parent with one or more children. It is projected that the number of single parents will double within the next five years. "The current trend indicates that of all children born in 1990, six out of ten (60 percent) will live in a single-parent household for some period of time before they reach the age of eighteen."[5] One out of every five children lives in poverty, and the number is increasing. The rate is twice as high among blacks and Hispanics.

An astonishing two thirds of all mothers are in the labor force, which is double the rate in 1955, and more than half of all mothers of newborn infants are in the work force. "The increasing prevalence of divorce and working mothers has turned child care into a major growth industry."[6]

According to a *Newsweek* poll, we find the family worse than it was a decade ago, and we are uneasy about the '90s. Parents are torn between work, careers and family obligations; economic uncertainties and skyrocketing teen pregnancies cloud the horizon. Marriage has become a fragile and expedient institution, not something anyone can depend on. Getting married two or three times will be normal and commonplace during the '90s.[7]

Divorce has produced an emotional wasteland, leaving a devastated generation in its wake. The pain is multiplied by poverty and abuse.

"Although we think of the 'Woodstock Generation' as the era in which couples were most likely to live together outside of marriage, cohabitation is more prevalent today than ever. Half of all adults under the age of thirty will live with someone before they get married."[8]

The fear of divorce is one of the major reasons that an increasing number of young adults cohabit outside marriage. Sixty percent of recently married adults lived with their new spouse before getting married. While unmarried, cohabitating adults constitute a small percentage of all households, it is the fastest growing household arrangement. The proportion of households headed by unmarried people living together has quadrupled since 1970.[9]

Most couples who cohabit eventually get married, but it has been found that their marriages are more fragile and problematic than those of couples who don't cohabit before marriage.

A good family life remains the number one desire in survey after survey for the last thirty years among teens as well as adults. Ninety percent of teens in a recent Gallup poll cited the family as the most important thing in their lives. And in all the research survey findings, family is reported to be teens' as well as adults' greatest source of happiness in life. The flip side is that research studies cite that family is the greatest source of pain, anger and disappointment for teens and adults.

Let s Talk Tomorrow

Accelerated life-styles and rapid relationships have resulted in distorted priorities and less and less available time, making it difficult for parents to focus on the priority of the present in their family relationships. Parents are hurried and harried by hectic schedules, demanding personal goals, financial problems, marital pressures and teens who must stand in line for their time. In recent research studies, it was found that American parents spend less time per week communicating with their teens (an average of four to five minutes a day) than any other parents in the industrialized world. This trend has remained constant for the last ten years. Parents are simply too busy;

there is never any time for parent-teen relationships. "Let's talk tomorrow" is a typically heard promise to teens. The tragedy is it becomes only empty words to so many teens who are still waiting and desperately wanting it to happen.

Young people are very aware that the amount of time we spend on something or someone reflects the value we place on that person or object. In this shortcut society, we are spending less time than ever in family relationships. This fast-paced, high-stress culture has created an urgent pursuit for the trivial as the really important things are pushed aside. We live suspended between the urgent and the important; sadly, busy parents more often respond to the urgent rather than the important. The result is less and less time spent together in a meaningful way. Millions of teens and parents are strangers in their own homes. We get no deeper than surface relationships; we're afraid it might take too much time and effort. "We spend a lot of time buying time," observes economist James Smith of the Rand Corporation. What we're doing is contracting out for family care, but there's a limit. If you contract out everything, you have an enterprise, not a family.[10]

The media and the fast-food industry have conditioned family relationships for shorter time spans, as TV commercials explode for fifteen-second flashes and popular novels contain paragraphs no longer than two sentences. We order supper at the drive-through at McDonald's or Taco Bell because we believe faster is better. Rarely do we sit down together and have supper the way it was done twenty years ago; everybody's got something they must do or some place they should be. All these trends translate into a significant decline in the quantity and quality of time parents spend with their children. Parents are devoting much more time to earning a living or pursuing personal goals and much less time with their children than they did a generation ago.

We have an entire generation of "aliens," teens who are alienated from their parents.

The Divorce Epidemic

During the last twenty years, America has seen more than a million couples divorce each year. Over twenty-two million couples have divorced, profoundly affecting forty-four million men and women and over forty million children. Experts estimate that as many as one hundred million people have been directly affected by the emotionally devastating experience of divorce just in the last twenty years.

Millions of men and women, age twenty-something, thirty-something and some forty-something, are adult children of divorce. The current generation of children and teens are growing up "divorced"; fragmented, multiple marriages and blended families is the norm. "Even though the divorce rate began to rise dramatically in the early '70s and has remained high, for a full generation, there is an unusual reluctance to acknowledge its seriousness and its enormous impact on all of our lives. We are afraid as a culture to look and honestly confront what is happening in our midst."[11]

Divorce and its characteristic confusion, pain and impoverishment became the central fear of children born from the mid-'70s to the present as youth faced twice the risk of parental divorce that a boomer child did in the mid to late '60s.

When reality is painful, we avoid, deny, rationalize and justify. In looking at divorce, we examine our most fundamental moral and spiritual values, by which we measure commitment, meaning, the importance of relationships and the family itself. "Divorce is the mirror image of marriage."[12]

Relationship images in America could be characterized as short-term, self-fulfilling, convenient and disposable. *Throwaway* is a term Toffler said could be used to describe the relationship mind-set of the high-tech society of the '90s that used up relationships much like consumable products and got rid of them when they had used them up.

Divorce in America reflects our culture's attitudes, morality and the erosion of the moral commitment to our children. Today, we expect more from marriage than previous generations, and we respect it less. The divorce/marriage mirror also has a spiritual parallel not only reflecting our relationships with each other but our relationship with God. We in the church must be more compassionate and understanding toward couples who are divorced. But we must not embrace a secular psychology that endorses or encourages a casual attitude toward divorce—an attitude that glosses over sin and uses psychological explanations to excuse unfaithfulness, disobedience and self-centered life-styles. In our desire to be relevant, we must not seek to alter Biblical truth to fit the thinking of popular culture.

Marriage/divorce and the family is the ultimate barometer of relationships in America and particularly the youth culture. Mass divorce has set in motion a cycle of distorted, dysfunctional and destructive relationships for many teens and adults. The disintegrating family is symptomatic of a society that has lost its moral and spiritual bearings.

Decreasing Family Stability

There are some marriages that are so abusive, destructive and even dangerous that divorce becomes necessary just for survival. But this is the exception rather than the norm. In this era of noncommittal relationships, too many marriages are being sacrificed too easily.

Sometimes a single-parent household can bring more security than an extremely volatile and chaotic two-parent household. However, single-parent families generally have many more pressures because one parent is trying to fill the role of both parents. Increased financial stresses lead to extra work for one parent and much less time with the children. Divorce also produces enormous amounts of emotional pain for years and multiplies dysfunctional relationships for children and teens as well as adults.

The Pop Psychology Mind-set

As a society, we have come to accept, tolerate and encourage divorce as a viable alternative; it is viewed as normal and even desirable to get divorced today. Starting around 1965, a new "therapeutic mentality" took root in contemporary culture. The quest for personal growth, self-fulfillment and self-realization became the goal for millions of adults and college students. Psychotherapists became the new gurus as Americans turned inward and started focusing on their own needs and desires.

The pop psychology mentality focuses on self rather than on a set of external obligations or commitments. It encourages an individual to find and assert his or her true self, and to define this as the only source of genuine relationships to other people. Commitments, self-sacrifice, loyalty or other obligations — whether to parents, children or God — are to be severely limited because they interfere with a person's capacity for self-love and fulfillment. In its purest form, the therapeutic pop psychology mentality denies all forms of duty or commitments in relationships with God, marriage and family, replacing these values with the ideal of full, open, honest communication among self-actualized individuals. "A whole generation became newly determined to consume every dish on the smorgasbord of human experience."[13]

During the last twenty years with the rise of pop psychology, Christianity has lost much of its influence and credibility with the American public. This has created a "moral vacuum" with respect to moral principles including those pertaining to child rearing, sexuality and the family. This "new enlightenment" through humanistic psychological personal development and understanding has filled the vacuum by providing core moral values and temporary fulfillment for many adults and teens.

Commitment to Jesus Christ is viewed by the humanistic therapeutic psychological community as oppressive, outdated, demanding nonsense based on beliefs that guarantee to get in the way of personal goals and personal pleasures. The search for immediate self-fulfillment in America has reduced our enthusiasm for self-denial, delayed gratification and long-term commitments. When therapists speak of the need for meaning and love, they define love and meaning simply as the fulfillment of a person's emotional needs and desires, without any constraints or obligations to anyone or anything else, without any guilt. The new enlightenment has come to mean the overthrow of inhibitions and the immediate gratification of every impulse.

No-Fault Divorce

As an "enlightened culture," we have approached divorce/marriage with casual indifference. Marriage is disposable for the first time in American history. The stigma of divorce has been drastically reduced in recent years. In fact, it is now widely accepted that men and women have the right to expect a happy marriage and if that marriage does not work out, no one has to "stay trapped." If marriage or family stifles your freedom, creativity and individual fulfillment, just walk away; you deserve happiness, even at the expense of others.

No Fault, No Guilt

In 1970, the "no-fault divorce" law was instituted in California. This was hailed as a milestone in the modernization of laws relating to marriage and divorce. This legitimized divorce and redefined marriage as a time-limited, conditional arrangement rather than a lifelong commitment. "No fault," a term borrowed from the car insurance industry, meant that the courts would simply accept a spouse's claim that there were irreconcilable differences. Under this new practice, if both spouses wished to terminate a marriage, regardless of the reasons or of the potential of their relationships, they were allowed to do so.[14]

The emergence and popularity of the self-awareness movement and the no-fault divorce became a perfect catalyst for no responsibility/no guilt divorces. Divorce is increasingly seen as "morally neutral, just another option, a life choice, no better or worse than staying married."[15]

We try to maintain the illusion that our society is as it was before. We try to convince ourselves that the family is intact and that commitment is forever (at least until we change our minds). The truth is that we refuse to acknowledge the widening gap between our belief systems and everyday lives. But the family has changed; the illusion is not reality, and every parent, child and teen in America knows this; divorce is both cause and effect.

The scenario that divorce has produced is one of societal confusion and emotional insecurity in relationships. Adults are alienated and detached from children, while children are baffled and frustrated by adults. Many adults are too busy, too unhappy, guilt-ridden and self-absorbed to be intimate with their children.

Divorce can be a powerful long-range catalyst for destructive psychological, emotional, social and economic change; however, most mental health experts until recently disregarded any long-term effects of divorce. The negative effects of divorce on children and teens would take no longer than two years at the most to get over — that was the general consensus of the humanistic psychological intelligentsia. The view that divorce would not cause any long-lasting problems and pain was embraced by a society that found comfort and rationalization for their actions. We didn't really want to know if there was long-range pain involved, because it would make us feel more guilty.

The National Center for Health Statistics found that "children/teens from single-parent homes were 150 to 250 percent more likely than children from two-parent families to have emotional and behavioral problems." Most disturbingly "the most reliable predictor of crime is neither poverty nor race but growing up fatherless."[16]

The Ten-Year Cycle of Pain

"The findings at the end of ten years after divorce were surprising, shocking and unexpected," says Wallerstein. "To our astonishment, divorce continues to occupy a central, emotional position in the lives of many adults ten to fifteen years later. They are not back on track but are grappling with the aching consequences of a decade-old divorce. Many continue to have very strong feelings about the failed marriage and have not given up the hopes and disappointments attached to it. They still have deep-seated feelings of hurt, depression, failure, anger and outrage ten years later."[17]

The responses and feelings of children and teens ten years after divorce are sobering, grim reminders of the emotional ripping they suffered and live with. Half of these children were six, seven, eight and nine years old and are now sixteen to nineteen years old; the other half were nine to eighteen and are now nineteen to twenty-eight years old.

"In myriad ways, they tell us that growing up is harder for children/teens of divorce, every step of the way. They say their lives have been overshadowed by their parents' divorces and they feel deprived of a range of economic and emotional supports. Their sense of loss and wistful yearning persists, and their emotions run deep and strong. These now teens and young people in their twenties share vivid gut-wrenching memories of their parents' divorces."[18] The ripple effect of divorce on our society is devastating for adults-children-teens caught in divorce's cycle of pain. Also, for couples involved, nobody gets away from its agony.

Divorce sets in motion a cycle of unimaginable human pain and fears, sometimes a never-ending chain of events, relocations and radically shifting insecure relationships strung through time, a process that forever changes the lives of the people involved. Children's and teens' basic attitudes and perceptions about society, relationships and about themselves can be forever changed by divorce. These changes can greatly affect their identities and personalities.

Traumatized Children/Teens

The death of a parent is far less a destructive experience for children and teens than the divorce of a parent. Loss due to death is final; the dead person cannot be retrieved. Also, in death most children do not feel responsible, as they often do with divorce. With divorce, they stay in a suspended state of hope, hurt and frustration, and feel powerless to change what is happening.

Wallerstein feels it would be very difficult "to find any other group of children, except the victims of natural disasters (earthquakes, floods, fires, etc.), who suffered such a rate of sudden psychological shock as divorced children. As in natural disasters, divorce creates feelings of total helplessness, vulnerability and a terrible sense of abandonment and powerlessness."[19]

The Divorce Effect

In this landmark study, more than half of the children/teens of divorce entered adulthood as worried, under-achieving, self-deprecating and angry young men and women.

- Half saw their mother or father get a second divorce during the ten-year period.[20]
- Teens from divorced families are less optimistic and have more psychological problems than those whose parents stayed together.
- Half grew up in families where parents stayed angry (fighting, arguing) with each other, even after the divorce.
- Three in five felt rejected by at least one of the parents, sensing they reminded them of a bad experience they would rather forget.[21]
- A full 60 percent of the young people are on a downward educational course compared with their parents.
- Many young people who grow up in divorced families are not climbing the economic ladder as high as their parents did.[22]

- The research evidence is overwhelming: Divorce sentences a significant proportion of this generation of American children-teens to periods of real economic hardship. Financial insecurity follows the children of divorce into adult life, derailing college and compromising careers.[23]
- Children of divorce grow up with more profound anxieties and greater feelings of anger, isolation, frustration and self-blame.
- Over a third of these young men and women of divorce, now between the ages of nineteen and twenty-nine, have little or no ambition ten years after their parents' divorce. They are drifting through life with no set goals, limited education and a sense of helplessness. Some stay home well into their twenties; others leave and wander without purpose. They don't make long-term plans and are aiming below the intellectual and educational achievements of their fathers and mothers. They drifted in and out of college, jobs and relationships.
- Divorce has been for many kids the single most significant cause of stress and pain.
- Young people are getting married much later than ever, due to the rampant divorce rate. According to the Census Bureau, the majority of American women age twenty to twenty-four (66 percent) have never been married. That's up sharply since 1960, when just 28 percent of women in that age group had never wed. Among men age twenty to twenty-four, the proportion of those who have never wed is up too — from 53 percent in 1960 to 80 percent in 1992.[24]
- Divorce has been a major factor in such at-risk behaviors among youth as suicide, drug abuse, crime, violence, teen pregnancy and dropping out of school.[25]

Research reveals that male youth whose parents divorced during their teen years were twice as likely to commit crimes as peers who did not experience parental divorce during adolescence. Young men who not only saw their parents divorce during their teen years but who experienced further instability and uncertainty in their homes during their teen years were especially prone to commit crime: A remarkable 65 percent of young men with such backgrounds had committed one or more crimes.[26]

Children of parents who divorce are twice as likely to cohabit before marriage than children of parents whose marriages endure. Research studies predict more and more young people will decide to cohabit during the '90s.

Teens living in single-parent or stepparent households suffer from a number of serious psychological and emotional problems not seen among peers in intact stable families.

Experts found that adolescents from disrupted families reported higher levels of general health problems, were more neurotic, more withdrawn, felt less able in relating to peers and had distorted, low self-perceptions of their bodies, were more impulsive, irresponsible and had more negative views of their school performances and relationships.[27]

Divorce and the Missing Father

Escalating divorce rates combined with epidemic teen pregnancy has created father-absent households. During the '70s and '80s, the over one million divorces a year were paralleled by the over one million out-of-wedlock teen pregnancies. The teen pregnancy rate for all teens has increased 300 percent in the United States over the last twenty years. The rate is three times higher (600 percent) for black teen girls as compared to white teen girls. One out of every three black mothers is an unwed teenager, and a third of these go on to have a second child while still in their teens. Marriage has become an almost forgotten institution among black teens, as cohabitation is an acceptable norm. Sixty-two percent of all black babies are born out of wedlock. In whole sections of the black community, children are being raised almost exclusively by very young mothers without any male role models.[28]

Over fifteen million American children — one quarter of all children under eighteen — are now growing up with little or no contact with their fathers. This is twice as common as it was a generation ago, and future projections say that in the '90s, the number will nearly double. For most children, the partial or complete loss of a father produces long-lasting feelings of betrayal, abandonment, rage, guilt and pain. The absence of the father for males has been a major factor in causing some boys to be excessively violent and has produced antisocial behavior. The missing father for girls creates the need for attention and affection from a male; sexual activity becomes the panacea for their father insecurity. In reality, this only produces more insecurity, as too many times they end up with a baby who doesn't have a father either. The search for intimacy and security through sex has perpetuated the cycle of pain. "Also, 70 percent of teenage mothers drop out of school, and their lifetime earnings are less than half of those women who wait until age twenty before having their first child. To compound the problem, children born to teens achieve academically and economically at rates substantially below those born to adults."[29]

"Wallerstein, in her ten-year study, shows how children yearn for their fathers in the years after divorce, and how this longing is infused with new intensity at adolescence, even among the children who have considerable contact with their fathers. Nevertheless, three out of four of these teens still feel rejected by their fathers.[30] The "father vacuum" in America has produced a "father hunger" among many youth where anger, bitterness, rejection, fear and a constant wish to know their fathers dominate their lives.

Over the last twenty-five years, the proportion of mothers in the paid labor force has tripled, and the number of children growing up without a father is twice as great. By and large, the vacuum left in children's lives by the disappearance of the traditional mother has not been filled by attentive fathers, and in many cases there have been no fathers at all. Children have been left to fend for themselves in a society that is increasingly isolated, indifferent and hostile to children.

The economic harm to children from divorce revolves around the fact that fathers generally earn a good deal more than mothers, but in 90 percent of divorce cases, children remain with their mothers. It seems that in moving toward no fault/no responsibility divorce, we have created an economic crunch for most women and children involved in the split family. Since no-fault eliminates guilt or innocence, it usually deprives the mother and children of divorce some economic privileges.

The Census Bureau reports that there are now ten million households with sixteen million children living without fathers. More than half of the fathers who owe child support don't pay, and they also can't or don't see their children. The new census numbers "are a striking alarm for our children and our society," says Health and

Human Services Secretary Louis Sullivan. "Divorce for many children/teens and women produces severe economic financial hardships. Half of all divorced fathers fail to see their children in the wake of divorce and two thirds fail to pay child support."[31] For some children, divorce means financial insecurity and much less fathering. For others, it means poverty and complete loss of their father.

The New Poverty

In the 1980s, it became clear that poverty is now linked to a social revolution involving changing cultural attitudes about marriage, family life and morality. It is also clear that families headed by females have become the focus of the "new poverty." In fact, 2 percent of the families still form just under half of the households below the poverty line at any given time; but they seldom stay in poverty for more than one or two years.[32]

A recent research study in *USA Today* stated that poverty is rapidly rising in America. One in seven is poor; 33.5 million people are living in poverty. Over fourteen million children/teens are poor.

- Single-mother households are the majority of poor families, 53.1 percent.
- One in five children/teens is poor.
- One in three blacks is poor.
- Among children younger than six, almost one in four is poor.

The poverty rate for children under six is now higher than for any other age group in America. It's more than double the rate for adults.[33]

In an article in *USA Today* titled "Runaway Parents," a description is given of the scenario where thousands of parents simply disappear after divorces. These parents, 95 percent of them men, owe $5 billion in unpaid child support each year. This is leaving a legacy of poverty and pain for eleven million children/teens and a national crisis that is forcing thousands of families onto welfare. The consequences for the families left behind can be devastating, but the impact doesn't stop there. If you are a taxpayer, you will pay the child support that is not being paid by parents on the run. Divorce pushes many middle-class women and children into poverty.[34]

Crises in the Black Family

The state of the African-American family has reached a critical stage. A recent feature story in *Newsweek* titled "A World Without Fathers" (August 1993) paints a disturbing and bleak portrait of the struggle to save the black family in America.

For blacks, the institution of marriage has been devastated in the last generation. Two out of three first births to black women under thirty-five are out of wedlock. In 1960 the number was two out of five. And the situation is only getting worse. A black child born today has only a one-in-five chance of growing up with two parents until the age of sixteen (generally without a father), according to research. The impact, of course, is not only on black families but on all of society. Fatherless homes increase crime, violence rates, teenage pregnancies, and lower educational attainment and breed poverty for black youth.

Thirty years ago one quarter of black families were headed by women. Today the situation has deteriorated rapidly, as now 62 percent of black families are headed by one parent. The result is what Johns Hopkins University sociologist Andrew Chaplin calls an almost complete separation of marriage and childbearing among African Americans. It was not always so. Before 1950, black and white marriage patterns were similar.

Since the sexual revolution the rate has shot up for both whites and blacks. But the numbers of out-of-wedlock births are much higher for black women than whites. Between 1960 and 1989, the proportion of young white women giving birth out of wedlock rose from 9 percent to 24 percent, markedly faster than it did for blacks. However, blacks' rate at 42 percent was already so high by 1960 that if it had kept pace with the white rate, it would have topped 100 percent by now. It currently stands at 70 percent compared to 24 percent for white women.

Also, the economic transition that began in the '70s, when the nation shifted from an industrial to a service-based economy, was particularly devastating to black men. Their ability to qualify for good jobs was greatly diminished. Their ability to adapt was hampered by years of racial discrimination, which still exists in the workplace. "When men lose their ability to earn a living, their sense of self-worth declines dramatically. They lose rapport with their children," says University of Oklahoma historian Robert Griswold (quoted in *Newsweek*).

Traditionally the extended family has served as a safety net, but now the extended black family is breaking down. With the soaring number of teenage mothers, grandparents today are getting younger and are more likely to be working themselves. A grandmother in her early thirties isn't necessarily eager or able to raise a grandchild when she is also trying to survive herself.

And after two generations of no fathers, there are no grandfathers either. Many black families are now severely fragmented and isolated, especially in the inner cities. And traditional neighborhoods are disappearing quickly due to the fears of violence and the need for survival.

Today's world without black fathers is one that is increasingly desperate, extremely tragic and frighteningly brutal. More young black girls seek love and security and become pregnant out of wedlock. More young black males shoot to kill or get killed to prove their manhood and vent their vengeance. This is the grim legacy for too many black youth today.

Throwaway Teens

There are over one million homeless teens who are runaways and throwaways that live on the streets of America. Nearly 50 percent of the runaways said their parents didn't want them. Kids often become throwaways when their families are under economic stress or relationship pressure through divorce. These youth live in abandoned buildings, in makeshift cardboard homes, bus terminals, alleyways, under bridges or wherever they can find a place. They get involved in prostitution, drugs, crime (mostly stealing) and other at-risk behaviors to survive. "Dumpster diving" is scavenging for food in garbage dumps. In addition, there is more pregnancy, sickness and disease; the AIDS risk is five times greater for street kids.

The majority of throwaways come from families in which only one biological parent is present. Divorce has resulted in either a single-parent household or the remarriage of one parent in the step-family setting. The step-family has helped create a violent, more stressed situation in the family with stepparent and stepsibling relationships.

At least half report having suffered incidents of physical abuse at the hands of their parents, and an increasing number report sexual abuse.

- Seventy percent are white, 16 percent are black, the rest Hispanic and other ethnic groups.
- Forty-four percent of runaways or throwaways are due to constant family problems and stress.
- More than half of all throwaways come from households where one or both parents are alcoholic.[35]

Latch-Key Children

Through the 1970s, the number of latch-key children, age six to thirteen, who go home to an empty house after school, doubled. During the '80s, the number of latch-key kids more than tripled as more mothers joined the work force.

On any given day in America, as many as ten million kids carry their own key and come home to an empty house. Latch-key children are the fallout of a society that over-emphasizes material success and personal fulfillment. They are the consequence of the influx into the labor market of working mothers. Today, thirty-five million children, over 60 percent of all children under eighteen, have mothers who work.[36]

As single-parent families are continuing to increase, mostly headed by women, an economic survival mentality has been created where the mother has to work, sometimes even two jobs, to make ends meet.

As a result, the children and teens suffer as the time spent in meaningful relationships with a parent is nonexistent. They don't just lose one parent through divorce; they lose them both in many ways, due to the financial burden left on mothers who must work to survive.

- Today's grade schools report their students' number one fear is being left alone at home.
- Thirty-three percent of youth in detention centers come from the ranks of the frequently unsupervised and unattended.
- The numbers of kids who expressed fear, loneliness and boredom are in the millions. These kids were also more likely to be involved in drinking, sex, crime and general rebelliousness.

Latch-key children are the victims of a society that replaces the extended traditional family with fragmented families. It mirrors a profound change in the structure and attitudes of our society. Family relationships and values that brought stability are tossed aside. They are products of a culture that wants children to mature rapidly but not to take a productive, meaningful place in society — mature, yet immature. They act world-wise and self-reliant as they withdraw into themselves, or they explode in anger or frustration in at-risk behavior. They make us believe that they need us only as much as we are willing to be present for them. They project a grown-up image of confidence and contentment while hurting and longing for their parents' attention and security.

The Noncommitment Effect

Rooted in Divorce. The noncommitment mentality of this generation is rooted in the divorce epidemic; youth fear and avoid making long-term commitments today. "How can you believe in commitment when anyone can change their mind at any time, and usually does?" says one young man whose parents divorced. Due to divorce, the noncommittal attitude permeates our entire culture as it undermines and subconsciously affects every relationship we have and commitment we make. For this generation, "I love you forever" is a definite maybe.

In the world of divorce, relationships today are short-term, self-gratifying, convenient and disposable. Uncertainty and insecurity are the norm, especially in those most basic and crucial relationships teens and young adults desperately need.

Without commitment, love is really irrelevant, a word that just describes our selfish desires. "I'm afraid to use the word *love*," says a young lady in her twenties who remembers her parent's divorce as if it were yesterday. "You can hope for love, but you can't expect it."

In research surveys 95 percent of teens, when asked about marriage, said they wanted to be married for life to one person. They wanted romantic love, faithfulness and commitment from these partners. By the year 2000, nearly 50 percent of the United States population will be adult children of divorce.[37] With divorce comes a weakening of our unspoken moral commitment to an entire generation.

Concept of Relationships. Young people's concepts of

relationships are shaped and determined by marriage and the family. When divorce destroys that bond, it creates a distorted view of love relationships. The disillusionment and disappointment of their parents' failed relationship produces on the one hand an obsession to find real love and commitment. They vow that "what happened to my parents won't happen to me." On the other hand is a deep-seated fear that a happy fulfilling relationship is really not possible. Many who experience divorce as children and teens approach girl-boy relationships with the feeling that the deck is stacked against them. Both attitudes create distorted and desperate relationships. Children and teens who grow up in divorced families are more eager and determined to have quality relationships and more worried about ever achieving them. Children of divorce grow up to have more troubled relationships with the opposite sex and are four times more likely to divorce than those from intact homes, says the American Psychological Association.

A twenty-year study of three hundred families finds adult children of divorce with more dating anxiety and earlier marriages. It also showed that young adults of divorce were more hostile and more fearful of getting close to anyone.[38]

Fears from Divorce. Divorce is an emotionally ripping, traumatic experience that leaves children/teens with deeply entrenched fears that profoundly affect their lives. Divorce mass produces fears and anxieties that are still present with young adults ten years after the actual divorce.

Two traits were common among adult children of divorce: the fear of rejection and betrayal, and a lifelong vulnerability to experience loss. The children of divorce find that their search for love and intimate relationships is haunted by their parents' divorce.

Many teens and young adults of divorce get involved in destructive relationships, which include living together, multiple relationships and premature teen marriages. Seventy percent of all teen marriages end within the first five years. These relationships are based on their fears and emotional pain from divorce that perpetuate the cycle of pain.

For young adults, anxiety about these issues hits full force. They fear betrayal. They fear abandonment. They fear loss. They draw an inescapable conclusion: Relationships can't be trusted; betrayal and infidelity and unfaithfulness are the accepted norm and probably will happen. The suspicion that betrayal can come at any time without warning permeates contemporary society.

Despite the widespread acceptance of divorce, there remains something frightening at its core. It is as if married people are afraid that another's divorce will illuminate the cracks and fears in their own relationships. On an emotional/spiritual level, every divorce threatens to erode and undermine every marriage.

Rite of Passage into Adulthood. The entry of children and teens of divorce into young adulthood is encumbered by an inescapable need to reexamine the past. The changing roles of men and women, greater sexual freedom, confusion and the high rate of divorce make relationships much riskier and uncertain. Children of divorce are afraid of repeating their parents' failure to maintain a loving relationship. The extent to which this fear dominates their lives and relationships as a constant undercurrent is pervasive and intense. The behavior of children of divorce is often at odds with their philosophy of high hopes and high morality. They seem propelled by despair and anxiety as they search for what they fear they will never find.

Young adulthood is the time to venture forth, to trust and to make commitments, yet the children of divorce find their search for love and intimacy is ghost-ridden. Even those children of divorce who have done well in high school and who have many friends and stable relationships say that they experience rising anxiety and uncertainties in their late teens and in their twenties. Young adults' lives are dominated by these fearful feelings and painful memories of divorce and fragmented relationships. The children of divorce constantly fear they are doomed to repeat their parents' mistakes.

The fragmented family has produced a fragmented culture, with fragmented identities and destructive relationships.

Chapter 15

I Love You to Death: The Destructive Family

But whoever causes one of these little ones who believe in Me to sin, it would be better for him if a millstone were hung around his neck, and he were drowned in the depth of the sea (Matt. 18:6 NKJ).

We most fear violence in the streets, which is frightening and increasing each year, and there is a very real danger in the streets of America. But the cruel irony is Americans are more likely to be physically assaulted, beaten and killed in their own homes at the hands of a family member than any place else or by anyone else. Family violence is the most underreported crime in America.

"Americans are 100 times more likely to experience violence in the family/home setting than in our crime-ridden streets. The family is society's most violent institution with the exception of the police and the military in times of war."[1]

We are hearing more and more shocking stories about bizarre family violence: child abuse, wife battering, husband battering, sexual abuse, marital rape and calculating vicious murders where members of the family have been strangled, shot, axed, dismembered, stabbed or bludgeoned to death. One man chopped up his wife and put her body through a wood chipper. Investigators recovered less than one ounce of her remains.

The incidents are widespread, chilling stories of brutal, cold-blooded murders of husbands, wives, children and teens in every imaginable method. Despite all the pictures of missing children on shopping bags and milk cartons, 90 percent of the 1.5 million child/teen kidnappings are abductions by parents or a family member; hundreds of children are snatched by parents embroiled in custody disputes. While the public is focused on and fears children being abducted or harmed by strangers, the real danger is in the home. A brutal and grisly incident that occurred several years ago underscores the point. When a thirteen-year-old girl was missing and her father orchestrated and organized the search for his missing daughter, the father later admitted that he had sexually abused his daughter for years. He confessed that when his daughter fought his sexual advances, he had stabbed her to death. He hid her body for a few days and then buried it in a field, a tragic ending to an already sad story.[2]

Enduring Violence

One of the saddest lessons in all the research on family violence is the amount of outrageous abuse and violence human beings can absorb over long periods of time with barely a whimper and rarely a cry for help. Battered women have endured brutal beatings from their husbands for ten to twenty years before killing them out of sheer desperation and fear.

Millions of children and teens have been victimized by a parent or parents through physical, emotional or sexual abuse. "That violence and love can actually coexist in families is perhaps the most insidious aspect of intimate violence because it means that, unlike violence in the streets, we are tied to our abusers by the bonds of love, attachment and affection."[3]

National Family Violence Survey

These are research findings on intimate violence.

- 2.4 million children age three to seventeen years were victims of physical abuse. This means that one child in fifteen was a victim of physical abuse. "Every forty-seven seconds a child is abused or neglected."

- Over three million children-teens age three to seventeen are victims of sexual abuse each year, with girls ten times more likely than boys to be sexually molested. Experts believe another one million cases go unreported each year.
- 1.5 million women each year are battered.
- One woman in twenty-two is the victim of physical, abusive violence.
- The FBI reports that a woman is battered every eighteen seconds in the U.S.
- Two million husbands have been victims of physical, abusive violence by wives.[4]

The actual numbers for physical and sexual abuse in the home is projected to be two to three times higher than the documented statistics.

Child abuse is, and has been, a major hidden epidemic in America for years, only recently coming more to the surface during the last ten to twelve years. A recent in-depth survey found that one in six adults across America was physically abused as a child and one in seven confess that they were a victim of sexual abuse.

These numbers far exceed the official statistics of the Department of Health and Human Services, which were based on official reported incidents of abuse. The complete anonymity of the new survey revealed vast numbers of adults whose abuse went unreported and totally unrecognized.[5]

Research shows one in three girls and one in five boys will be sexually abused or molested in America before reaching eighteen years of age.[6]

There are more than thirty-six million individual cases of sibling violence each year. More than 100,000 children annually face brothers or sisters with guns or knives in their hands.

On the other side of the coin, parents are beaten and abused by their teens. Research study reveals that 3 percent of parents report being victimized at least once by a severe form of violence from children older than eleven. This translates to 900,000 parental victims of serious violence each year.[7]

National Rape Study

Rape is the fastest growing violent crime in America. The frightening specter of a monstrous stranger lurking in the shadows ready to attack is a deep-seated fear and potential reality for many women in America.

Rape is rampant, as "one in four women will be raped in her lifetime, less than 10 percent will report the assault, and less than 5 percent of the rapists will go to jail."[8]

There are 683,000 women forcibly raped every year in the U.S.A. — more than three times the number reported by the Justice Department according to the definitive new national study on rape.

"Ours is the only study that has looked at rape over a lifetime with a national sample of adult women," says Dean Kilpatrick, study coauthor.

Perhaps the most disturbing finding, the study says, "sixty-one percent of the rape victims surveyed said they were seventeen or younger when attacked. The dimensions of the sexual abuse problem may be the most staggering when it comes to children and teens."

Dean Kilpatrick says, "We have severely underestimated the scope and degree of violence in the sexual assault of our youth." What this survey proves is that the problem of sexual abuse in America is an enormous tragedy.

The most common widespread teen and college crime committed is date rape; it has reached epidemic proportions. This action and attitude would have been unthinkable and outrageous twenty years ago; but today it occurs with frightening frequency among high school and college youth. A number of research studies on dating and violence reveal that 27 percent, more than one in four, dating relationships have involved "date rape."[9] The average age of both victim and rapist is eighteen. The fears, shame, embarrassment and peer pressures of youth help explain why so few cases are reported. Nearly 60 percent of the victims of date rape tell no one, and only one in twenty goes to the police, so the epidemic gains momentum. Twenty-five percent, or one in four, have been raped on a date. Projected nationally, that figure means that as many as twenty million women have been the victim of date rape in America. College students returning to campus this week have more to worry about than tough courses, finances and grades: Every two hours, one of them will be the victim of murder, rape or violent assault.[10]

The term "date rape" was coined during the '80s to describe the increasing incidents of rape. College administrations have attempted to cover up these incidents because it would generate negative publicity for their schools.

Emotional Abuse

The most hidden, most insidious, least researched and, in the long run, most damaging form of intimate victimization may be emotional abuse of loved ones. Defining physical and sexual abuse is relatively easy, compared to the formidable task of determining what constitutes emotional abuse.

Millions of children and teens are the objects of continual degrading, humiliating, criticizing and vicious verbal attacks. The invisible wounds produced by such emotional battering has a devastating effect on the emotional well-being of children and teens.

Young people and children bear the brunt of emotional abuse that ranges from verbal abuse to outright brutal acts of cruelty. Many parents call their children "stupid, idiots, ugly," and say, "Can't you do anything right?" "You're so worthless," and even curse them. Many times parents cloak their insulting criticism with humor in front of people and say, "They know I'm only kidding."

Millions of children and teens are branded by insults from parents who are unaffectionate, cruel and completely insensitive to their pain or feelings. These parents use guilt, shame and fear to motivate their children, which only creates emotional scarring, crippling and a destructive long-range effect on future relationships.

The Alcoholic Family

Alcohol abuse has a devastating ripple effect, causing a long-range cycle of pain within the family and young people that is staggering. Latest research shows alcohol abuse affects far more people than previously thought and appears to play a major role in the failure of many marriages. The report says that fifteen million Americans are alcoholics, and another four million have serious drinking problems.[11]

The cycle of pain set in motion through alcohol abuse affects seventy-eight million adults, children and teens—including those married to an alcoholic or problem drinker and those who grew up with one.[12] The sheer magnitude of people affected is overwhelming, says the National Center for Health Statistics. Alcohol abuse is a major contributing factor in murder, suicide, rape, fatal car accidents, domestic violence and abuse, crime and other destructive behaviors. The alcohol-related death toll each year in America is over 100,000.

- Most research studies show that over one third of murders are alcohol-related.
- More than half of rapists were drinking immediately before their crimes.
- Mothers convicted of child abuse are three times more likely than other mothers to be alcoholics; fathers convicted of child abuse are ten times more likely to be alcoholics than are non-abusing fathers. Up to 36 percent of suicide victims have a history of alcohol abuse or were drinking shortly before their suicides.[13]

Incest the Ultimate Betrayal

Incest is perhaps the cruelest, most baffling of human experiences. It is a betrayal of the most basic trust between child and parent. The young victims are totally dependent on their aggressors and totally exploited by them, so they have nowhere to run, no one to run to or trust. Protectors become persecutors and reality becomes a prison of dirty, shameful secrets. Incest betrays the very heart of childhood; its innocence is shattered. Incest is not just the act of sexual intercourse between blood relations. The psychological impact of incest covers a much wider range of behaviors and relationships. "Incest includes physical contact with a child's mouth, breasts, genitals, anus, or any other body part, that is done for the purpose of sexually arousing the aggressor. The aggressor does not have to be a blood relative. He or she can be anyone whom the child perceives as a family member, such as a stepparent or an in-law."[14] The divorce explosion and remarriage has multiplied the number of stepparents, increasing the potential risk of incest.

It wasn't until the early '80s that we as a culture began to realize just how epidemic incest is. The U.S. Department of Human Services shows that at least three in ten children are molested by age eighteen. Since 90 percent of all incest victims never tell anyone what has happened or what is happening to them, the actual number of incest victims is said to be three to four times higher than documented incidents listed in research. Prior to the last ten years, most people believed that incest occurred in no more than one out of 100,000 families.[15] The majority of sexual crimes committed against children are perpetrated by trusted family members. Most incest families maintain a facade of normalcy for many years, sometimes forever.

The perpetrator of incest dramatically distorts, thereby disrupting the normal emotional developmental stages of childhood and adolescence. Incest creates trauma, a deep-seated guilt and shame, self-loathing and a psychological cover-up, pushing these horrible memories so far beneath conscious awareness that they may not surface for years.

What Teens Need From Parents

The need for time and attention. Time pressures affect how we behave and relate to each other as a family. Time with each other is a rare commodity these days as families get caught in the "rushing relationships cycle." As a parent, when was the last time you sat down and just listened to your teen talk about the fears and frustrations of being a young person without being quick to offer advice or criticism? If you haven't given them time and understanding, you haven't earned the right to be heard. If you haven't given them time and acceptance, why should they believe you understand or really care about their problems? Why should they accept your solutions? Teens need quality time with their parents. The lack of time together creates hostility, loneliness, frustration and deep insecurity.

Teens get their sense of importance, confidence and self-worth from the amount of time spent with parents. Today's parents are spending less time with their young people than ever. Time is passing quickly; take time to know your teen. Don't look back and say, "I really should've . . ." or "If only I would've . . ."

Attention. Spending time with young people is important; but it's not just spending time, it's time with your undivided attention that's critical. Time without attention is like love without commitment — it's nothing. Teens know when we pretend to pay attention and act interested but really aren't.

Young people need to be listened to, not just heard but understood and taken seriously. Our kids aren't going to confide in us unless they believe we're really interested. Inattentive parents motivate our youth to use something negative or destructive to get parental attention. Teens need to feel they are a priority and that parents aren't just filling a time slot but are acutely aware of what is happening in their teens' lives and what their teens feel.

Respond, don't react. Parent-teen relationships are constantly in a state of reaction rather than response. Screaming with confidence might seem effective, but it causes more problems than it solves. It's not just what you say, it's how you say it that is crucial. A parent's tone of voice communicates an attitude. Too often the attitude of parents is one of, "I brought you into this world, I can take you out." "You did what?" or "Because I said so, that's why." Parents tend to react in anger out of fear, which magnifies the anger, confusion, fear and hurt feelings.

Parents too often major in the minors; we are constantly nagging, lecturing or criticizing, which causes more reaction from teens and further separates us. Too much time is spent arguing and fighting over things that don't really matter.

The harsh, condemning, reactionary attitudes and words of parents can wound and close a young person's spirit. This produces angry, bitter and rebellious attitudes toward parents. Words have incredible power to bring love and healing or hate and destruction.

Parents need to respond and communicate an attitude of love, acceptance and patience to their teens instead of reacting. Teens react to parents who react.

Admitting when you're wrong. Being a parent doesn't make us automatically right; parents aren't perfect. They make mistakes. But sometimes we feel we cannot admit to our teens when we're wrong.

Parents willing to admit their mistakes or to say, "I was wrong, forgive me," teach kids honesty and forgiveness, opening the lines of communication; teens then feel they can share their problems and shortcomings without fear of condemnation.

Too often, parents are afraid that if they admit to failing, they will appear weak, lose control and then all will be lost. The attitude of parents that "I'm never wrong and if I am, I shouldn't have to admit it to you" creates frustration, anger and bitterness in teens. This teaches teens to be unforgiving, critical and inflexible.

Young people who learn from their parents to admit mistakes and start over again live happier lives than those who maintain the "I'm always right" attitude. The words, "I'm sorry, I was wrong, please forgive me," are the hardest words to say. But, teens who never hear them will carry the negative unforgiving cycle to the next generation.

Be a consistent role model. What you say is important, but what you do is essential. "I'd rather see a sermon than hear one any day." Teens know that talk is cheap. If parents want what they say to have significance, they must show kids, not just tell them. "Do as I say, not as I do" just doesn't cut it with teens. Being genuine and consistent is very important to young people. Failure to see a positive, consistent role model produces shallowness, inconsistency and noncommitment in the lives of youth.

Parents who live out love, forgiveness, commitment and godliness in their lives demonstrate to teens a consistent Christian life-style, not just in theory but in reality. Parents' negative, inconsistent actions speak so loudly that teens don't listen to or respect what they say. Teens can't stand hypocrisy. Many youth have turned off Christianity completely because they see a double life-style lived by their parents. They say, "If this is what being a Christian means, I don't want any part of it." Being a consistent role model teaches youth moral responsibility which includes character, commitment, honesty and trust. Many youth are only modeling what they see in their parents' relationships and life-styles.

Trust and respect. Trust and respect go hand in hand. If you don't trust someone, you don't respect them either. Trust and respect are essential in developing and maintaining meaningful relationships. Distrust breeds disrespect. Parents want teens to trust them without reservation; they say, "Believe me; this is for your own good." Even though parents often suspect the worst from their teens, that suspicion is based on fears rather than reality and on the lack of a close relationship with their teen. The FBI — or "Family Bureau of Investigation" — is always watching and waiting. Their motto is: Remember, anything you do or say can and will be used against you. Teens tend to live up to your expectations. If you don't trust them, they will give you a reason not to.

Parents want and even demand respect from their teens, but they will get only the respect they give. If parents are doing things that demonstrate a disrespectful attitude, that will diminish teens' respect for them. Embarrassing your teen in front of their friends or in public by criticizing or making fun of them is insulting to them. Failing to approve of your teenager's friends before you even get to know them communicates that you don't trust their judgment. Even when we have legitimate concerns about our teens' friends, it is best to refrain from open criticism. Immediately rejecting their friends is taken as rejecting them and not respecting their opinion. There will be a time to approach the issue in a sensitive, respectful way.

Many parents believe they don't really owe their teens respect. After all, they're just teenagers; what do they know? When a teen doesn't feel you trust and respect him or her, this produces distrust, disrespect and rebellion.

Unconditional love and acceptance. Young people are starving for a love that they can always depend on, no matter what. Many relationships between parents and teens are conditional, self-centered and manipulating. Without realizing it, parents give their love with strings attached. Their love is always based on meeting certain conditions or on their teens' performance.

Teens need parents' unconditional love; even when they fail or do something wrong, they still need to feel their parents' love and acceptance. The lack of intimate relationships at home causes teens to look elsewhere for love and security — relationships with the opposite sex, using sex to fulfill the need for intimacy or with the peer group through reckless and risky behavior to fill the void of parents' acceptance, approval and affection.

Too many times these relationships provide a temporary, false sense of security that only leads to greater disillusionment and desperation for young people. In this uncertain and fast-changing world, youth need the stability, acceptance and security of parental relationships more than ever. Unconditional love doesn't change its mind or walk away; today so many relationships just aren't there for teens anymore. Too many parent/teen relationships are based on guilt and fear.

An atmosphere of unconditional agape love and acceptance and approval helps teens develop their real identity, their sense of significance and a positive concept of relationships. There are many adults today who still long for their parents' love and approval and strive desperately to get it.

Generational Anxiety

During the last twenty-five years, America has experienced a revolution in the family and a redefining of sexual morality and relationships. The plight of children and teens growing up today is often focused on the disintegrating family. The family has become the mirror of popular culture and particularly the youth culture.

The family shapes, reflects and profoundly affects every relationship youth have. Today, we not only have disintegrating families, but we also have multiplied families where young people must now adapt and adjust to two or three sets of stepparents, and stepbrothers and -sisters. This can be stressful, frustrating and even traumatic for them.

According to a 1991 American Medical Association report, today's children "are having trouble coping with three times the stresses in their lives and have many more serious psychological problems than a generation ago."[16] An entire generation is emotionally crippled through these toxic family relationships that are exploitative, self-centered, abusive and destructive.

Recent research by the National Commission on the Family states: "Too many of our children-teens have lost their way and are engaged in destructive behavior that imperils their future and their prospects for a fulfilling life. This is not only confined to low-income communities that are suffering from poverty, pregnancies and crime; but also involves millions of mainstream middle-class youth across the nation, who seem to have everything in a materialistic sense, and yet are having severe problems coping and functioning in today's culture."

Generational Discontinuity

The lost family has created a generational discontinuity where a generation of youth are disconnected from any extended stable family. Lost is the once-cherished family legacy, heritage and a commitment to future generations. The only legacy we're leaving today's generation is isolation, hostility, abandonment and noncommitment.

The electronic media, new peer power and surface sexual relationships have filled the vacuum left by the family, as young people are looking elsewhere for direction, guidance and love. In popular culture, adults have lost their role in transmitting the meaning and purpose of life.

Several destructive trends — epidemic divorce, rising numbers of single-parent families and step-families, widespread abuse and neglect, rampant teen pregnancies and missing fathers — have produced a "generational disconnectedness," where there is no healthy, stable, secure or extended family roots or valued heritage.

Children and teens feel alienated, disconnected, betrayed and disposable in too many family settings today. The most consistent barometer and the most significant factor in at-risk or problematic teen behavior is the family. Disintegrating and destructive family relationships have produced generational discontinuity — a rootlessness, insecurity and uncertainty about their identity, relationships and the future.

"Same old song. Just a drop of water in an endless sea. All we do crumbles to the ground, though we refuse to see. Dust in the wind. All we are is dust in the wind. Don't hang on. Nothing lasts forever but the earth and sky. Slips away and all your money won't another minute buy. Everything is dust in the wind."

"Dust in the Wind"
Kansas

Chapter 16

Fatal Attraction: The Suicide Solution

Hope deferred makes the heart sick
(Prov. 13:12 NKJ).

Death Wish

The atmosphere at West High School was heavy as I stepped to the microphone to speak to 1,500 students, who were still reeling in the wake of the recent suicide of a fellow classmate. Her name was Heather. She was fifteen years old. You could feel the pain in the air. A sense of confusion, disbelief and shock permeated the auditorium. Heather was very popular among her classmates. Her death came crashing down on her parents, friends and classmates like an unbelievable nightmare. There had been none of the typical warning signs that psychologists describe: no spells of depression; no withdrawal from friends, family and activities; no neglect of appearance; no outward expressions of anger, hopelessness, persistent boredom. That's what made this suicide all the more horrifying to Heather's classmates and family.

Heather told her parents she had been molested, but that had occurred five years before. By all indications, she was over that now. She projected this happy, carefree image like everything was fine, which matched her bubbly personality. Her parents had no idea there was anything wrong.

One day after school, her father entered the house and thought it strange when he called out and his daughter didn't answer. He decided to check upstairs in Heather's room; he found no one. Then, as if strangely compelled, he looked in the bathroom and found his daughter. With methodical perfection, Heather had folded back the rug, lined up the shampoo bottles on the floor, crawled into the tub, pulled the shower curtain closed and shot herself in the head with a .22 caliber pistol.

On the dining room table lay a suicide note Heather had earlier read to a friend, telling her it was a report on suicide and young people. It read: "Dear Mom and Dad, It's not your fault. You did not do anything wrong. I just don't like my life. I guess I better go. Y'all are going to be home soon. I'm up in the bathtub because I thought that maybe the blood would not mess up much in there. Also, I put on old clothes so I would not ruin good clothes, and I took out my contacts so that you could maybe get your money back. I love y'all. Forever, Heather."

The emotional devastation that followed is unimaginable, but it occurs thousands of times each year for families and classmates of teen suicides. I felt engulfed by the tidal wave of pain being multiplied by Heather's 1,500 classmates and wondered which young person sitting out there was contemplating suicide now.

Tragic Phenomenon

The current epidemic of teen suicide in America is an alarming and frighteningly ominous trend. Never in history have so many youth, age thirteen to nineteen, decided to take their lives. The suicide rate among teens has increased 300 percent over the last thirty years. In 1960, there were 1,239 suicides among teens age fourteen to nineteen. In 1970, there were 3,128. By 1980, youth suicides had risen to 5,239, and we know that's underreported.[1] During the decade of the '80s, there were over five thousand teen suicides each year. Tragically, more than fifty thousand teens committed suicide over this ten-year period. The '90s finds the suicidal trend still drastically on the rise. Recent research shows more teens than ever are contemplating how, when and why they might commit suicide. "Michael Peck, a Los Angeles psychiatrist who has studied adolescent suicide for more than two decades, asserts that up to 10 percent of the teens in any high school classroom may be considered at some risk for suicide; he believes more than one million teens enter suicidal crises each year."[2]

Suicide is the third leading cause of death for teens, surpassed only by alcohol-related car accidents and homicides. Research indicates that half a million teens attempt suicide in the U.S. each year. A recent study said, "More than two million youths, one in every ten, will attempt suicide before finishing high school."[3] Every day 1,500 young people in America attempt suicide.

So many teens are committing suicide today that a representative of the U.S. Centers for Disease Control in Atlanta said, "If people in society were dying from a disease at the same rate that teenagers are dying from suicide, it would be considered a major epidemic."[4] There are more youth thinking about, obsessed with and attracted to suicide than ever before.

Teen suicide cuts a destructive path across every geographic, racial and socioeconomic strata in the youth culture. Suddenly, suicide seems to be snatching the best and brightest teens who had everything to live for, star athletes, academic over-achievers, the most popular, as well as teens who seemingly have very little to live for, the loner, the abused, the drug user, the delinquent youth. There is no group in American society that has been more profoundly affected by suicide than the teen culture.

Why is the teenage suicide rate increasing so rapidly? Why are young people so unhappy? Why are they choosing death rather than life?

Tip of Suicide Iceberg

The five thousand teen suicides reported each year have sadly become the norm in America. Experts, however, believe the actual number of suicides is four times higher than reported, because thousands more may be mistakenly or intentionally listed as accidents and homicides. Mitch Anthony, director of National Suicide Help Center, says, "It is impossible to accurately calculate the actual number of victims because many suicides are not reported as such. The accuracy of statistics is affected by the social stigma of suicide. For example, it would be impossible to prove that a sole-occupant car accident was a suicide."[5] Yet, forensics experts believe as many as one quarter of youth-involved car accidents are deliberate teen suicides. "Those determining the cause of death may want to spare a family the stigma, shame and confusion identified with suicide by simply reporting it as accidental or undetermined."[6]

It is a common practice to list car accident fatalities, drug overdoses and gun deaths as accidents rather than suicides to cover up and protect families from pain and embarrassment, and for insurance purposes. *Newsweek* says, "Every year in America, five thousand unidentified young people are buried in unmarked graves, youth who got lost in the system and became just another statistic. The cause of death for many of these teens is suicide."[7]

Suicide Is Symptomatic

Young people's perceptions, motivations and choices are ultimately based on their needs and fears. All the major visible problems facing the youth culture today — drug abuse, teen pregnancy, gangs, violence, satanism, suicide — are really symptoms of much deeper problems. Suicide is a symptom that youth's critical emotional and spiritual needs are not being fulfilled and their fears are being magnified. The powerful emotional needs and fears represent the root causes behind the dangerous trends affecting today's youth culture and have remained constant for this generation — the need for intimacy, identity, meaning, significance, ability to cope with pain and problems, hope in the future and spiritual fulfillment. When teens' essential emotional needs aren't being met, they focus on their fears to meet their needs. Their fears:

- Create illusions and distort reality.
- Intensify their needs.
- Magnify their pain and problems.
- Produce extreme destructive behavior and a vicious cycle of false hope.

Suicide and other destructive trends have become epidemic today among teens because contemporary culture has failed to recognize, confront and effectively deal with the root causes of the problems.

Cultural Forces

Today's culture has created a self-destructive mind-set for youth; dangerous life-styles are promoted, condoned and viewed as normal. Let's look at these societal forces that have encouraged and fueled suicide among youth.

Accelerated Change. This high-tech society is rocketing youth into a brave new world where they feel overwhelmed, inadequate and confused. Youth are in a constant state of transition, which further frustrates their attempts to achieve intimacy, a sense of identity and a meaningful role in the culture. They are exposed to more lethal pressures and confronted with more totally new situations, more critical choices at a faster pace than ever. The speedup of change is a powerful social and psychological force that can have emotionally crippling effects. The deadly combination of accelerated change socially, morally and technically, with less security and guidance, becomes a catalyst for suicide. As youth feel increasingly disoriented, a sense of helplessness and being out of control dominates. Faced with a magnified sense of impotence, a teen may believe that the one thing he still owns is his life and suicide is the only way he can take control over his world. As one teen said, "If I can't control my life, I can control my death."

A Highly Stressed Generation

Popular culture has rendered teens more vulnerable while exposing them to new and more powerful stresses than were ever faced by previous generations. This makes teens much more susceptible to self-destructive solutions. All of today's stresses converging at once paralyze youth leaving them unable to cope with everyday problems and situations. They are traumatized and totally unprepared, unable to adapt, function and make positive choices. Too much stress creates an illusion; this can make suicide appear as a viable alternative, a deadly illusion.

Popular culture's obsession with competition generates a stress-filled atmosphere. Youth are taught to compete with and dominate their classmates rather than be compassionate or make a connection with them. This performance-oriented culture puts teens under enormous pressure to achieve, succeed and be number one at all costs, which further isolates and desensitizes them to each other's needs and pain.

Young people are told from grammar school, "You'd better start running — and fast — because the pie is shrinking." Teens are not only driven to succeed but also compelled to measure their success against the accomplishments of others. Society effectively pits youth against each other rather than helping each other, producing frustration and loneliness in living.

Moral Suicide

A generation in transition has an acute need for stability, security and certainty. However, the deteriorating moral foundation intensifies instability, insecurity and uncertainty. Rapid change in what is ethical has created a moral vacuum where right and wrong is now relative. Moral suicide occurs when a culture rejects God's truth and principles as obsolete and irrelevant, and embraces immorality and perversion as truth.

This amoral (neutral) mentality has produced confusion, despair and a meaningless drift among today's youth. Society is committing "moral suicide" by rejecting and ridiculing Biblical standards as outdated and irrelevant. The collapse of a moral value system has helped fuel the suicide rate among teens.

In times of accelerated social and moral flux, even committed parents are confused about what limits to set and what values to advocate and enforce. Baby-boomer parents are in disarray when being more permissive is considered progressive; it's easier to say yes than no.

Ironically, the boomer generation set in motion the personal morality and liberated life-style in the '60s that is in vogue today. Awash in a rising tide of critical choices and more dangerous consequences, parents are as confused as teens. Parents are paralyzed by ambivalence, which further magnifies the uncertainty among youth.

The narcissistic philosophy — living life only for yourself — ultimately leaves youth feeling disillusioned, desperate and depressed. These hyper-self-indulgent conditions set them up for the final stage of futility and nihilism. As significance and meaning continue to elude them, they believe there is nothing in life worthwhile.

Rolling Stone Magazine, in a classic feature article on suicide entitled "What Makes Johnny More Prone to Kill Himself Today Than in 1960," stated: "Youth don't know what rules are valid anymore. Everything in the world is negotiable now; everything is shades of gray, and all that matters is green. All is uncertain, nothing is shocking, everything is tolerated. Even suicide, with each passing example, becomes less taboo."[8]

Disconnected Relationships

The impermanence in relationships creates deep insecurities and fears among youth. The fast-paced transient society produces "transient relationships" where faster, shorter and easily disposable relationships are viewed as progressive.

The fragmented family and increased sexual relationships among teens create deep feelings of "disconnectedness" in popular culture. The media and our sex-saturated society, promoting and encouraging safe sex, have produced emotionally devastated youth. The tremendous increase in sexual activity among teens at an earlier age only intensifies their need for intimacy.

Sexual promiscuity among teens is definitely a factor contributing to teen suicide. Premarital sex can cause extreme emotional damage, producing deep feelings of guilt, failure, self-hate and depression.

In this high-tech, emotionally detached atmosphere, loneliness and uncertainty multiply concerning relationships. The feeling of betrayal and a tremendous fear of intimate relationships permeate our culture. Youth and adults feel more isolated and alienated from each other than ever. Too many disconnected teens are becoming intimately connected with suicide.

Appetite for Destruction

Today's youth culture has a morbid fascination with themes of death, destruction and hopelessness. The media — through music, movies, videos, TV and games — promotes, packages and sells these messages of destruction. The electronic media not only reflects dangerous new realities, but also has helped create a new self-destructive mind-set among youth.

The fantasy role-playing game, *Dungeons and Dragons (D & D)*, has helped fuel self-destructive tendencies among teens. *D & D* replaces reality with fantasy power; teens believe they have the ability to alter events, even death. Youth who become obsessed with *D & D* believe if they die there are spells that can bring them back.

In the *Dungeon Master's Guide,* one finds this description of "Suicidal Mania": "This form of insanity causes the afflicted character to have overwhelming urges to destroy himself or herself whenever means are presented. The more dangerous the situation or item, the more likely the individual is to react self-destructively."[9] *Dungeons and Dragons* has been cited as the major factor in numerous teen suicides. (See Chapters 17 and 18 for more details.)

Heavy Metal Mania

Heavy metal is "white hot," thanks to bands like Guns 'N' Roses and Metallica, who defy the establishment. Guns 'N' Roses recently came out with "Use Your Illusion I & II." This multimillion-dollar seller taps into the dark anger and vengeance that make it dangerously provocative and outrageous. Axel Rose, lead singer for Guns 'N' Roses, said, "I'm wired on indignation." What is so alarming is that the subject matter of the album includes bondage and brutality of women, the lure of murder, mindless violence, sexual promiscuity, perversion, suicide and the pleasures of drug-induced comas.[10] "'Coma' is a disturbing life-death odyssey of suicidal impulses and emergency room drama, heightened by eerie special effects and abruptly shifting tempos," says *USA Today.*[11]

The heavy metal group, Metallica, with a best-selling album by the same name ("Metallica") entered Billboard charts at number one and stayed there four weeks. In one of their recent earlier albums that went gold ("Masters of Puppets"), they hinted at suicide: "Nothing matters, no one else, I have lost the will to live. Simply nothing more to give. There is nothing more for me. Need the end to set me free."[12]

These heavy metal messiahs spew out radical raw lyrics espousing "total anarchy" through violence, death and destruction; they exude a rebellious, destructive defiance that touches a nerve among many teens today. These metal heroes to a generation now have massive appeal to a mostly white male teen audience; however, their popularity is growing with white female teens as well.

What is disturbing about this dangerous trend is that it is the voice of an increasingly angry group of disillusioned and alienated youth. A teenager who is hurt is vulnerable to self-destructiveness. "A teen who is angry is vulnerable. A teen who feels powerless and overwhelmed, a teen who is hopeless and despondent, is vulnerable, and a teen who lives through a separation and divorce situation will experience hurt, anger, betrayal and despondence."[13]

The Rap Subculture

Rap music is another cultural phenomenon that exploded on the music scene in the '80s, a social force for black teens that expresses their outrage against a hypocritical and apathetic establishment. Rap groups — like Public Enemy, Ice-T, Snoop Doggy Dog and Ice Cube — reflect the deep distrust, discontent and hostility among black youth. The dark side of "gangsta" rap music promotes revenge, rape, sadomasochism and glorifies degradation, brutality and hatred toward women, gang violence, racist attitudes, gang rapes and murders. The destructive gangsta rap mind-set advocates an angry, militant attitude where violence and death is what occurs when you "fight the power."

Songs like "Death Certificate," "Endangered Species," "Cop Killer" and "On Dead Homies" describe the brutal and deadly gang life-style in black America. Gang-related death and destruction have engulfed every segment of our culture, no longer just the inner cities; hundreds of innocent people have been killed or maimed by random gang violence.

The gang life-style is "suicidal" for many black teens. The normal life expectancy for gang members is two to four years or less; very few gang members live beyond the age of nineteen or twenty years. The gang life-style becomes a black hole of despair, where too many black youth get swallowed up by hopelessness and death.

An L.A. Crips gang member said: "If you die, you die. Most gangbangers don't have nothin' to live for no more anyway. That's why some of them gang-bangin'. . . . I tell you this . . . you see dyin', then you be ready to die yourself, just so you don't have to see no more of death."[14]

The Triggering Event

The causes for each suicide are a complex and unique combination of stresses and traumas.[15] Too many teens today are ill-equipped and unprepared to deal with the pressures, problems and pain that have multiplied over the past thirty years.

There are myriad causes that have contributed to the epidemic youth suicide, which include the deteriorating moral foundation, disintegrating family relationships, drug and alcohol abuse, rampant youth violence and murder, divorce, rootlessness, meaninglessness, loneliness, excessive freedom, sexual promiscuity, new peer pressure, hyper-competition, delinquency, runaways, gangs, media illusions, lack of spiritual commitment and alienation from God, unrealistic expectations, self-hatred, satanism, racism, fantasy mentality, boredom, disillusionment and fear of the future, recent loss, narcissism, increased school pressure, abuse and other causes that correlate with the rising rate of teen suicide.

Sociological, interpersonal, psychological, emotional and spiritual factors all play a role in youth suicide. These multiple factors usually converge to trigger the suicide.

The "triggering event" is what pushes them over the edge; it is the totality of their pain. "For the depressed and suicidal teen, the break-up of a romantic relationship could be the precipitating or triggering event. This event can be a bad grade, failing a driver's test, an argument, the death of a friend or pet, being rejected or embarrassed at school, divorce, moving to another city, being a victim of an assault or rape."[16]

The triggering event for a deeply troubled and confused teen may be listening to heavy metal music groups like Slayer's song, "Mandatory Suicide," Suicidal Tendencies singing "Suicide's an Alternative," Ozzy Osborne's "Suicide Solution" or Pink Floyd's song, "Good-bye Cruel World." All of these groups with their fatalistic lyrics have been linked to numerous teen suicides. Many experts state that "death metal" music that promotes and advocates suicide has helped fuel teen depression and self-destructive behavior. After listening to such music, the teen may feel he has failed and that his failure is unacceptable to parents, peers or himself.

The triggering event need not be momentous. Teens have killed themselves for seemingly trivial reasons: the fourteen-year-old boy who, according to his parents, shot himself because he was upset about getting braces for his teeth that afternoon; the girl who killed herself moments after her father refused to let her watch *Camelot* on television; for Justin Spoonhour, not receiving a flower on Valentine's Day became the final straw. Such incidents are often misinterpreted as the "reason" for a suicide, but they are usually the culmination of a longer series of painful experiences and intensified feelings of frustration and desperation.[17] The triggering event may seem to verify the low self-worth or self-hatred the teen has felt all along.

"In all the teen suicides we see," says Judy Pollatek, a counselor in Washington, D.C., "the kids always have some secret and are terrified that someone is about to find out."[18] To a teen in pain, suicide seems like the ultimate solution or the instant cure to their problem.

Failure Perception

Teens' perception of failure is critical in determining their sense of self-worth and meaning, and in developing relationships. Our achievement-oriented society has created a failure complex among many teens. They believe one failure means they are a total failure. Failures in relationships with peers, boyfriends, girlfriends and parents have left them feeling rejected, inadequate and inferior.

If success only means achieving, performing, competing and accomplishing, then they will be totally obsessed with self-interest, which produces a false sense of significance, rather than helping or reaching out and caring for others. On the other hand, "Many suicidal teens express frantic frustration about the pressures that are bombarding them: 'It seems like I am living my life for everyone but me.'"[19]

The fear of failure is a powerful driving force that confuses and distorts youth's perception of reality. The constant massive cultural pressure to succeed has produced a paralyzing, traumatizing effect that has led to an epidemic inability to cope with failure.

Youth specialist Mitch Anthony says, "The issue of failure blends two major motivators for suicide: the lack of self-worth and the inability to cope with problems and pain. Failure, more accurately defined as the inability to process failure correctly, takes a heavy toll on one's self-esteem."[20]

Youth who believe they are failures are especially vulnerable to constant depression and eventually suicide. Too many young people just aren't emotionally prepared to deal with the accelerated failures, stresses and unprecedented situations this high-tech culture is assaulting them with.

Rootlessness

More youth are being uprooted from relationships and familiar environments than ever before. They are being exposed to a harsh, uncertain and even dangerous atmosphere. Previous predictable factors — such as security, safety and nurturing — are no longer there for them. This mobile culture in constant transition and the impermanence of relationships are sadly becoming the norm for many teens today.

The Census Bureau reports that millions of families move as often as three to four times within a five-year period. This transient life-style and lack of quality family relationships leave youth floundering for secure roots. Combined with all the pressures youth face, they must keep adapting to new environments and new relationships.

Many teens don't know what it is to have a secure, caring family or the experience of predictability in their lives. There is a sense of rootlessness in today's youth culture, producing prime candidates for delinquency, under-achievement and, ultimately, suicide. The fear of unpredictability is causing youth to feel more vulnerable and less able to cope.

"Predictability is recognized as a vital environmental factor that contributes to a child/teen's emotional well-being. Without the stabilizing influence of predictability, the resulting frustration and confusion may lead to thoughts of death. Many youth who have been affected by the transient life-styles of their parents have remarked that they do not feel they are as important as their parents' personal interests and careers."[21]

Youth today desperately need a sense of roots and belonging. "A sixteen-year-old male, whose family had just moved again, hanged himself from an oak tree in the backyard, leaving a note: 'This is the only thing around here that has any roots.'"[22]

Worthlessness

Teens who feel worthless are vulnerable to self-destructive solutions. New peer power is filling the vacuum left by the negative and neglectful parental relationships. Teens are looking to friends and the opposite sex for identity. Due to the fragmented family, these relationships are more important than ever.

Peer acceptance and approval by the opposite sex is crucial for so many teens' sense of worth. Teens base their self-worth on how they think others perceive them. Sadly, after a period of time, the teen experiences enough betrayal and rejection from friends and the opposite sex which produces even greater disillusionment and desperation. Now, the teen is engulfed in deeper feelings of inadequacy and worthlessness. Teens base their entire existence and sense of worth on that relationship. When it goes, they believe as one suicide note read, "without him, I'm nothing. I'm nobody."

Loneliness

"All the lonely people, where do they all come from? All the lonely people, where do they all belong?" These Beatles lyrics from "Eleanor Rigby" describe perfectly the "crowded loneliness" that pervades popular culture today.

The vacuum of meaningful relationships has created a monster of loneliness that feeds off pain and desperation. "Experts estimate that loneliness in America has reached epidemic proportions and, if it continues, could erode the emotional strength of our nation."[23] Nobody has felt this rampant loneliness more acutely than the youth culture. Researcher John Woodward of the University of Nebraska has researched loneliness for twenty years. He states that high school girls are the loneliest people in America, according to the study.[24]

The deepest loneliness teens experience is not just being by themselves, which is certainly painful, but it's constantly being surrounded by and involved with people, and still feeling alone.

Statements made by lonely youth: "There is no one I can turn to." "I am no longer close to anyone." "I feel left out." "I don't fit in." "I need someone." "No one really knows me well." "People are around me but not with me." These statements reflect the isolation and loneliness common within the youth culture.

Lonely teens are extremely vulnerable to "illusions of love," and they will do anything to avoid being alone. Consuming loneliness is being at a party, in a crowd or involved in relationships, and not feeling close or intimately connected to that person or persons.

The fear of loneliness pushes teens to superficial relationships or a paranoid isolation. Breaking up isn't just hard to do; for some teens, it's unthinkable. Relationship breakups have become tragic suicide scenarios for many lonely teens.

Depression

There is a cloud of depression hovering over today's youth culture. We all experience depression to some degree at one time or another. However, millions of children and teens (as many as 15 percent of adolescents) are experiencing severe paralyzing depression, and it's taking a devastating toll on their lives. At the individual level, the rate of emotional depression over the last two generations has multiplied tenfold![25]

Here are some multifaceted dimensions of depression: sadness, hopelessness, loneliness, withdrawal, apathy, despair, disorientation, paranoia, over-sensitivity, vulnerability, self-hatred, worthlessness, guilt, gloom, discouragement, anxiety and anger.

The two most common causes of depression are repressed anger and a deep sense of loss. Both of these feelings feed off each other, increasing the intensity of depression. Many young people experience deep-seated anger toward parents who are divorced. Rooted in a sense of having been exploited, betrayed and rejected by their parents, they experience intense anger and loss.

The loss of a steady girlfriend or boyfriend can produce anger toward the person they trusted, leaving them feeling foolish and humiliated because they opened themselves up to that person and were rejected. They resent the person and somehow want to get even but also feel sad that the relationship has ended. Related to the anger is a sense of powerlessness. Just as in divorce, they feel they have no way to influence or change this major event in their lives.

There is a driving desire to make them pay for what they did, the hostile attitude of "I'll show them," to lash out at the source of their pain. Significant loss and anger produce deep depression that can turn to suicidal revenge, which has led numerous teens to end their life.

Significant loss (deep sense of loss) comes through the death of a family member or friend, divorce or separation, or the breakup of a romantic relationship. "These scenarios have led to innumerable suicides."[26]

Destructive depression is the result of anger turned inward, experiencing extreme loss and feeling frustrated and powerless to change the situation. "This devastating combination may cause youth to feel irrational guilt, self-hatred, shame or helplessness, finally leading to feelings of hopelessness. At this point, some feel the compulsion to kill themselves, as though suicide is the only thing that makes sense. Others feel suicidal because their internalized anger begins 'leaking out,' and they desperately want some way to let important others know just how angry and hurt they really are." This anger becomes the self-directed hate that is found in depressive symptoms, such as suicidal impulses, or a variety of self-destructive behaviors, such as drugs, sex, violence or running away.[27]

When a person is depressed, they lose perspective. Depression distorts youth's perception of reality. "It is not only the severity of the actual loss itself that is important to judge when attempting to understand youth's depression; rather, it is the person's perception of that loss and the meaning they assigned to it."[28]

Depression intensifies youth's fears and produces a distorted negative perception, where everything is viewed from a gloomy, hopeless mind-set. Focusing on despair, desperation and fears will always distort reality. Depression blurs the line between fantasy and reality, making it indistinguishable. Author Norm Wright says, "Once a person becomes depressed, he tends to behave in a way that reinforces and perpetuates the depression."[29] The longer and deeper the depression, the more extreme the distortion and confusion.

Perfectionism

Our performance-oriented culture promotes and fuels perfectionism. Perfectionists derive a sense of identity, meaning and self-esteem from what they accomplish, achieve or produce.

Performance perfectionists are driven by a powerful need to prove to themselves and others that they are valuable, lovable, capable people. Perfectionists believe, "I am what I do." The inability to accomplish tasks or perform perfectly creates self-doubt and insecurity.

Perfectionists have ultra-high expectations and excessive standards that invite depression into their lives. However, no matter what the perfectionists accomplish or achieve, it's never enough; they never quite measure up to their own hyper-expectations because they expect the impossible. To be perfect, complete and flawless in all respects, perfectionists spend a great deal of time feeling worthless and disappointed in themselves. "When perfectionists fail to live up to their unrealistic, unattainable standards, this creates either anger or depression, or both."[30] Perfectionists get trapped in an endless self-defeating cycle of disappointment, self-hatred, failure and depression.

Perfectionism can lead to self-destructive behavior: girls who are "appearance perfectionists" become anorexic or bulimic, trying for the perfect look. But they can never achieve their goal because their perception of reality is distorted by their fears and insecurities. Tunnel vision blinds them to everything but their imperfections and an almost incurable dissatisfaction with themselves. Perfectionists have an inferiority complex because they can never satisfy their driving need to be perfect, which only intensifies their feelings of inferiority, a floating bitterness and increased compulsiveness.

The star athlete who must reach another level of performance to get bigger, stronger and faster, uses steroids to achieve his goal. The perfectionist uses drugs and alcohol to escape feelings of disappointment, frustration and imperfection. Perfectionism is a major catalyst for depression and even suicide.

The most baffling and disturbing youth suicide is when the most popular, best-looking, outstanding star athlete or student that most kids would give their right arm to trade places with kills themselves. Teens think, *If they weren't happy, who can be? What does it take?*

Youth have experienced so much today, yet still feel this confusing emptiness. On the one hand, they are overpowered by a high-tech, impersonal culture that makes them feel insignificant and irrelevant. The electronic media has created an "over-stimulation effect" by exposing teens to too much, too fast, too soon, producing a deep apathy, depression and aimless drift.

On the other hand, a monotonous, repetitious and boring environment can be just as stressful and depressive as a fast-paced, pressure-filled, and ultra-competitive atmosphere. Youth feel under-challenged, and real meaning gets lost in a sea of trivial pursuit.

Many young people feel they can't make a difference in their world and they don't really matter. At that point, suicide becomes the answer.

Hopelessness

Young people's perception of the future powerfully affects their expectations, attitudes, motivations and behavior. If they view the future as bleak, gloomy and hopeless, self-destructive behavior will increase dramatically.

Pain distorts youth's concept of time. They believe the present pain will only get worse and never end. For teens, the moment is everything. They think, "I've got pain, and the pain is lasting for more than two minutes; that means the pain will last forever."

When reality is too painful, too stressful and too traumatic, escaping the pain becomes an inviting alternative. They want to escape problems and painful feelings of failure, guilt, loss, helplessness, shame, rejection, loneliness, self-hatred, humiliation and fear.

Hopelessness is projecting the futility and despair of the present into the future. The spiritual void in their lives is the major cause for the deep-seated feelings of meaningless activity and purposeless existence. Their sense of meaning and destiny is directly related to their relationship with Jesus Christ. Youth are experiencing a false sense of significance, which increases the suicidal behavior.

Their pain distorts and creates an illusion where the suicidal teen can't see past the moment. They only want relief from their present agony. Teens may feel, in the words of the theme song from *Mash,* that "suicide is painless" and what comes afterward is pleasant.[31] Many young people believe death is the only way to escape an intolerable situation and unbearable pain. They don't see any other option or solution to their problems and hopelessness besides escaping through suicide. Emotional pain not only distorts but produces confusion and delusion. Suicide is a permanent solution to a temporary problem.

"Suicidal teens suffer from tunnel vision," says psychologist Pamela Cantor. They are looking down a long tunnel, and all they see is darkness. They don't know where they are in the tunnel; they think it goes on forever. They don't know there is light at the other end.

"Perhaps more accurately, at a certain point, the suicidal teen believes that there is light at the end of the tunnel, and that light is suicide which is the ultimate delusion."[31]

Hopelessness is the final stage of desperation, when loneliness, meaninglessness, despair and depression converge, producing massive inescapable pain.

Author Jerry Johnston describes the deep hopelessness of a sixteen-year-old named Jay. "His parents found his lifeless body on the floor of his bedroom. There was a bullet wound in his head. Lying nearby was the gun he used to kill himself. There was also a suicide note. It read simply: 'Dear world, I don't want to get my hair cut. I don't want to tend kids or see Tina at school on Monday. I don't want to do my biology assignment or English or history or anything. I don't want to be sad or lonely or depressed anymore. I don't want to talk, sleep, move, feel, live or breathe anymore. Tina, it's not your fault. Mom and Dad, it's not your fault. I'm not free. I feel ill. I'm sad. I'm lonely. One last request . . . all my worldly possessions go to Debbie as a wedding present."[32]

That tragic letter reflects the terminal hopelessness that too many young people are experiencing.

Tara the Survivor

After an assembly presentation at a major high school in Northern California, an attractive emotionally intense girl approached me. She said, "Eric, could I talk with you for a minute?" Tara, a seventeen-year-old senior, had almost died six months earlier from an overdose of pills. She spent weeks in intensive care in a comatose state, on the edge of death.

She said emphatically, "Eric, please keep telling kids to reach out to each other, to care and be sensitive. The doctors told me I should have had brain damage or be dead; I'm so grateful neither occurred."

Tara said, "I thought tomorrow wouldn't get better, but it did! I thought I couldn't cope or deal with the pain, but I can. I thought I was the only one, and nobody else understood or cared, but they do! I would have missed so many wonderful and exciting things.

"Sure, I still have pain and problems. Sometimes I get depressed, but I know I can make it with Christ's help. We all have to deal with reality and pain; it makes us better, more compassionate people."

In extensive major research concerning American teens in crisis, teens were asked, "If you were having serious problems, who would you talk to?" Not surprisingly, 85 to 90 percent of the teenagers surveyed responded that they would most likely talk to a teen friend, not an adult. Teenagers almost exclusively turn to other teenagers for help. Because of this, teens are in the most strategic position to help their peers.[33] The number one deterrent to teenage suicide is young people who are caring, compassionate and sensitive to the needs and pain of others.

A Generation Searching for Hope

Hope represents a promising, exciting, anticipated future, believing the best is yet to come. However, if teens believe the future means increased pain, gloominess and despair, the result will be disastrous. When youth lose their hopes and dreams, America is a nation at risk. Too many teens today view the future negatively; they are all dressed up with no place to go. Young people feel they have no control over their lives or their future.

"A person can live approximately forty days without food, about three days without water, but only one second without hope" (Orson Welles).

There are two equal and opposite errors into which our race can fall about the devils. One is to disbelieve in their existence. The other is to believe and to feel an excessive and unhealthy interest in them. They themselves [demons] are equally pleased by both errors.

C.S. Lewis
The Screwtape Letters

Chapter 17

The Seduction of Evil: The Satanic Phenomenon

For we do not wrestle against flesh and blood, but against principalities, against powers, against the rulers of the darkness of this age, against spiritual hosts of wickedness in the heavenly places (Eph. 6:12 NKJ).

Recruiting a Generation

I received a frantic phone call from a mother who said she needed to talk to me immediately about a very serious matter that she wouldn't discuss over the phone.

When I arrived, she looked desperate and very frightened. She said nervously, "A few days earlier my son came home from school, changed clothes and said he was going to hang out with his friends and would be home later. He had been acting a little strange recently, very secretive and was unusually evasive. I didn't know exactly what it was, but I knew something wasn't right. I decided to go through his room, thinking maybe I'd find something to give me some explanation for his attitude and behavior. What I found was so frightening." She was trembling as she handed me a letter.

The following are excerpts from a letter given to me by a mother whose fifteen-year-old son was being recruited by youth on a high school campus who were involved to some degree in satanism.

The Power of Satan

"Welcome to good times ahead! Satan and his organization would like to thank you for showing faith and solidarity. We are sure through our mutual commitment of one another and the power of evil, we will defeat the diseased minds of the pastors and priests of the Christian churches of the world that seek to slander our mighty lord, Lucifer. Eventually, our mighty leader Satan will regain his position of prominence: Those who help in our crusade will be richly rewarded, your every dream will be fulfilled. Those who oppose our master will be destroyed."

The letter describes in detail the rituals involved in making contact with Satan and the forces of darkness. "In the name of Satan, the ruler of the earth, the king of the world, I command the forces of darkness to bestow their infernal power upon me. Open wide the gates of hell and come forth from the abyss to greet me as your brother and friend. Grant me the indulgences of which I speak. I have taken thy name as part of myself. I live as the beasts of the fields, rejoicing in the fleshly life. By all that is evil, I command that these things of which I speak shall come to pass. Hail Satan, Hail Satan, Hail Satan."

Satan is making an all-out bid for this generation; a foreboding evil is spreading across North America, stalking and destroying young people. Satanism is offering a searching, cynical and desperate generation emotional, sensual and spiritual fulfillment through power and self-indulgence.

There is so much disillusionment, confusion and emotional devastation in the lives of millions of youth that the occult experience becomes very attractive and enticing. Satanism is seducing young people while promising to meet their real needs and fulfill their desires now; it effectively exploits and ultimately devours them.

Former satanists talk about the youth satanic recruitment process. They refer to it as "progressive entrapment."

"Step by step and little by little we would lead them into deeper involvement with the occult. If they continued to show interest, we would show them even deeper satanic secrets. This is known as 'progressive entrapment' because the individuals didn't realize that we were setting them up, whetting their appetites, conditioning them, feeding and creating a craving and desire for devil's food."[1]

Teens Especially Vulnerable to Satanism

According to Shane Westhoelter, president of the National Information Network, as many as 30 to 40 percent of high school students are involved in some form of the occult.[2]

Several national cult awareness networks concur with the increased involvement, activity and significance of teenage satanism today. Here are prime candidates for satanism:

The Loner. The kid that doesn't fit in or belong to any group or clique, has few friends if any, and has difficulty relating to others. He is the invisible youth on the campus. Loneliness and low self-esteem magnify his need for acceptance and a sense of belonging.

The Intellectual. This is the classic high I.Q. over-achiever, a very successful youth who is extremely creative and bored with the status quo. He is looking for something challenging, novel, on the edge, avant-garde to push him to the limit. These kids are honor students, student council members and outstanding athletes.

The Abused Kid. Many teens have been physically, emotionally and sexually abused by a parent or parents. They have a deep sense of betrayal, worthlessness, guilt and rage toward authority and are extremely alienated and hostile toward family.

Mainstream America. Middle- and upper-class suburbanite youth are much more prone to get involved than urban kids. More mainstream kids are dabbling into satanism than ever before; it has become a trendy status symbol and a very dangerous fad. These kids have been so overexposed, they are jaded and cynical, and it takes more and more to shock, impress, excite and thrill them. They are intelligent, curious and bored.

The Underachiever. This youth does not necessarily have a low I.Q., although he can have. He is not motivated by anything other than what pleases him. He excels in not excelling. The "metal head" is a classic underachiever, only concerned with the immediate present; he worships a particular heavy metal rock group, buys all their albums, wears their T-shirts. He is only concerned with making the next rock concert, learning what his band has to say and getting wasted with his head-banging buddies.

The Addictive Personality. Youths who have obsessive-compulsive tendencies (they do everything to extreme) are motivated by intense irrational fears: fear of rejection, fear of not measuring up, fear of betrayal and abandonment, which makes them particularly susceptible to the occult experience.

The Religiously Alienated. These young people come from Christian backgrounds where they experienced harsh, condemning, critical and unforgiving attitudes. They experienced manipulating love, hypocrisy and relationships based on guilt, fear and shame rather than unconditional love and forgiveness. These youth view Christianity as uncompassionate, impersonal and irrelevant. They turn to the evil alternative — satanism — that offers acceptance, power and instant gratification.

Antisocial Personality. This is the most frightening personality and the most susceptible to satanism. These are young people without a conscience, and they have the capacity to hurt and even brutally kill others without guilt or remorse. They are commonly referred to as psychopaths or antisocials, and they possess a poisonous mix of personality traits. They are arrogant, shameless, immoral, impulsive, superficial, cold, charming, callous, irresponsible, irreverent, cunning and self-assured. This pathological personality is characterized by attention seeking, uninhibited indiscriminate friendliness, lack of guilt, an ability to con, an inability to follow rules and an inability to establish and maintain deep significant relationships. Without conscience, these are emotionally detached, affectionless individuals who are reckless, aggressive, cruel and deadly destructive. They leave in their wake a huge amount of human suffering. These are your mass murderers: serial-killer types Ted Bundy, Charles Manson, "Son of Sam" David Berkowitz, Jeffrey Dahmer.

What's really scary is that criminologists, sociologists and mental health experts say we have more antisocial and psychopathic types in America than ever before. Based on conservative estimates if you consider 5 percent of the population, there could be as many as thirteen million psychopaths.[3] They are prime candidates for satanism.

Three Kinds of Satanic Groups

Traditional Religious Satanists

Religious satanists belong to the highly organized, orthodox "Church of Satan" who are incorporated and recognized as a nonprofit, tax-exempt religious organization. This is a very high-profile, visible satanist group whose members advocate egotism, indulgence, self-interest and the acquisition and use of personal and political power. They are very structured, have a spiritual base and have set up their group to worship Satan in some particular ceremony and form. Satan is perceived not as evil but as the ultimate symbol of man's carnality, potential and rationality. Religious satanists have as their ultimate aim the restoration of Lucifer to a position they believe is his rightful place as ruler of the universe.[4]

Rites, rituals and ceremonies are strictly adhered to and conducted by a satanic priest. These traditional satanists are very formal, intense and precise in their rituals, worship and practice of satanism. Currently, at least two formal satanic churches provide services to their congregation: the Church of Satan, founded by Anton LaVey, and the Temple of Set, founded by a dissident member of LaVey's flock, Michael Aquino. Taking the name of his organization from the Egyptian mythological god of death, Aquino is a highly visible spokesperson for Satan. The Temple of Set (another name for Satan) is inaugurating his own eon, a time of satanic spiritual and intellectual enlightenment.[5]

It is interesting to note that almost all publicly recognized satanic organizations claim noninvolvement in any criminal activity. Anton LaVey, high priest of the Church of Satan, has made the claim that true satanists would never harm an animal or baby, nor would they harm anyone else, except for people who wish or deserve to be hurt. Despite satanists claims of noninvolvement in violent criminal activities, occult-motivated crimes continue to grow.[6]

Many experts believe the Church of Satan is just a front or cover for what's really happening below the surface. Don't forget that the real mode of satanic operation is deception.

Self-Styled Satanists

These are satanists who are individually involved or belong to a small, loosely organized cult group, apart from traditional mainstream satanism. They are called self-styled satanists because they create their own rites, rituals and philosophies, based on their understanding and perceptions of occultic concepts. Their rituals can encompass a wide range of activities, from a particular wish or desire, fulfillment through the acquisition of money, popularity, sex or success, to sadistic physical beatings, and cutting and scarring themselves, especially their genitals; it also may include sacrificing animals such as dogs, cats and chickens and drinking their blood.

Self-styled satanists are involved in human sacrifice, murders, rituals, drinking human blood, eating feces and eating human flesh. These individuals are dedicated, calculating and cold-blooded, capable of bizarre and ghastly acts.

Richard Ramirez, the "Night Stalker," was a self-styled satanist who left a trail of human carnage and terror; he butchered, raped, sodomized and murdered fourteen people, all in the name of Satan. In the courtroom one day, Ramirez flashed a pentagram drawn on the palm of his hand and shouted, "Hail Satan!" Before he was sentenced, he proclaimed, "Lucifer dwells within us all. You don't understand me. You are not expected to. You are not capable of it," he said. "I am beyond good and evil—legions of the night breed. Repeat not the errors of the night prowler, and show no mercy. I will be avenged."[7]

Youth Subculture Satanists

Like their adult self-styled counterparts, youth subculture satanists are teens who are alienated, bored, angry, anti-social, intelligent, creative and have low self-worth and emotional and family problems. They also have intense curiosity about the unknown and mysterious and are looking for power and control over their lives. Youth satanists create their own dark world by producing their own rules, values, dress, language and life-style through a satanic subculture. Like their adult counterparts, youth subculture satanists are involved individually or belong to a small loosely organized group that has its own rites and rituals. "Most teenagers don't participate in highly structured, traditional satanic ceremonies; they prefer the spontaneity and freedom of self-styled ritualism as opposed to more formal worship of Lucifer. Instead, teen satanists make up their own style and protocol of evil with only a general outline to guide them. They are more likely to have informal evolving beliefs. The intent of 'self-styled' and 'youth subculture' satanists is generally to provide an excuse or justification to indulge in criminal and morally depraved conduct."[8]

Youth satanists are involved in ritual murders, human sacrifice, drinking of blood, the killing of parents or a classmate for Satan, sexual orgies, body mutilations and/or suicide and other bizarre and brutal behavior. Youth satanists are often conditioned by heavy "black metal" music, fantasy role-playing games like *Dungeons and Dragons* and dabbling with *The Satanic Bible.*

Other criminal activities by youth satanists include rape, arson, kidnapping, animal sacrifice, the taking of blood and body parts from hospitals, grave robbing, theft of human cadavers from morgues and funeral homes and vandalizing and robbing churches of sacred objects like crucifixes, communion wafers and chalices.

Law enforcement officials and cult experts currently believe the youth satanists are more at risk and prone to serious criminal involvement than any other occult group. Sandi Gallant, a veteran occult investigator for the San Francisco Police Department, has compiled a general profile of the youth subculture satanist.

"*Youth subculture satanists* are primarily male, Caucasian adolescents who exhibit various behavior problems that have gone unnoticed or undiagnosed; are intelligent, but underachieve; are creative and have high levels of curiosity; have low self-esteem; come from middle- to upper-middle-class families, some of whom may be dysfunctional or detached; have difficulty relating to peers; and who seek power and attention. Their belief system allows them to become involved in crime without having to accept any internal responsibility or guilt for it."[9]

Tommy Sullivan Teen Satanist

Fourteen-year-old Tommy Sullivan was a hard-core youth satanist who plunged deeply into a dark, evil satanic world. His favorite rock group was Suicidal Tendencies. His bedroom wall was covered with occult paraphernalia and posters of Ozzy Osborne. He spent days listening to a growing collection of heavy metal music and became absorbed with playing *Dungeon and Dragons*. Tommy learned to write backwards and inscribed in his Book of Shadows the words, "Evil of all mankind dwells within my soul. If you want in, let me know." Tommy made a pact with Satan. He writes: "To the greatest of demons, I would like to make a solemn exchange with you. If you will give me the most extreme of all magical powers, I will kill many Christian followers. Exactly twenty years from this day, I will promise to commit suicide. I will tempt teenagers on earth to have sex, have incest, do drugs and worship you. I believe that evil will once again rise and conquer the love of God."[10]

Finally, Tommy told his friends about a dream in which Satan appeared to him. "Satan had my face," he said. "He was carrying a knife, and he told me to preach satanism to other kids and then kill everyone in your family. I'm going to do this."[11]

One night, shortly after that, Tommy headed for the downstairs' den to watch the horror movie *Friday the 13th* on the VCR. When authorities arrived, they found a grisly and shocking, blood-spattered scene. Tommy's mother was discovered with her throat slit and dozens of slashes made with a knife. In a driven satanic viciousness, Tommy had tried to gouge her eyes out, and her hands were partially severed.

The next day, authorities found Tommy buried in a snow drift. His wrists were cut and his throat had been slashed from ear to ear with a ferocity that nearly decapitated him. Tommy's satanic madness ended in a murder-suicide pact to his master of evil, Satan.[12]

The Satanic Church

In 1966, Anton LaVey founded the Church of Satan in San Francisco for the purpose of worshiping Satan and self. To the satanist, the self is the highest embodiment of human life and is sacred. It is narcissism taken to the extreme, where self-interest and self-indulgence overshadow everything else in life.

The Church of Satan not only exalts Satan but is essentially a human potential movement, and members are encouraged to develop capabilities by which they might excel or obtain whatever they want. They are, however, cautioned to realize their limitations, an important factor in this philosophy of rational self-interest.

LaVey defines practicing magic as the art of changing with one's will situations or events that would, using normally accepted methods, be impossible and unchangeable.[13]

"To LaVey, man's true enemy is guilt, instilled by Christianity, and the path to individual freedom and fulfillment is through pursuing sin on a regular basis." The Church of Satan has little direct influence on current satanism as practiced among youths. Even though most teens never affiliate with LaVey, they are heavily influenced by the rituals, beliefs and ideology set forth in *The Satanic Bible*. Teen satanists do attribute the teachings of LaVey that paved the way for the present occult explosion. "Church of Satan theology is integral to teens' ideas and concepts about Lucifer, although most youth consider organized satanism as too restrictive and outdated."[14]

Satanic Beliefs

The Satanic Bible, written by Anton LaVey and published in 1969, became an instant best-seller and is widely read by many curious youth and is a source book for many satanists.

Radio talk show host and author Bob Larson says many teens who call his radio show mention *The Satanic Bible* as their source of information. Sean Sellers, perhaps the youngest man on death row, at fifteen years of age brutally and sadistically committed multiple murders in a satanic frenzy. "Halfway through my sophomore year, I learned about *The Satanic Bible*," Sean said. "It seemed like it was all true. I would go around quoting the nine satanic statements. I was really studying hard the magical formulas."[15]

Sean described vividly the final effects of satanism that caused him to kill. "It took away the love for my parents and my girlfriend," he explained. "Eventually, I had no love, no mercy, no conscience. It was subtle; it happened little by little."[16]

In order to understand the principles, practices and beliefs associated with modern satanism, we will look at the nine satanic statements in *The Satanic Bible*. Although the book does not openly advocate any illegal activity, its hedonistic philosophy of self-indulgence and self-interest has undoubtedly contributed to the rise of satanically motivated crimes in the '80s and '90s. Much of the hatred, perversity and deadly violence that are a part of youth subculture satanism comes from *The Satanic Bible*.

Here are the nine satanic statements:

1. Satan represents indulgence instead of abstinence.
2. Satan represents vital existence instead of spiritual pipe dreams.
3. Satan represents undefiled wisdom instead of hypocritical self-deceits.
4. Satan represents kindness to those who deserve it instead of love wasted on ingrates.
5. Satan represents vengeance instead of turning the other cheek.
6. Satan represents responsibility to the responsible instead of concern for psychic vampires.
7. Satan represents man as just another animal — sometimes better, more often worse, than those that walk on all fours

— who because of his "divine spiritual and intellectual development" has become the most vicious animal of all.

8. Satan represents all the so-called sins, as they all lead to physical, mental or emotional gratification.
9. Satan has been the best friend the church has ever had, as he has kept it in business all these years.[17]

These nine creeds form the basis of the satanic philosophy and belief system, which is the total antithesis of Christian beliefs. These teachings are diametrically opposed to and mock the Christian principles and life-style Jesus taught and commanded.

LaVey himself stated: "We feel a person should be free to indulge in all the so-called fetishes that they would desire, as long as they don't hurt anyone that doesn't deserve or wish to be hurt. This is a very selfish religion. We believe in greed, we believe in selfishness, we believe in all the lustful thoughts that motivate man because this is man's natural feeling. This is based on what man naturally would do."[18]

Simply stated, the laws of satanism are:

1. Practice indulgence.
2. Seek vengeance when someone wrongs you.
3. Look for sensual and emotional gratification.
4. Come from self-interest at all times.[19]

LaVey goes on to say, "Self-preservation is the highest law. He who turns the other cheek is a cowardly dog."[20]

Lying, selfishness, vengeance and other deadly beliefs are taught, condoned and rationalized throughout *The Satanic Bible*.

LaVey's ideology is based on constant and immediate gratification. "Life is the great indulgence; death the great abstinence," LaVey proclaims. "There is no heaven of glory bright, and no hell where sinners roast. . . . no redeemer liveth."[21]

But *The Satanic Bible* goes much further since blasphemy is an integral part of worshiping Satan. LaVey includes outrageous insults and vicious denunciations hurled against God. "I dip my forefinger in the watery blood of your impotent, mad redeemer, and write over his thorn-torn brow: the true prince of evil — the king of all slaves. I gaze into the glassy eye of your fearsome Jehovah and pluck him by the beard; I uplift a broad axe and split open his worm-eaten skull."[22]

Imagine thousands of teens studying, believing and repeating these satanic statements and other blasphemous, wicked beliefs contained in *The Satanic Bible* over and over again like Sean Sellers.

The Pathological Narcissist

The satanic philosophy produces the "pathological narcissist." This is a person who is totally self-consumed and self-motivated. He has a remarkable inability to empathize with or feel compassion for other people. His value system is perverted and corrupted, and his goal is self-fulfillment and being in control. His relationships with others are manipulating, calculating, even destructive and vengeful. It is as if the satanic narcissist has the right to control and possess others for personal gratification and self-interest, and to exploit — even kill — without guilt.

Nothing is more important than fulfilling their wish or desire, even at the expense or pain of others. Satanists believe everyone exists for their personal exploitation. This elitist attitude believes the world is comprised of half-wits and fools that deserve to be used. Satanic narcissism intensifies this dehumanizing effect as they are unable to feel for or care for or love others; they become youth without a conscience.

The pathological narcissist fears above all depending on, trusting in and loving others. To do that would render them vulnerable and weak. "Although even satanists want to be loved, they believe love is unattainable, and so they choose evil. In their lives, love has been uncertain and disillusioning. To the satanist, hate is dependable and predictable. It's always there, and you know the effect of its application."[23] Their commitment is only to themselves. They project a superficial love and possess a calloused indifference and a tremendous capacity for treachery and destruction.

The pathological narcissist has little tolerance for feelings of boredom, delayed gratification, restlessness. He is unable to accept the mundane nature of ordinary life and searches constantly for gratification by striving for importance, wealth, the ultimate rush and power!

Dungeons and Dragons

Fantasy has become a major preoccupation with young people today. In a culture where reality is boring, overwhelming and too painful, escaping to a fantasy world becomes an enchanting alternative.

Dungeons and Dragons, the fantasy role-playing (FRP) game, offers an excitement and "fantasy power" to many teens today. *Dungeons and Dragons* burst on the scene in 1975 and became very popular on college campuses. Today, there are more than four million *Dungeons and Dragons* (*D & D*) players in America, with teens being the main participants. The sales of *D & D* and other fantasy games is well over $150 million each year, and growing. *Dungeons and Dragons* is an elaborate fantasy game played essentially in the mind, using one's creative imagination, and based on occult powers and principles.[24]

The first requirement of players is to lose touch with reality, to become lost in a fantasy-created, supernatural realm of magical adventure.

"Gary Gygax, the originator of *Dungeons*, discarded the typical game components — like cards, boards and six-sided dice — and created a game with no rules or time limits. A single game of *D & D* can last for hours, days, weeks, months or even years. At least three people must play. One is the dungeon master, a controlling figure who devises the dungeon map and directs the game's flow. The other players are pitted against each other. They roll poly-sided dice to determine the intelligence and dexterity ratings of their alter-ego characters, which are given fictitious names." *D & D* players consult the dead wizards, witches, demons, magicians, deities and other unseen spiritual forces to get power and hidden knowledge. They cast spells, recite magical incantations, conjure up demons, use astral projection and other occult practices in order to develop their spiritual powers, which they use to conquer their adversaries and reach their goals. "However, no one wins. The object is to survive and become a more powerful character to play in the next *Dungeons and Dragons* game."[25]

On their magical journey, they are confronted with violent tactics and occult spells. *D & D* players become obsessed in the mazes, obstacles, sorcery and fantasy of the medieval world of *Dungeons and Dragons*. They use murder, rape, torture, robbery, arson, occult curses and spells to survive, create and destroy, as they battle monsters, demons, dragons, evil warriors and spiritual powers. This is all standard procedure for *D & D* players in their quest for the dungeon.

Fantasy Role-Playing

Another major requirement of *D & D* players is to assume the identity of such fantasy characters as Druid, magic user, fighter, illusionist, thief, assassin and cleric. Intense imagination is required to merge with your *D & D* character in developing an alter ego. Identifying and expanding your character makes you a better and more powerful player, as the player's imagination heightens.

D & D role-playing can have a very detrimental and dangerous effect on the identity formation of young people. The *D & D* character becomes an emotional extension of the player. Many teens with low self-esteem become vulnerable and more susceptible to changing their identity. What effect will creating this more appealing and desirable alter ego have on the development of a youth's self-image and personality? There is danger in the psychological and emotional fusion of teens and their *D & D* character. The possibility of carrying one's role-playing into everyday life is always present, combined with the fact that in *D & D* the line separating fantasy from reality becomes nonexistent.

In the original edition of *Dungeons and Dragons,* creator Gary Gygax says: "We invite you to read on and enjoy a world where the fantastic is fact and magic really works. If you dare, I will take you to such a world — but beware! You will find that this is somewhat more than just a clever computer game, that the characters you create may contain a tiny bit of yourself, and that the urge to return and explore just one more level down, if not carefully controlled, can begin to take precedence over work, family, eating and sleeping." The game is meant for simple entertainment, but even its creator recognizes the allure of fantasy role-playing for young people today.[26]

Satanism and Dungeons and Dragons

"The role-playing fantasy game, *Dungeons and Dragons,* has frequently been reported as a major factor and initial contact for introducing some youth to satanism."[27] Those who have come out of the occult tell us that *D & D* is one of the most comprehensive and effective training materials used to prepare young people for entrance into satanism. Sean Sellers entered the frightening world of satanism by playing *Dungeons and Dragons* and studying *The Satanic Bible.*

The growth and popularity of *Dungeons and Dragons* has increased over the years. But so has concern about the dangers and criminal activities linked to *D & D.*

Experts cite *D & D* fantasy role-playing as a major factor in suicides, murders, demon possession, over-identification with characters, and the inability to distinguish between fantasy and reality or good and evil.

The National Coalition on Television Violence describes a typical *D & D* scenario: "The *D & D* game is played in groups, mainly by boys ages ten to twenty-one. Each player creates his own character to fight in a medieval fantasy world of monsters, devils, sorcery and combat. The goal of the game is to amass power by finding treasure and killing opponents. Violence is a constant element of the game with assassination, sadism, poisoning, premeditated murder, curses of insanity, demonology and combat with all sorts of medieval weaponry. Satanic and horror violence is common to the game, even including human sacrifice, the drinking of blood, detailed descriptions of brutal killings, commanding the undead and creating zombies and desecrating religious forts by urination. The game requires many hours of fantasy development from the players and usually lasts for weeks and months."[28]

The Deadly Game

National attention has focused on numerous incidents where death and destruction have engulfed the lives of young people who were obsessed with *Dungeons and Dragons.* Critics blamed the game's influence for the devastating aftermath. Here are a few of the tragedies:

Item: Classmates stunned by youth's suicide in front of his drama class, Arlington, Texas (UPI). A teenager who killed himself with a sawed-off shotgun in front of his drama class was a devotee of the fantasy game, *Dungeons and Dragons,* and had a lead role in this weekend's school play, friends said. . . .[29]

Item: In Colorado, a twelve-year-old boy fatally shot his sixteen-year-old brother in a suicide fantasy associated with *Dungeons and Dragons,* then killed himself. The incident was linked to deep involvement with *D & D.*[30]

Item: (*USA Today*) In Kansas, a fourteen-year-old Eagle Scout candidate walked into his junior high school and opened fire with a rifle, killing his principal and three others. He was totally absorbed with *D & D*.[31]

Item: Straight-A student, Irving Lee Pulling II, put a loaded gun to his heart and pulled the trigger because he'd been cursed by a wizard in the eerie game of *Dungeons and Dragons*.[32]

Item: Juan DeCarlos Kimbrough, fourteen, was shot and killed by his fifteen-year-old brother, Antony Kimbrough. Oakland police homicide detective Jerry Harris stated, "It was really a tragic thing. The brothers were playing *Dungeons and Dragons,* a fantasy game set in medieval times that involves role-playing and fantasy death. Juan had assumed the role of dungeon master, a powerful individual who directs the play of the game." Detective Harris said, "I'm told that to die in combat while playing the game is nothing because there are spells which can be cast to bring you back. . . . Unfortunately, that's not the way it works in real life."[33]

Item: Lafayette, Colorado. Timothy Grice, twenty years old, committed suicide by shotgun. A detective report noted, "*Dungeons and Dragons* became reality. . . . He thought he was not constrained to this life, but could leave and return because of the game."[34]

Dr. Thomas Radecki, psychiatrist, college professor and research director of the National Coalition on Television Violence, has documented 123 cases of homicides and suicides for which he blames *D & D*. He has testified as an expert in eight murder trials in which *D & D* was criminally implicated. Radecki claimed brutal murders, rapes, crimes and suicides have been patterned after characters *D & D* players concoct in the game.

He cited one example in which a nineteen-year-old Utah boy choked, raped and sadistically disposed of a fourteen-year-old girl. Radecki surmised that the murder/rapist, who slaughtered evil female *D & D* characters to survive in the game, was unable to distinguish fantasy from reality when he committed the horrible crime.[35]

In a spiritual vacuum, spiritual hunger and spiritual deception increase drastically.

Yes, there are two paths you can go by
But in the long run
There's still time to change the road you're on.

"Stairway to Heaven"
Led Zeppelin

Chapter 18

Dark Power: The Spiritual Vacuum

For Satan himself transforms himself into an angel of light (2 Cor. 11:14 NKJ).

Satanic Rituals

All occult rituals revolve around one theme: summoning of supernatural power that can be used to effect a change.

In his book, *Satanic Rituals,* a companion to *The Satanic Bible,* Anton LaVey offers a how-to guide for satanists. Claiming that we are living in the age of Satan, he promises followers the ability to call the names of the gods of the abyss with freedom from guilt and immunity from harm; by following the rites and ceremonies outlined, he offers the participant power and control over his destiny.[1]

LaVey explains that "the productions contained (within satanic rituals) fall into two categories: rituals which are directed toward a specific end that the performer desires; and ceremonies that pay homage, declare faith and worship. Generally, a ritual is used to attain, while a ceremony serves to sustain." Most people have a love of ceremony, love of ritual, love of imagination and a deep desire for roots.[2]

According to Anton LaVey's writings, three different types of rituals are performed.

The first, the sex ritual, is used to fulfill an erotic desire, satisfy your lustful longings or to put a spell on someone you want, to create a desire on the part of the person whom you desire.[3]

The second, the compassionate ritual, is performed to help someone else in situations such as health, finances, happiness, education or material success.[4]

The third is the hex or destructive ritual, which is used to destroy, to get revenge. "The person to whom the destructive forces are aimed does not have to be a believer in magical forces of any kind, or even know that any curse is being put on him."[5]

Sex Magick

Magick spelled with a "k" means the art of producing a desired effect through the use of incantations, rituals and other arcane techniques, as opposed to *magic* without a "k," which is what sleight-of-hand artists like Houdini performed.[6]

The sex magick ritual is where members of the satanic group get involved in sexual orgies. Satanists believe the sexual energy released during sexual climax can be harnessed and used for rituals. These orgies include every imaginable and detestable sexual perversion such as: lesbianism and homosexual activity, sadomasochism (sex and pain), chains, knives, whips, bestiality (sex with animals), pedophilia (sex with children), necrophilism (sex with a dead corpse), rape and gang rape of children and sexual torture.

The satanic members believe sex magick increases the group's power and magical energy. Members are dressed in red robes for sex rituals and use red candles. Open sexual orgies (fertility rituals) are a major dimension in the practice of satanism. *The Satanic Bible* describes an "invocation for the conjuration of lust." In this section, LaVey offers sexual invocations for both men and women.

In sexual rituals, LaVey calls upon ancient pagan rites such as the seventh satanic statement in which participants "regress willingly to an animal level, assuming animal attributes."[7] In satanic religion, the sex organs are supposed to contain power. Satanism is based on hedonistic indulgence and the belief that the release of sexual energy is one way to reach a higher consciousness. By taking the sexual organs of an animal, you have energy for your use. You want anything that can add power to your rituals.

Satan represents indulgence, sensual gratification and sexual power as they gorge themselves on fleshly erotic pleasures and perversion.

Blood Rituals

The use of blood in satanic rituals is very important. According to the belief, blood contains and releases the life force. If you have it, you have power. That's why satanists drink it in their rituals and pour it over themselves. Blood heightens the ritual's magic and the power of participants. "Many ceremonies are centered around the shedding and consumption of blood, both animal and human. Satanists believe the ingesting of blood increases the individual's power and supremacy over others. An animal is sacrificed and the blood is collected in a chalice and shared ritualistically in mockery of Christian communion."[8]

Large animals (cattle, horses) are killed and drained of all their blood to be used in satanic baptism rituals where the individual is totally submerged in blood and baptized unto Satan, and everyone drinks the blood.

Youth satanist Sean Sellers was obsessed with using human blood in his rituals. Sellers said, "I started carrying little vials of blood with me all the time. I kept some in the refrigerator and would take it to school and drink it. Blood gave me an eerie sensation, like in the horror movies where people say that wickedness is delicious. But, that's not all. Part of the idea of drinking blood came from the attitude among satanists that the more bizarre and depraved something is, the more evil it is. Drinking blood was something that was detestable, abhorrent and condemned by God. So, it fit in perfectly with the things I was doing. At first, it was like a thrill. As I got more into it, I began to crave blood."[9]

During his murder trial, Sellers told of how he had a ceremony in his room, alone, in which he wrote in his own blood: "I renounce God, I renounce Christ, I will serve only Satan. Hail Satan!" He became addicted to satanic rituals, often staying up late into the night practicing and reading about them.[10]

Animal Sacrifice

In the '70s and '80s, America was hit with an epidemic of bizarre animal mutilations. Cattle, sheep and horses were found drained of all their blood, and their reproductive organs were removed. These animals were killed and mutilated in a deliberate, surgically skillful manner; law enforcement officials were eventually convinced these animal mutilations were committed by satanic cults. The ceremonial slaughter of livestock is a clear trademark of satanic black magic killings for ritual purposes. "As more became known about the mutilations, the occult groups realized they would be discovered and, therefore, changed their ritualistic practices. Those who once participated in satanic ceremonies unquestionably reveal that killing animals is an integral part of appeasing dark forces." Satanists also use dogs, cats, rabbits and goats for sacrificial killings. The blood from the animals is drunk, and body parts such as eyes and sex organs are eaten in satanic rituals for power.[11]

Animal sacrifice is done to increase and release their psychic or magical powers and intensifies the psychological high from the savage act of slaughter. "For some, the ritual killing of an animal may serve as a step on the way to becoming capable of murdering a human being."[12]

Ritual Murder

In *Black Arts,* Richard Cavendish cites three reasons ritual murder can play a vital part in satanic ceremonies.

First, he points out that a common satanic belief is that the shedding of blood releases the life force of a victim that can be used as power. Second, the emotional state of the victim can provide a type of "psychic fuel" for a magical spell. Third, and perhaps the most important, is that the act of sacrifice produces an intense psychological rush for the satanist.[13]

Many satanic philosophies teach that the magician must transcend both good and evil through experience in order to gain true power. The satanist feels that he or she needs to experience good and evil in order to set themselves above these influences. Hence, murder, cannibalism or any other horrible evil act can be rationalized and justified as good, right and appropriate.[14] The most effective and sacred sacrifice to demons is the killing of a human being.

Fiendish Fascinations

Satanists believe when you sacrifice someone, in the instant just before they die, they supposedly emit their life energy. That power can be harnessed to increase their magical abilities. Satanists believe babies are best for sacrifice because babies are pure innocence and precious to God. They haven't sinned or been corrupted so they possess a higher power than adults. One of the most prized possessions of a satanist is a candle made from the fat of an unbaptized baby.[15]

Satanists believe that specific body parts contain power and will enhance their rituals. Cemeteries are prime targets; skeletal body remains are stolen from graves all the time by youth satanists. The stealing of recently buried bodies from cemeteries is done because they need something having to do with death and the defilement of consecrated ground. Satanists use dirt from cemeteries to sprinkle around when they perform rituals.

Probation Officer Darlyne Pettinicchio said, "I talk to kids who tell me, 'I need a human skull for my rituals.' I've seen youth who carry body parts like fingers around with them for the power they're supposed to contain. Yeah, it's nuts, but the kids believe in it."[16]

The skull is the symbol of death, and satanists believe great power remains in the skull. The skull contains the spirit of a person, the heart contains the soul. Having them would allow them to be in control. "They will steal the left hand from morgues and cemeteries as the left hand is referred to as the 'hand of glory.' This pays homage and honor to the devil because the left hand is the path of Satan and the right hand represents God and the path of righteousness."[17]

These secret satanic rituals create their own ghoulish and ghastly dimensions of evil; every imaginable wicked and repulsive act is performed in a satanic frenzy. Hundreds of identical, terrifying stories are beginning to surface all across the country as children, teens, adults, law enforcement officials and therapists are telling of frightening and bloodthirsty stories of satanic slaughter and perversion. They reveal unbelievable accounts of animal and human sacrifice: human torture; mutilation and dismemberment of bodies; sacrifice of babies; ritualistic rape of children; sex with animals; drinking of blood and urine; eating of feces; the ritualistic eating of human flesh and body parts, mutilation, torture and murdering of children for ritualistic or sacrificial purposes; bottles of human flesh preserved in formaldehyde; vats of blood; orgies between adults, children and animals performing every imaginable sexual perversion; the forcing of children to help murder a sacrifice victim; also, children are forced to lie in coffins with dead people.

Ritualistic Abuse

Dr. Lawrence Paxder is a pioneer in the field of ritualized abuse. He defines ritualistic abuse as "repeated physical, emotional, psychological and spiritual assaults, combined with a systematic use of occult symbols, ceremonies and devices of terror designed and orchestrated to attain evil effects."[18]

Ritual abuse of a sexual nature has two purposes for those who engage in it. "First, it gives the participants an opportunity to exert control over another individual and to perceive themselves as being in a position of dominance. Secondly, the emotional response of the victim is considered to be a source of power for the magician. Participants in black magic regard the emotions of fear and pain as being equally potent. Thus, the emotional anguish and terror of the victim and the emotions of the person performing the ritual provide a form of fuel for the magical spell."[19]

There is a maniacal blood lust and savagery in satanic rituals that thrives on terror and pain. "The most important reason for sacrifice is the psychological charge which the magician obtains from it. The frenzy which he induces in himself by ceremonious preparations, by concentration, by incantations, by burning fumes, is heightened by the savage act of slaughter." These ceremonies instill a fiendish terror and a ghastly ritualistic atmosphere.[20]

One father wrote concerning his two children who were victimized through ritual abuse: "Our two beautiful kids were sexually and physically molested. They also had to participate in satanic rituals."[21] The horrifying accounts of satanic ritual abuse described previously have been documented by law officers, therapists, mental health professionals, parents of abused children and adults who were abused as children.

The children represent innocence, and this is a way for satanists to show their contempt and disdain for God. The more blasphemous and perverted the act, the more power they obtain and the more pleasing they are to Satan.

As Boise, Idaho's police occult investigator, Larry Jones, and many other investigators have pointed out, the statements made by ritual victims from different parts of the country, the terminology used and the specific incidents all concur with each other and are being corroborated by therapists.[22]

Satanic Crime

There is a shocking wave of occult crime sweeping across America. It is the most discussed issue in law enforcement circles today. Occult crime encompasses ceremonial actions and/or ritualistic acts, involves occult-related behavior patterns and is motivated by a belief in some occult ideology. Despite growing evidence of occult incidents, it wasn't until the late '80s that the law enforcement establishment even acknowledged and confronted satanic crime as legitimate. Previously, anything even remotely connected to satanically motivated crime was labeled ridiculous, absurd, paranoid and bordering on lunacy. Through the '70s and '80s, police investigators began to encounter more and more eerie crime scenes, mutilated animals, inverted pentagrams, satanic messages and symbols written in blood: "666," "Lucifer," "Hail Satan," "Evil is with you," upside-down crosses and other bizarre satanic evidence.

Police kept hearing chilling stories from children, teens and adult occult survivors about human sacrifices, killing babies and children, torture, mutilation, drinking blood, all kinds of ritualized sexual perversion and abuse, blood baptisms, bestiality, satanic communions, and cannibalism, all in the name of Satan.

In addition to grisly murders, there were other shocking stories of grave robbings, animal sacrifices, kidnappings, drug and sex rings, rape, arson, incest and necrophilism.

There is now a group of police officers all over the country known as "cult cops" or "ghost busters." They specialize in occult crime and are overwhelmed with requests to analyze satanic cases and lecture before other law enforcement agencies.

With the dramatic rise in satanic crime, many major cities have now implemented an occult department or division to effectively address all satanic-oriented crime. The rapid increase in occult crime is so pervasive that investigative procedures and occult awareness information is being taught in police academies across the U.S.

Experts say that "satanic felony and murder will be the crime of the '90s." Investigative reporter Larry Kahaner, author of *Cults That Kill,* says, "There is a frightening new element threatening the peace and safety of us all. It is the hidden, powerful, dark underworld of occult crime."[23]

Murder in the Name of Satan

Ritual murder and human sacrifice become a very essential element for hard-core satanists. It is estimated that thousands of people are killed in ritual homicides in the U.S. each year. The belief system of certain satanists leads them to think that specific aspects of supernatural power are available only through criminal activity.

Item: Newsweek reports, Northport, Long Island—Police arrested Ricky Kasso, seventeen, and James Troiano, eighteen, on charges of second degree murder. Teenage members of a group, called the "Knights of the Black Circle," had been spray-painting satanic symbols in a local park for several years.

The members of the youth satanists group led Gary Lauwers, seventeen, into the woods and conducted a four-hour ritual in which they burned Lauwers's clothing and hair, and then stabbed him to death. "I love you, Mom," Lauwers shouted during the attack. But one of his assailants, Ricky Kasso, commanded, "No! Say you love Satan." Two days after his arrest, Ricky Kasso was found hanged in his cell.[24]

Item: Carl Junction, Missouri—Pete Roland was considered the all-American boy, tall, handsome, and basic all-around good guy. On December 6, 1987, Pete and three other boys, James Hardy, Ron Clements and Steven Newberry, drove to a wooded area for a satanic ceremony. They sacrificed a cat to honor the devil. Suddenly, three of them turned on Steven Newberry. "Sacrifice for Satan," they chanted. Frightened, Newberry started running. The three picked up baseball bats, which were part of the ritual, and began hitting Steve. Steve pleaded, "Why me, you guys? Why me?" Jim remembers Ron saying, "Because it's fun, Steve." Seventy blows later, Newberry was dead. Pete and his friends dragged the body to a cistern — "the well of hell," they called it. Along with the dead cat they had sacrificed earlier, the young satanic slayers tossed Newberry's body in the well.

When it was over, Pete said he had expected the devil to appear and grant all of them great powers. Instead, Pete and his two satanic comrades got life in prison without parole.[25]

Item: Sanford, Maine—The bizarre story of a devil worshipper who killed a twelve-year-old girl began last year when Scott Waterhouse walked into a bookstore and bought a copy of *The Satanic Bible.* It ended last week when a jury convicted Waterhouse, eighteen, of luring Gycelle Cote into the woods and strangling her "for the thrill of it." Between the time Waterhouse bought the book and his conviction, he experimented with LSD, got heavily involved in satanic worship, became obsessed with a fifteen-year-old girl and allegedly threatened to kill her and finally murdered Cote.[26]

"The satanism bit just changed him," Doug Waterhouse, the killer's brother, said when the trial ended. It was sometime last year that Waterhouse, then a junior at Sanford High School, bought *The Satanic Bible* by Anton LaVey. "He studied it and started calling satanism his religion."[27]

Why Teens Get into Satanism

1. The Need for Power and Control

Young people feel increasingly powerless, vulnerable and out of control of their lives. "When a person realizes the stress and anxiety he is experiencing in his life, his perception of that stress causes him to seek ways to overcome and resolve it." Youth's perception of stress is a "predisposing condition"[28] — the enormous stresses and problems make them especially susceptible to satanic philosophies and solutions.

Young people who are engulfed with endless pressures, expectations and fears are looking for power and control over their situations and lives. Power means control. Satanism promises them incredible power and control of their lives, situations, problems and the lives of others.

"The love of power is the most fundamental of all human motives."[29] It is this craving for personal, supernatural power that drives many youth to enter the world of occultism.

2. Boredom and Curiosity

There is an innate curiosity within all of us, especially teens, to know what's behind the forbidden door. Boredom fuels their curiosity to experience something they've never felt or known before. This boredom factor increases tremendously as it takes more and more to get the same emotional thrill.

The word *occult* means hidden, mysterious, unexplainable, mystical and secret — which is very appealing to youth. Captivated by the desire for a supernatural experience, and wanting to escape their monotonous, boring and even depressing existence, teens plunge into the dark and deadly world of the occult. As the obsession for knowledge, power and magic increases, so does their curiosity level.

3. Magical Thinking

We've all felt at times, "If I could only magically change something or someone, or have power over a situation." In this uncertain, high-stress, rapidly changing atmosphere, "magical power" promises youth a sense of control and order in a chaotic fearful world. Magical thinking becomes a way for youth to deal with their problems and pain. Wishing, hoping and magical solutions are their devices for coping.

Believing in magical powers helps them to escape threatening or intolerable situations and problems, at least temporarily. Satanism, through spells, ceremonies, rituals, incantations and symbols, promises them a way to tap into this hidden magical power. The occult offers them a magical force they believe can alter situations or circumstances to obtain a desired wish or specific result.

Magical thinking means they believe they have the power to change events, people, situations, the future—an appealing thought for young people. Magical thinking puts the individual magician or youth satanist at the center of his or her own universe. Youth become obsessed with this supernatural realm of satanic power and magical solutions.

4. Self-Indulgence

To teen satanists, the devil is a friend who offers money, drugs, sex, nonstop party excess, excitement and whatever their selfish desires fancy. The trivialization of evil is one of the most serious and least-discussed effects of hedonism gone to seed. The continual pursuit of personal pleasure eventually produces a moral numbness — a desensitization to the finality and pain of death and the meaning of life.

Satanism promises to instantly fulfill their desires, lusts and wishes, appealing to their immediate gratification as opposed to delayed fulfillment of the so-called real happiness in the future.

Satanism advocates no restraints, no inhibitions, no delayed gratification, no wrong, no sin, no perversion or immorality. Everything is permissible and right if it is satisfying, enjoyable and self-gratifying. Satanism offers to grant youth their every desire, every immoral instinct and imagination — now!

5. Rebellion and Alienation

We live in a violent, sensual, negative and perverted society. As a result, kids are prone to greater extremes than ever — murder, suicide and satanism. Actions and life-styles that were previously considered rebellious are now viewed as normal behavior, such as drug use, violence, premarital sex, dropping out of school, joining gangs and getting pregnant. Teens must go to greater extremes to get our attention or to shock us; satanism becomes the perfect vehicle.

The ultimate rebellious act against God, parents, peers and society is satanism. Through satanism, they find a way to justify all their feelings of alienation, hostility and rebellious behaviors. It offers them a social context in which to express their pent-up frustrations and animosities. Satanism becomes the means to vent their vengeance, rage and rebellion. They become rebels with a cause — evil.

6. The Need for Identity and Significance

Satanism offers low self-image teens a unique sense of identity, feelings of acceptance, personal power and confidence. This is so incredibly inviting to kids who believe they are losers, misfits and nobodies; suddenly and distinctively, they become someone special. Members of a satanic cult feel they have special abilities, knowledge, a rare persona, and exclusive privileges and power.

The teen satanist may dress in black, wear various occult paraphernalia — such as upside-down crosses, inverted pentagrams, satanic heavy metal rock T-shirts — and will flash the satanic hand signs to appear forbidding, mysterious and powerful. This gives youth a unique sense of identity combined with a tremendous ego-gratification rush that is temporarily very fulfilling.

Low self-worth is the driving motivation for teens to exchange virtue for evil! They reason that if being good didn't bring happiness, then being bad — exceedingly bad — will at least lead to power, lustful gratification and self-importance.[30]

Teens who feel they are not impacting their world and who believe they don't really matter see satanism as a way of achieving significance and meaning in their lives.

7. Religiously Alienated Youth

Many mainstream young people who are attracted to satanism come from traditional Christian backgrounds. They are searching for the power, excitement and reality they didn't experience in their churches. Many teens view organized religion as boring, irrelevant and unchallenging. Today's pseudo-Christianity is an apathetic, surface, dead ritual of religious form without power, involvement, purpose or passion.

Young people have a spiritual hunger in their lives. They secretly and subconsciously crave to be committed to someone who is bigger and more powerful than themselves and their problems so they can feel love, meaning and fulfillment. Youth try to fill the spiritual emptiness in their lives with sex, drugs, materialism, popularity, success and even satanism. Bored and desperate teens desire spiritual reality and fulfillment—if not through the power of God and good, then through the power of Satan and evil. The spiritual vacuum must be filled.

Another reason youth have become alienated from Christianity is because their concept of God is distorted. Youth have been taught that being a Christian means only keeping certain rules; a faith system based on performance and a list of "don'ts" rather than a faith centered on a personal relationship with Christ. "Toxic faith is a destructive and dangerous relationship with organized religion that allows the religion, not the relationship with God, to control a person's life. This produces a legalistic system of rules where what you do is valued more than who you are."[31]

This distorted Christianity is viewed by teens as an impersonal, insensitive, degrading, condemning and enslaving life-style. They see God as a judgmental tyrant always waiting for them to make a mistake so He can punish and shame them. Young people come to believe the lie that God is withholding real happiness and fulfillment from them by demanding they live a specific way.

These descriptions of our loving, just God are, of course, totally inaccurate and distorted misconceptions. However, through "man-centered" religion, young people believe them to be true.

Youth are alienated from Christianity because they have seen the double standards, the hypocrisy and fake facade of religion, without real commitment, compassion and self-sacrifice. Teens hate phoniness; they know when someone is real and they know when they are fake. The "do as I say and not as I do" Christianity will not cut it with youth who want to believe in something that is real.

Another reason youth are alienated from God is because they have been disillusioned, disappointed and ripped off by people they trusted. They blame God for the frustrating situations, problems and pain in their lives. Deep-seated feelings of anger and bitterness lead to rebellion against family values, God and Christian teachings, as youth turn to satanism.

Satanic Seduction

Satanism becomes more and more enticing and alluring to teens by promising fulfillment of their dreams, desires and immediate happiness. But it ultimately proves to be a cruel deception as the powers of darkness only mock their desperation and intensify their pain, sorrow and devastation.

Satanism is based totally on lies, projecting illusions of reality, which only leads to more distortion, deception and destruction. Everything and everyone in the occult world is counterfeit.

Satanism gives young people an illusion of power. The power is real; but this dark, evil power is designed to devour and destroy them, not give them the power it promises.

Satanism gives teens the illusion of control; even as they feel in control, they are actually being controlled, manipulated, exploited and being set up for treachery.

Satanism offers an illusion of happiness. While giving immediate gratification and temporary fulfillment, it produces future pain, misery and tragedy. Satan's goal is to destroy future happiness and eternal fulfillment with God by damning the souls of human beings.

Satanism feeds off our desperate need for spiritual fulfillment with God. The least understood and most powerful facet of our being is the spiritual dimension. God created us as spiritual beings; without a relationship with Jesus Christ, there will be an ever-deepening emptiness in our lives. The key to confronting our fears and experiencing total fulfillment and ultimate happiness as individuals is found in knowing Jesus Christ as Lord.

The Battle for the Soul of a Generation

This generation is caught in a perilous time of accelerating cultural change, moral upheaval and chaos, with rising uncertainties about their future. The extreme has become the norm. Decadence, confusion and deception are rampant. Satanism thrives in this kind of atmosphere.

Much of the Christian church is spiritually apathetic, distracted, superficial, overwhelmed and self-centered, lacking conviction, commitment, compassion and vision, which produces a spiritually powerless religious organization.

Youth are facing unprecedented problems and enormous pressures to conform and change. Combined with the media-generated, secularized humanistic mind-set that permeates popular culture, a spiritual vacuum has been created.

Teens become increasingly susceptible to the darker side of life. They are searching for something powerful, something mysterious, something supernatural, a spiritual experience or encounter to fill the void in their lives. There is a growing hunger for spiritual reality and power among young people today.

In an attempt to fill the spiritual void, youth are turning to Ouija boards, seances, communication with spirits, astral projection (soul travel), fantasy role-playing games like *Dungeons and Dragons*, black metal or death metal rock groups who promote death and Satan and the ultimate extreme spiritual experience — satanism!

The lack of power, reality and relevance of the church has further intensified teens' spiritual frustration and desperation. There is widespread cynicism and skepticism with organized religion in America. While the world is becoming more dangerous and threatening, youth's future hopes are becoming lost in foreboding fears and feelings of powerlessness.

This high-tech, impersonal society has created a deep disenchantment with man's scientific logic, vast technology and intellectual rationalism, a feeling reflected in our culture's growing fascination with the mystical, paranormal, psychic, new age philosophies and the occult. There is a massive spiritual vacuum in America that must be filled with something. The question is, who or what will fill this void?

Apocalypse 90s

America is a spiritually destitute and spiritually vulnerable society, creating a deadly, dangerous and deceptive scenario. If current trends continue unabated, what could occur in the next ten to fifteen years will be apocalyptic! Powerful forces are converging in the '90s that could set the stage for the ultimate confrontation between good and evil.

The battle is for the soul of a generation.

Chapter 19

Spiritual Drift: Cultural Crisis

America has been in a state of spiritual drift for the past thirty-five years, creating a post-Christian culture for this generation. Recent findings by Barna Research reveal the chilling effects of this dangerous drift in the current belief system in America.

Youth and adults are making moral and ethical decisions based on self-interest, situational ethics and convenience rather than a biblical belief system.

- Nearly 70 percent of Americans reject the notion of absolute truth.
- Over 40 percent of people believe Jesus made mistakes or was imperfect.
- Sixty percent of adults do not believe in Satan.
- Fifty percent of all Americans believe that all religious faiths are basically the same.
- One out of three adults believe that God is something or

someone other than the perfect, all-powerful, omniscient Creator of the universe who rules the world today.[1]

These beliefs reflect a disturbing departure from a biblical perspective concerning truth and morality. Barna Research poses the question, "Who has lost ground as a change agent in our society?" According to the public, churches wield less influence today than five years earlier. Also, according to the American people, the powerful mass media has gained more influence than five years earlier.

What is more alarming is the state of the Evangelical Church in America. In survey after survey "born-again Christians" are literally indistinguishable from non-Christians in their life-styles. Faith in America could be defined as extremely superficial and convenient rather than obedient and committed. There is a vast difference between the way we think of ourselves and the way we actually are. We've created a kind of "schizophrenic spirituality." The Evangelical Church has lost the desire and ability to discern between the secular and the spiritual.

Cultural Christianity is defined as almost anything that accommodates our life-styles, personal theology and current social trends, where everything is rationalized and accepted as enlightened and even godly.

Today's Christianity is being redefined in America, "where faith is now understood more in terms of its benefits than its cost, emphasizing God's responsibilities more than our own sacrifice. Sanctification is now merely a matter of personal choice rather than an alignment with eternal truth." [2] Cultural Christianity is where man creates a god in his own image and likeness.

The new cultural morality forces the Bible to conform to our felt needs and desires rather than submitting our lives to the demands of the Scripture. Much of today's Christianity is designed from a recreational entertainment approach, sort of a massage theology. Make us laugh—make us cry—make us sing. But don't dare make us think or change.[3]

Much of the Evangelical Church in America is in a massive comfort zone. While we are witnessing the disintegration of the social and moral foundations of American society, the comfort zone produces an illusion of reality where we deceive ourselves daily about where we are and where we're headed. Spiritual drift produces spiritual deception.

If there is hope, it is to be found in a renewed and repentant people, guided by the God of the Scriptures and revealed in the life, death and resurrection of Jesus Christ. This is the only chance of restoring and reclaiming this generation. This rising generation of Christian youth, like those of the '60s, see the shallow and empty nature of casual Christianity. My fear is that in rightfully rejecting the current superficial Christianity, they will also reject the genuine faith that it has perverted.

The Evangelical Church must begin to reestablish—restore and renew authentic radical Christianity, not just in words, but through action. Authentic Christianity will always produce a true counterculture that stands in total contrast to the cultural system. We offer this generation no distinct alternative.

If the church is in danger of losing this generation, it will be because we failed to live what we say we believe. This generation reasons no commitment—no reality. The Evangelical Church teaches and preaches to change society, but in reality it only reflects the life-styles and mind-set of popular culture. Also the Evangelical Church refuses to acknowledge there is a spiritual crisis in the church today. This only intensifies and fuels the cultural crisis.

The major change for the church in America is that she has forgotten her identity in relation to the world. We have abandoned our unique identity and have pursued another identity, that of the cultural Christian. When the church loses her identity, she also loses her sense of purpose or destiny; without identity and purpose she has no power.

Before the Evangelical Church can begin to reclaim a generation at risk, it must first heal itself.

20

The Positive Affects of Crisis

Actually crisis has always served as a catalyst to make the church a true force for God. Throughout the Bible, including the ministry of Jesus Christ, was born our of crisis. Historically even the most wicked and ungodly cultures have been powerfully impacted by radical Christianity. That doesn't mean Christians converted the entire culture because they did not and neither will we, but we can impact our world.

The early church suffered extreme persecution and alienation from the world, but their affect was undeniable. The Bible clearly states that intensifying evil would co-exist with a mighty outpouring and anointing of God's spirit on true believers in the last days.

However, the real danger for the Christian community is that we've become crisis hardened, being conditioned to and jaded by a decadent culture. Christians continually confront and assure ourselves that we are still in control and everything will be alright; thus, minimizing the depth of the cultural crisis we face, and the self-absorbed and apathetic state of the church in America today.

Crisis can be our greatest motivation for spiritual fulfillment and maturity or our deadliest means to spiritual destruction. The difference depends on our response. Crisis represents any exciting opportunity for Christians to fulfill God's purpose and experience His love in a new way.

Crisis is God s way of getting our attention

We've become so preoccupied and obsessed with the cares of this world, our plans, goals and desires. God wants our attention. When crisis comes, we are suddenly confronted with pressures and problems too big for us to deal with. We are forced to look to God for answers (Isa. 40:31). Crises causes us to wait upon the Lord—the benefits of waiting upon the Lord are renewed strength, fresh insight into problems and power over sinful habits.

Crisis is a warning that God s principles have been violated

The law of gravity was established by God and involves forces which have predictable results, when the same circumstances are in effect. The law of gravity is universal. The same results will take place anywhere on the planet. You can defy the law of gravity, but you can't deny it, eventually reality will hit you in the face. God wants us to see the devastation and painful consequences of our sinful life-styles—how it has robbed us of our potential for achieving and enjoying what God has planned for us. Because of the dynamics of crisis, it may occur from a culture who mocks God's principles, or because Christians are violating God's principles or both. God wants us to understand that His principles were designed for a purpose - to protect us from destructive consequences, bless us and minister to our needs (Gal. 6:7-8).

Crisis is God s method of revealing the futility of human effort and abilities

When humans attempt to do what only God can do, the results are disasterous. Our enlightened, humanistic, cultural approach to solving current problems has actually increased and intensified them. The pseudo solutions look good on paper, but in reality serve both as a delusion and distraction. The crisis we face today is far too complex and massive for human abilities and solutions. We must look to God for solutions or continue to wander through the maze of confusion (1 Cor. 1:19, 25-27).

Crisis gives us new perspective with increased spiritual insight and discernment

There isn't anything that changes our attitudes like a fresh perspective. Crisis awakens us to unresolved conflict in our lives and God causes us to focus on the root causes of the problems. Our image-oriented culture tends to focus on the symptoms of the problems, never dealing with the root causes. The result is obvious and deadly. Crisis is God's method of revealing to us His wisdom and understanding, causing us to focus on the motivating needs and fears (Prov. 4:7; 1 Cor. 2:14).

Crisis is God s signal to re-evaluate our priorities

What's really important gets lost in this fast-paced, immediate-oriented society. Our culture is driven by materialism, success and self-gratification at all costs. Wrong priorities may result in painful problems, not only for us, but also for those who are affected by our lives. When we fail to spend quality, consistent time with the Lord in His Word, in praise and prayer, we create a spiritual void in our lives, which produces a spiritual vacuum for society—robbing others of spiritual encouragement and direction. We tend to pursue things that don't really matter, sacrificing the significant for the trivial or most urgent. Wrong priorities produce crisis situations which are God's way of telling us He wants to deepen the relationship with us. They cause us to re-evaluate what's really important in our lives (Matt. 6:33; 16:26).

Crisis is God s method of creating opportunity for Christians to take action

Crisis can have two effects: we either become increasingly self-centered and survival oriented, only looking out for number one, or we get involved in the lives of people by serving, ministering to their needs and evangelizing our communities with the gospel. The power of compassion breaks down walls and changes lives: Jesus was moved with compassion for the masses of people. Compassion is love in action It's always focused on the needs and pain of others: people don't care how much you know till they know how much you care. Crisis is a double-edged sword, representing both "danger and opportunity." The word *crisis* immediately brings to mind the possibility of physical, emotional or relational harm. We aren't particularly excited about experiencing pain or discomfort, but it is actually through pain, discomfort and threatening situations, or some other seemingly negative experience in our lives, that we grow. Crisis can have a paralyzing effect, leaving us feeling helpless and hopeless, afraid to seize the opportunity. Throughout biblical history the greatest danger always represented the greatest opportunity for Christians (Luke 11:10; Matt. 5:13-16)

Crisis is God s way of bringing unity among the body of Christ

There is power in unity, nothing can cause the Christian community to rally together like crisis situations. Throughout the Bible crisies have galvanized God's people into a spiritual force. Crisis is an opportunity for the Christian community under the guidance of the Holy Spirit, to develop specific strategies to address the critical issues. Crisis produces a unifying cause, where Christians put aside our petty differences and spiritual pride, thus demonstrating to the world that we are Jesus' disciples because we have love for one another. Division, jealousy and bitterness only fuel and intensify the cultural problems. Crisis is God's way of fulfilling His plan and purpose through His people for His glory (Eph. 4:3,12-13; Ps. 133:1).

Crisis is God s call for self-examination

Can you imagine not looking in a mirror for a month to check your appearance. Yet we go longer periods of time without actually seeing our true spiritual condition. We also tend to focus on everybody else's faults and problems rather than really dealing with our own. God wants us to focus on the wrong attitudes, motives and actions that are negatively affecting our lives and our relationship with Him. God's mirror is His Word; as we study and meditate on it, it reflects and reveals our spiritual condition. Personal crisis requires real change, not just lip service! The result of spiritual health is love, joy and peace in the Holy Spirit (1 Cor. 11:31-32; Prov. 28:13).

Crisis is God s method of revealing the need for spiritual warfare

Our typical response to crisis is to focus on the obvious outward circumstances. However, God wants us to understand that we are dealing with unseen spiritual principalities, powers and spiritual wickedness in high places (Eph. 6:11-18). Any attempt to solve spiritual problems from a humanistic surface mind-set will result in deadly consequences. The current cultural atmosphere of confusion, deception, and spiritual hunger has created a dangerous scenario. God is calling Christians to put on spiritual armor and be guided by spiritual discernment in order to battle and expose darkness and be a warrior for Jesus Christ. Crisis is God's call to prepare us for spiritual warfare.

Crisis is God s way of exposing cultural Christianity from true Christianity

Both in the Old and New Testaments crisis always separated true believers from those who just professed to know God. Crisis has always confronted people with a choice concerning their relationship or belief about Jesus Christ. Crisis will cause them to either become committed or walk away from God. Crisis has a way of revealing religious activity and humanistic-centered spirituality for what it is—counterfeit. Desperation can produce a deep desire to know God, driving out casualness, easy believism and indifference. Crisis can produce a new desire for God or we can ignore the promptings of the Holy Spirit, and become more hardened to what is actually happening. Crisis can become a powerful motivation to seek God with all our heart, because everything else around us has failed. In a non-commital society only deep commitment to Christ brings real freedom and happiness (Matt. 10:38-39; 15:8-9).

Crisis is God s method for establishing accountability in the body of Christ

The moral irresponsibilities and total chaos of this generation are a result of a culture with no accountability. We shift the blame, we rationalize our actions, we make cheap excuses, we answer to nobody but ourselves. Recently, several of the biggest and best known ministries came crashing down. The major reason cited by people who worked closely with these powerful ministry personalities was—no accountability. Power without accountability is like a fire left unattended, it destroys everything in its path. When there is no accountability, we become desensitized to the Spirit of God and lose the ability to distinguish between right and wrong. Crisis awakens us to the need for accountability in our lives. Accountability is being responsible for all our actions, attitudes and motives. Accountability is God's way of protecting us from destructive forces in our lives and preserving our spiritual welfare (Matt. 18:23; Rom. 14:7,12).

Crisis is God s call to identify with Christ

Crisis was the very heart of Jesus' ministry. Christ's earthly ministry until His death and resurrection was a life engulfed by controversy and crisis. Crisis brings together the dynamics of Christ's life, death and resurrection, that we may know Him more intimately. Jesus was surrounded by hostility, lies and hatred, as everything He did infuriated the religious system of the day. Crisis is our motivation to identify with Christ. Jesus experienced human pain and suffering on a level that nobody has ever experienced. So we can take comfort that He does understand, He has felt our loneliness, rejection, grief and disappointments to the extreme. Identifying with Christ gives Christians the power to rise above the pressures, problems and temptations of life and to be victorious (Phil. 3:10; Rom. 8:1, 37-39).

Notes

Introduction

1. William Strauss and Neil Howe, *Generations* (NewYork: Morrow Publishing Company, 1991), 317.
2. Ibid., 320.
3. Ibid., 321.

Chapter 1

1. David Elkind, *All Grown Up and No Place to Go* (Menlo Park, CA: Addison Wesley Publishing, 1984), 3.
2. Mike Yaconelli and Jim Burns, *High School Ministry* (Grand Rapids: Zondervan Publishing, 1986), 16.
3. William Strauss and Neil Howe, *Generations* (New York: Morrow Publishing Company, 1991), 63.
4. Søren Kierkegaard, *This Present Age* translated by Alexander Dru (New York: Harper & Row, 1962), 83.
5. Landon Y. Jones, *Great Expectations: America and the Baby Boom Generation* (New York: Ballantine Books, 1980), 79.

6. Quentin J. Schultze, Roy M. Anker, James D. Bratt, William D. Romanowski, John W. Worst, and Lambert Zwidervaat, *Dancing in the Dark* (Grand Rapids: Eerdmans Publishing, 1991), 82.
7. Strauss and Howe, *Generations,* 303.
8. Tom Mathews, "The Sixties Complex," *Newsweek,* September 1988, 23.
9. Paul Perry, *On the Bus* (New York: Thunder's Mouth Press, 1990), 8.
10. Annie Gottlieb, *Do You Believe in Magic?* (New York: Simon & Schuster, 1987), 8.
11. Lance Morrow, "1968," *Time,* January 1988, 28.
12. Peter Collier and David Horowitz, *Destructive Generation: Second Thoughts About the Sixties* (New York: Summit Publishing, 1989), 72.

Chapter 2

1. David Gelman, "A Much Riskier Passage," *Newsweek* Special Edition, *The New Teens,* Summer/Fall 1991.
2. William Strauss and Neil Howe, *Generations* (New York: Morrow Publishing Co., 1991), 60.
3. Strauss and Howe, *Generations*, 61.
4. Gary R. Collins and Timothy E. Clinton, *Baby Boomer Blues* (Dallas: Word Publishing, 1992), 9.
5. Arnold M. Washton and Donna Boundy, *Will Power's Not Enough* (New York: Harper and Row Publishers, 1989), 130.
6. Landon Y. Jones, *Great Expectations: America and the Baby Boom Generations* (New York: Ballentine Books, 1980).
7. Washton and Boundy, *Will Power's Not Enough*, 135.
8. Annie Gottlieb, *"Do You Believe in Magic?"* (New York: Simon and Schuster, 1987), 192.
9. Fran Sciacca, *Generation at Risk* (Chicago: Moody Press, 1990), 73.
10. Mike Bellah, *Baby Boom Believers* (Wheaton: Tyndale Publishers, Inc., 1988), 45.
11. Gottlieb, *Do You Believe in Magic?* 234-35.
12. Chuck Raasch, "Coping with 'Virginity' As a Dirty Word," *USA Today,* 1991.
13. Ibid.
14. Jones, *Great Expectations,* 298.

15. Bellah, *Baby Boom Believers*, 387.
16. Ibid., 21.
17. Ibid., 21.
18. Collins and Clinton, *Baby Boomer Blues*, 170.
19. Strauss and Howe, *Generations*, 305.

Chapter 3

1. Tom Squitieri, "Television Shapes Our Lives," USA Today, May 1993.
2. Charles W. Conn, *The Anatomy of Evil* (Old Tappan, NJ: Fleming H. Revell, 1981), 69.
3. Gary R. Collins, *The Magnificent Mind* (Waco, TX: Word Books, 1985), 67.
4. Ibid., 67.
5. Daniel Lum and Susan E. Swedo, "Creating a Sexual Mindset," The American Academy of Pediatrics Research, Bethesda, MD, and the Center for the Study of Adolescents Newsletter, March 1991, 23.
6. Josh McDowell and Dick Day, *Why Wait? What You Need to Know About the Teen Sexuality Crisis* (San Bernardino: Here's Life Publishers, 1987), 40.
7. Ibid., 45.
8. National Institute on Alcohol Abuse and Alcoholism, Rockville, MD.
9. Peter Plagens and Mark Miller in New York; Donna Foote and Emily Yoffe in Los Angeles, "Violence Goes Mainstream," *Newsweek*, April 1991, 23.
10. Thomas Radecki, *Boys Will Be Boys*The National Coalition on Television Violence, Champaign, IL, 6.
11. Ibid.
12. Joan W. Moore, *Isolation and Stigmatization in the Development of the Underclass: The Case of Chicago Gangs in East L.A.* (Colorado Springs: Thom Schulte Publications, 1988), 188.
13. Mike Yaconelli and Jim Burns, *High School Ministry* (Grand Rapids: Zondervan Publishing, 1986), 21.
14. Gary Strauss, "The Vast Teen Market," *USA Today*, June 1993.
15. Anthony Campolo, *Growing Up in America* (Grand Rapids: Zondervan Publishing, 1989), 147-148.

16. Richard Corliss, "Dirty Words: America's Foul-Mouthed Pop Culture," *Time*, May 1990.
17. H. Stephen Glenn and Jane Nelson, Ed. D., *Raising Self-Reliant Children in a Self-Indulgent World* (Rockland, CA: Prima Pub., 1989), 41.
18. Neil Postman, *Amusing Ourselves to Death* (New York: Viking Penguin Inc., 1984), 11.

Chapter 4

1. Mike Yaconelli and Jim Burns, *High School Ministry* (Grand Rapids: Zondervan Publishing, 1986), 9.
2.
3. 1. David Elkind, *All Grown Up and No Place to Go* (Menlo Park, CA: Addison Wesley Publishing, 1984), 69
4. Alvin Toffler, *Future Shock* (New York: Bantam Books, 1970), 17.
5. George Barna, *The Frog in the Kettle* (Ventura, CA: Regal Books, 1990), 24.
6. Toffler, *Future Shock*, 34.
7. Judy Keen, "Student Searches Yield Fear," *USA Today*, November 1991.
8. Rod Norland, "Deadly Lessons," *Newsweek*, March 1992, 44.
9. Richard O. Saul Wurman, *Information Anxiety* (New York: Doubleday Publishers, 1989), 77.
10. "Toughen Gun Controls to Save Kids at School," *USA Today*, November 1991.
11. Wurman, *Information Anxiety*, 34.
12. John Naisbitt, *Megatrends* (New York: Warner Books, 1982), 24.
13. Victor Stursbugen, American Academy of Pediatrics Research, Bethesda, MD, and the Center for the Study of Adolescents Newsletter, February 1989, 138.
14. Barna, *The Frog in the Kettle*, 85.
15. Ibid., 82.
16. Robert Brody and Glenn Deutsch, "Virtual Reality: What a Concept!" *USA Today*, March 1992, 8.
17. Mike Yaconelli and Jim Burns, *High School Ministry*, 18.
18. Ibid., 19.
19. Ibid., 19.

Chapter 5

1. Francis A. Schaeffer, *The Complete Works of Francis A. Schaeffer* (Westchester, IL: Crossway Books, 1984), 5.
2. Fran Sciacca, *Generation ar Risk* (Moody Press, 1990-1991), 143.
3. Ibid.
4. Susanna McBee, "The State of American Values," *U.S. News and World Report,* December 1985, 25.
5. Fran Sciacca, Generation ar Risk (Moody Press, 1990-1991), 117.
6. Ibid.
7. Allan Bloom, *The Closing of the American Mind* (New York: Simon and Schuster, 1987), 39.
8. Greg Barna, The Invisible Generation: Baby Busters (Glendale, CA: Barna Research Group, 1992), 81.
9. Ibid.
10. David Brandt, *Is That All There Is?* (New York: Poseidon Press, 1984), 102.
11. Mike Yaconelli and Jim Burns, *High School Ministry* (Grand Rapids: Zondervan Publishing, 1986), 22.
12. Josh McDowell and Dick Day, *Why Wait? What You Need to Know About the Teenage Sexuality Crisis* (San Bernardino: Here's Life Publishers, 1987), 30.
13. Winkie Pratney, *Youth Aflame* (Minneapolis: Bethany House Publishers, 1983), 40.
14. Yaconelli and Burns, *High School Ministry,* 30.
15. Katherine Ramsland, "Hunger for the Marvelous — The Vampire Craze in the Computer Age," *Psychology Today,* November 1989, 24-28.
16. Ibid., 28.
17. Pete Axthelm, "Somebody Else's Kids," *Newsweek,* April 1988.

Chapter 6

1. Bryce J. Christenson, "Psychology and the Rise of Anti-Child Ideology," *The Family of America Newsletter,* Rockford Institute Center on the Family, Rockford, IL, August 1991, 2-6.
2. Ibid., 3.
3. Ibid., 6.
4. Jerry Adler, Linda Wright, and Patrick Houston, "Hey I'm

Terrific," *Newsweek,* April 1992, 40.

5. Charles Colson, *Against the Night* (Ann Arbor, MI: Vine Books, 1989), 33.
6. Carl F. Henry, *Twilight of a Great Civilization* (Westchester, IL: Crossway Books, 1988), 15.
7. D. Bruce Lockerbre, *The Cosmic Center* (Portland. OR: Multinomah Press, 1977), 88.
8. Daniel J. Boorstin, "History's Hidden Turning Points," *U.S. News and World Report*, April 1991, 28.
9. Ibid., 29.
10. Cal Thomas, "T.V.'s Overexposure Takes Joy Out of Sex," *USA Today*, April 1992.
11. Josh McDowell and Dick Day, *Why Wait? What You Need to Know About the Teenage Sexuality Crisis* (San Bernardino: Here's Life Publishers, 1987).
12. Kim Painter and Gary Boeck, "The Teenage Sexual Dilemma," *USA Today*, October 1993.
13. Margaret L. Usdansky, "Teens Birth Formula for Disaster," *USA Today*, February 1994.
14. Ibid.
15. Ibid.
16. Ibid.
17. Josh McDowell, *The Myths of Sex Education* (San Bernardino, CA: Here's Life Publishers, 1990), 121.
18. Ibid.
19. Ibid.
20. Ibid.
21. Patricia Feeny, "Next AIDS Epidemic Crisis Likely to Be Among Teens," *USA Today*, March 1992.
22. Ibid.
23. Sally Ann Stewart, "3 Million AIDS Victims Seen in the Americas," *USA Today*, April 1992.
24. Ibid.
25. David Hocking, *The Moral Catastrophe* (Eugene, OR: Harvest House, 1990), 29.
26. Gary Boeck, "Gay Sympathy in Prime Time," *Social Issues Resources*, May 1991.
27. Craig Wilson, "Assault on Homophobia Gains Ground," *USA Today,* April 1992.

28. Kim Painter, "Key Evidence More Maternal Kin Are Gay," *USA Today,* July 1993.
29. Ibid.
30. Elizabeth Snead, "Some Chafe at Media's Embrace," *USA Today,* October 1993.
31. Ibid.
32. Marian Wright Edelman, "Is This the Best America Can Do?" *USA Today,* May 1992.
33. Hocking, *The Moral Catastrophe.*
34. George Roche, *A World Without Heroes* (Hillsdale, MI: Hillsdale College Press, 1987), 58.
35. James Patterson and Peter Kim, *The Day America Told the Truth* (New York: Prentice Hall Press), 1991, 6.
36. John Elson, "The Dangerous World of Wannabes," *Time,* November 1991, 62.
37. Ibid.
38. Roche, *A World Without Heroes,* 7.
39. Ibid.
40. Ibid., 133.
41. Patterson and Kim, *The Day America Told the Truth,* 119.
42. Marty Baumann, (Snapshots) "Nightline Top Programs of 1990," *USA Today,* March 1991.
43. Adrian Deevoy, "Reveal Yourself," *US Entertainment Magazine,* June 1991, 28.
44. Patterson and Kim, *The Day America Told the Truth,* 31.
45. Ibid.
46. Ibid.
47. Ibid.
48. George Barna, *The Frog in the Kettle* (Ventura, CA: Regal Books, 1989), 35.
49. Ibid.
50. Ibid.

Chapter 7

1. Josh McDowell and Dick Day, *Why Wait? What You Need to Know About the Teenage Sexuality Crisis* (San Bernardino: Here's Life Publishers, 1987), 69.
2. Ibid.
3. Kim Painter, "Fewer Kids Save Sex for Adulthood," *USA Today,*

November 1991.
4. Mike Yaconelli and Jim Burns, *High School Ministry* (Grand Rapids: Zondervan Publishing Company, 1986), 23.
5. Painter, "Fewer Kids Save Sex for Adulthood."
6. Painter, Kim, "Moves to Keep Teens From Sex Not Working," *USA Today*, May 10, 1994.
7. McDowell and Day, *Why Wait?*, 168.
8. Ibid.
9. Ibid.
10. Ibid.
11. Ibid.

Chapter 8

1. George Gallup, Jr., *Religion in America* (Princeton, NJ: Princeton Research Center, 1990), 7.
2. Merton P. Strommen, *Five Cries of Youth* (San Francisco: Harper & Row Publishers, 1988), 4.
3. Zig Zigler, *See You At the Top* (Gretna, LA: Pelican Publishing, 1977), 87.
4. Robert S. McGee, Jim Craddock, and Pat Springle. *The Parent Factor* (Houston: Rapha Publishing, 1989), 9.
5. Josh McDowell, *His Image—My Image* (San Bernardino: Here's Life Publishers, 1984), 52.
6. Robert S. McGee, *Search For Significance* (Houston: Rapha Publishing, 1990), 122, 123, 215.
7. Marilyn Elias, "The Missing Parent," *USA Today*, November 1992.
8. McDowell, *His Image—My Image*, 20-21.
9. Marilyn Elias, "Most Girls Have a Weighty Self-Perception," *USA Today*, April 1992.
10. McGee, *Search For Significance*.
11. Ibid.
12. Ibid.
13. Miriam Elliot and Susan Meltsner, *The Perfectionist Predicament* (New York: Morrow Publishing, Inc., 1991), 113-114, 125.
14. Ibid., 97, 99.
15. Ibid., 108.
16. Ibid., 111.

17. Ibid., 108.
18. Maurice E. Wagner, *The Sensation of Being Somebody* (Grand Rapids: Zondervan Publishing, 1975), 32-33.
19. McDowell, *His Image*, 88.
20. Wagner, *The Sensation of Being Somebody*, 36.

Chapter 9

1. Elizabeth Sporkin and Tom Cunneff in Las Vegas; Todd Gold, Lois Armstrong and Doris Bacon in Los Angeles; Vickie Bane in Denver; and Lynn Emmerman in Chicago, "The Tragic Stars of Different Strokes," *People Magazine*, March 1991, 23-28.
2. Ibid.
3. Karen S. Peterson, "Speaking Out on Need for Role Models," *USA Today*, September 1993.
4. Ibid.
5. Ibid.
6. Ibid.
7. Anthony M. Casale, *Tracking Tomorrow's Trends* (New York: Andrews McNeel Parker, Inc., 1986).
8. John A. Curry and Richard Lapchick, *Research Brochure the Center for the Study of Sport in Society* (Boston: Northeastern University, 1990), 4-5.
9. H.G. Bissinger, *Friday Night Lights* (New York: Addison Wesley, 1990).
10. William Taylor, *The American College of Sports Medicine* (Boston: The Center for the Study of Sports in Society, 1991).
11. Yesalis, Charles, "Steroids and Society," *USA Today*, October 1992.
12. Ibid.
13. Charles Yesalis, "Steroids and Tragedy," *USA Today*, June 1989.
14. Jacques Ellul, *The Technological Bluff* (Grand Rapids, MI: Eerdmans Publishing, 1990), 365.
15. Ibid., 358.
16. Rick TeLander, "Senseless," *Sports Illustrated*, May 1990, 43.
17. Ibid., 43.
18. Ibid., 44.
19. Steve Thurman, "Life, Liberty and the Pursuit of Just a Little More," *Discipleship Journal*, Issue 53, 1989, 18.
20. Mike Yaconelli and Jim Burns, *High School Ministry* (Grand

Rapids: Zondervan Publishing, 1986), 21.
21. Anthony Campolo, *Growing Up in America* (Grand Rapids, MI: Zondervan Publishers, 1989), 19.
22. Pat Ordovensky, "Apathy, Alcohol, Drugs Are Problems of Students," *USA Today,* May 1991.
23. Josh McDowell and Dick Day, *Why Wait? What You Need to Know About The Teen Sexuality Crisis* (San Bernardino, CA: Here's Life Publishers, 1987).

Chapter 10

1. Fred Streit, Adolescent Problems People Science Research Newsletter, Highland Park, NJ, March 1987, 22-23.
2. Keith G. Olson, *Counseling Teenagers* (Loveland, CO: Thom Schulte Publications, 1984), 50-51.
3. Ibid.
4. Robert McGee, *Search for Significance* (Houston: Rapha Publishing, 1985 and 1990), 166-169.
5. Mike Bellah, *Baby Boom Believers* (Wheaton, IL: Tyndale House Publisher, Inc., 1988), 45.
6. Christopher Lasch, *The Culture of Narcissism* (New York: Warner Books, 1979), 30.
7. David Brandt, *Is That All There Is?* (New York: Simon and Schuster, Inc., 1984), 58-59.
8. Ibid.
9. George Barna, *The Frog in the Kettle* (Ventura, CA: Regal Books, 1989), 193.
10. Gary Strauss, "Reality 101," *USA Today*, February 1993.
11. Anthony Campolo, *Growing Up in America* (Grand Rapids, MI: Zondervan Publishing, 1989), 152.
12. George Gallup, Jr., *Religion in America* (Princeton, NJ: The Princeton Research Center, 1990), 10.
13. David Elkind, *All Grown Up and No Place to Go* (Redding, MAAddison-Wesley Publications, 1984), 17.
14. Josh McDowell and Dick Day, *Why Wait? What You Need to Know About The Teen Sexuality Crisis* (San Bernardino, CA: Here's Life Publishers, 1987), 33.
15. Alvin Toffler, *Future Shock* (New York: Bantam Books, 1970).
16. Barna, *The Frog in the Kettle*, 67-71.
17. Ibid.

18. Ibid.
19. Campolo, *Growing Up in America*, 16.
20. Ibid., 35-38.
21. Ibid.
22. M. Scott Peck, *The Road Less Traveled* (New York: Simon and Schuster, Inc., 1978), 19.
23. Alvin Toffler, *Future Shock* (New York: Bantam Books, 1970), 358.
24. Archibald D. Hart, *Overcoming Anxiety* (Dallas: Word Publishing, 1989), 7-8.
25. Ibid.
26. Marilyn Elias, "Anxiety-Ridden Teens," *USA Today*, March 1990.
27. Barna, *The Frog in the Kettle*, 26.
28. George Barna, *Absolute Confusion* (Ventura, CA: Regal Books, 1993), 13, 30.
29. Barna, *The Frog in the Kettle*, 26.

Chapter 11

1. Quentin Schultze, Roy Anker, James Bratt, William Romanowski, John Worst, and Lambert Zuidervant, *Dancing in the Dark* (Grand Rapids: Eerdmans Publishing, 1990), 51.
2. Ibid.
3. Landon Y. Jones, *Great Expectations: America and the Baby Boom Generation* (New York: Ballantine Books, 1980), 72.
4. Allan Bloom, *The Closing of the American Mind* (New York: Simon and Schuster, 1987), 68.
5. Edgar Z. Friendberg, *Adolescent Research* (Chicago, IL: The American Medical Association, May 1990), 188.
6. Gary Boeck, "Music Trends," Youth Articles, *Social Issues Resources* (Boca Raton, FL 1990-91), 5
7. Edna Gunderson, "The Medium That Made Music Visual," *USA Today*, June 1991.
8. Anker Schultze, *Dancing in the Dark*, 181.
9. Ibid., 195.
10. Ibid., 180.
11. Ibid., 204.
12. Sally Ann Steward, "Sex and Music Gives Thrills," *USA Today*, July 1987.

13. Josh McDowell and Dick Day, *Why Wait? What You Need to Know About The Teen Sexuality Crisis* (San Bernardino, CA: Here's Life Publishers, 1987), 107.
14. Gary Boeck, "Music and Mood," *USA Today*, October 1992.
15. Schultze, Anker, *Dancing in the Dark.*
16. Ibid., 204.
17. Ibid., 205.
18. Ibid., 199.
19. Ibid., 190.
20. Ibid., 205.
21. Ibid., 192.
22. Kerry Livegren, "Dust in the Wind," (EMI Blackwood Music Inc./Don Kirshner Music, Inc. BMI), ©1977, Used by permission.
23. Ibid., 204.
24. Anthony Campolo, "Christianity for Alienated Teenagers," *Youth Worker,* Summer 1991.
25. Friendberg, *Adolescent Research*, 189.
26. Anthony Campolo, *Growing Up in America* (Grand Rapids: MI: Zondervan Publishing, 1989), 202.
27. Schultze, Anker, *Dancing in the Dark*, 205.
28. Bloom, *The Closing of the American Mind,* 80.
29. Tipper Gore, *Raising (PG) Kids in an X-Rated Society* (Nashville: Abington Press, 1987), 53.
30. Thomas Radecki, "Do You Know What Your Children Are Listening To?" *U.S. News and World Report,* October 1985, 23.
31. Gore, *Raising (PG) Kids in an X-Rated Society,* 106.
32. Ibid., 107.
33. Ibid., 125.
34. Tom Jarriel, "Satanism in America," *20/20* transcript, May 1985.
35. Schultze, Anker, *Dancing in the Dark,* 187.

Chapter 12

1. Vincent T. Bugliosi, *Drugs in America* (Knights Bridge Publishing, New York 1991), 173.
2. Philip E. Converse, Institute for Social Research. University of Michigan, Ann Arbor, MI, 1990, 43.
3. "Society's Mixed Messages" *USA Today*, August 1991.

4. Jerry Johnston, *It's Killing Our Kids* (Dallas: Word Publishing, 1991), 16.
5. Stephen Arterburn, and Jim Burns, *Drug Proof Your Kids* (Ramona, CA: Focus on the Family Publishing, 1989), 23.
6. Johnston, *It's Killing Our Kids*, 16.
7. Arterburn and Burns, *Drug Proof Your Kids*, 14.
8. Johnston, *It's Killing our Kids*, 73.
9. Arterburn and Burns, *Drug Proof Your Kids*, 15.
10. Ibid., 15.
11. Ibid., 11.
12. Edward W. Desmond, Barbara Dolan, Andrea Dorfman, and Melissa Ludtke, "Out in the Open," *Time*, November 1987, 45–46.
13. Johnston, *It's Killing our Kids*, 73.
14. Desmond, Dolan, "Out in the Open," *Time*, April 1990, 46-47.
15. Ibid., 47.
16. Ibid.
17. Mike Snider, "Alcohol Use Tied to Over Teen Problems," *USA Today*.
18. Ibid.
19. Robert Hemfelt, Frank Minirth, and Paul Meir, *We Are Driven*, (Nashville: Thomas Nelson Publishers, 1991), 6.

Chapter 13

1. Tom Squitieri, "Murder Tide Is Still Rising," *USA Today*, April 1992.
2. Ibid.
3. Ibid.
4. Ibid.
5. Ibid.
6. "7 Deadly Days," *Time*, July 1989, 25.
7. Tom Squitieri, "Killings Occur at a Record Pace," *USA Today*, May 1991.
8. Gordon Witkin, Ted Gest, and Dorian Friedman, "Cops Under Fire," *U.S. News & World Report*, December 1990, 42–43.
9. Ibid.
10. Bruce Frankel, "Our Problem Cuts Across All Groups," *USA Today*, October 1993.
11. Ibid.

12. Jon D. Hull, "A Boy and His Gun," Time, August 1993.
13. John Murray, Roy Menninger, and Tom Grimes, "Yes, Mayhem Does Echo Our Lives," [[Author: Is this a book or an article? Need rest of citation.]]
14. Anita Manning, "Gunshot Kills One U.S. Child Every Two Hours," *USA Today,* January 1994.
15. Robert James Bidinotto, "Revolving Door Justice: Plague on America," *Reader's Digest,* February 1994, 33–37.
16. Squitieri, "Murder Tide Is Still Rising."
17. Jack Kelley, "More Male Teens Means More Killings," *USA Today,* July 1990.
18. Ibid.
19. Gordon Witkin, Stephen Hedges, Constance Johnson, Monika Guttman, Laura Thomas, "Kids Who Kill," *U.S. News & World Report,* April 1991, 42–45.
20. Ibid., 44.
21. Myriam Miedzian, *Boys Will Be Boys,* (New York: Doubleday Publishing, 1991), 5.
22. Tom Squitieri, "19 Cities Set Record for Murder," *USA Today,* May 1991.
23. James Patterson, and Peter Kim, *The Day America Told the Truth,* (Prentice Hall Press, 1991), 5–6.
24. Ibid., 5.
25. Ibid.
26. Edgar Z. Friendberg, *Adolescent Research* (The American Medical Association, May 1990), 293.
27. Anthony Campolo, *Growing Up in America,* (Grand Rapids: Zondervan Publishing, 1989).
28. Miedzian, *Boys Will Be Boys,* 214.
29. Donald E. Wildmon, *The Home Invaders* (Wheaton, IL: Victor Books, 1991).
30. Miedzian, *Boys Will Be Boys,* 214.
31. Plagens, Miller, etc. "Violence Goes Mainstream," *Newsweek,* April 1991, 35.
32. Ibid., 36.
33. Schultze, Anker, etc. *Dancing in the Dark,* 234.
34. Ibid., 234.
35. Ibid., 242.
36. Miedzian, *Boys Will Be Boys,* 241.

37. Ibid., 243.
39. Ibid., 84.
39. Ibid., 241.
40. Jason Scott Weinland, "Police Puzzled by Murder," *Shreveport Times*, Shreveport, LA.
41. Karen Doran, "Antisocial Acts Tied to Excess of Success," *Shreveport Times*, Shreveport, LA.
42. Mimi Swartz, "Blood in the Streets," *Texas Monthly*, November 1991, 78.
43. Jana Miller, and Sally Ann Stewart, "Town Discovers Ugly Side," *USA Today*, March 1992.
44. Rod Nordland, "Kids and Guns," *Newsweek*, March 1992, 37.
45. Sally Ann Stewart, "Gangs: It's Like Your Family," *USA Today*, December 1989.
46. Steve Valdivia, "Law Enforcement Doesn't Have the Solution," *USA Today*, December 1989.
47. Tom Squitieri, "19 Cities Set Records for Murder."
48. Sally Ann Stewart, "Drugs, Violence, Rituals, Slaves," *USA Today*, December 1989.
49. Leon Bing, *Do Or Die*, (New York: Harper Collins Publishing, 1991), 20, 33–37, 54–55.
50. Ibid., 121.
51. Miedzian, *Boys Will Be Boys*, 80.
52. Bing, *Do Or Die*, 126.
53. Ibid., 205–206.
54. Miedzian, *Boys Will Be Boys*, 86.
55. Ibid., 80.
56. Bing, *Do Or Die*, 207.

Chapter 14

1. Landon Y. Jones, *Great Expectations: America and The Baby Boom Generation*, (New York: Ballantine Books, 1980), 5.
2. George Barna, *The Frog in the Kettle*, (Ventura, CA: Regal Books, 1990), 66.
3. Ibid., 67.
4. Ibid., 67.
5. Ibid., 72.
6. Barbara Kantrowitz, Pat Wingert, DeBra Rosenberg, Vicki Quade, and Donna Foote, "Breaking the Divorce Cycle,"

Newsweek, January 1992, 27–28.
7. Ibid., 28.
8. Barna, *The Frog in the Kettle,* 68.
9. Nancy Gibbs, "How America Has Run Out of Time," *Time,* April 1989, 23–24.
10. Judith S. Wallerstein, *Second Chances,* (New York: Ticknor & Fields, 1990), 19.
11. Ibid., 15.
12. Sylvia Ann Hewlett, *When the Bough Breaks,* (New York: Basic Books, 1991), 104.
13. Ibid., 108.
14. Ibid., 108.
15. Deidrie Donahue, "The Marriage Mess," *USA Today,* July 1992.
16. Wallerstein, Second Chances, 29.
17. Ibid., 23.
18. Ibid., 79.
19. Ibid., 55.
20. Sally Ann Stewart, "Divorce Clouds Outlook for Teens," *USA Today,* 1992. Marilyn Elias, "Children of Divorce More Troubled," Gannett News Service, 1992.
21. Hewlett, *When the Bough Breaks,* 112.
22. Ibid., 111.
23. Karen S. Peterson, "Marrying Later," *USA Today,* November 1993.
24. Wallerstein, *Second Chances,* 149.
25. Bryce J. Christensen, *The Family in America,* (Rockford, IL: The Rockford Institute, May 1991), 4–5.
26. Ibid., 5.
27. Hewlett, *When the Bough Breaks,* 88.
28. Ibid., 89.
29. Wallerstein, *Second Chances,* 149.
30. Karen S. Peterson, "16 Million Children Are Without Fathers," Gannett News, April 1992.
31. Christensen, *The Family in America,* 7.
32. Keith Carter, "1 in 5 Children in Poverty, Says Study," *USA Today's Nationline.* The State of Children: Children Defense Fund, February 1992., Pat Ordovensky.
33. "Runaway Parent," *USA Today,* April 1992.
34. Patricia Hersch, "Coming of Age on the Streets," *Psychology*

Today, 1988, 35–37.

35. Barbara Katrowitz, Pat Wingert, Debra Rosenburg, Vicki Quade, Donna Foote, "Breaking the Cycle of Divorce," *Newsweek,* January 1992, 62.
36. Ibid., 63.
37. Marilyn Elias, "Children of Divorce More Troubled," *USA Today,* April 1992.
38. Ibid.

Chapter 15

1. Richard J. Gelles, and Murray R. Straus, *Intimate Violence* (New York: Simon and Schuster, 1988), 18, 106.
2. Ibid., 130–131.
3. Ibid., 101.
4. Ibid., 101, 104..
5. James Paterson, and Peter Kim, *The Day America Told the Truth* (New York: Prentice Hall Press, 1991), 7.
6. The Ninth National Conference on Child Abuse and Neglect. Denver, CO. Associated Press. October 1991.
7. Gelles and Straus, *Intimate Violence,* 60.
8. Nancy Gibbs, "When Is It Rape?" *Time,* June 1991, 41.
9. Carolyn Pesce, and Jacqueline Blais, "Rape Called Enormous Problem," *USA Today,* May 1992.
10. Gibbs, "When Is It Rape?", 42
11. Kim Painter, "The Alcohol Effect," *USA Today,* April 1992.
12. Ibid.
13. Mike Snider, "Alcohol Use Tied to Other Teen Problems," *USA Today,* May 1992.
14. Gelles and Straus, *Intimate Violence,* 100.
15. Ibid., 106.
16. Sylvia Ann Hewlett, *When the Bough Breaks* (New York: Basic Books, 1991), 188.

Chapter 16

1. Jerry Shiver, "Teen Suicide Is a Growing Problem," *USA Today,* May 1991.
2. George Howe Colt, *The Enigma of Suicide* (New York: Summit Books, 1991), 39.
3. Alfred DelBello, "Federal Help Needed to Stem Tragic Toll,"

USA Today, November 1990.
4. McDowell and Day, *Why Wait?* 31.
5. T. Mitchel Anthony, *Suicide: Knowing When Your Teen Is At Risk* (Ventura, CA: Regal Books, 1991), 21.
6. Ibid., 21–22.
7. David Breskin, "Dear Mom and Dad," *Rolling Stone,* November 1984, 36.
8. Mike Warnke, *Schemes of Satan* (Tulsa: Victory House, 1991), 211.
9. Edna Gunderson, Joe Queenan, Drew Master, "Explosive Guns N Roses," *USA Today,* March 1992. April 1992. "Misfit Metal Bands." *Time.* "Bad Boys Music Express."
10. Ibid.
11. Ibid.
12. Anthony, *Suicide: Knowing When Your Teen Is at Risk,* 47.
13. Leon Bing, *Do Or Die* (New York: Harper Collins Publishers, 1991), 44.
14. Anthony, *Suicide: Knowing When Your Teen Is at Risk,* 79.
15. Colt, *The Enigma of Suicide,* 46.
16. Ibid., 47.
17. Ibid., 46.
18. Anthony, *Suicide: Knowing When Your Teen Is at Risk,* 79.
19. Ibid., 71.
20. Ibid., 73.
21. Colt, *The Enigma of Suicide,* 50.
22. Robert McGee, *Search for Significance* (Houston: Rapha Publishing, 1990), 215.
23. McDowell and Day, *Why Wait,* 289.
24. David Bushman, "Teen Suicide," Gannett News Service, February 1992.
25. Anthony, *Suicide: Knowing When Your Teen Is at Risk,* 76.
26. Steven W. Spotts, *Learning More About Depression* (Houston: Rapha Publishing, 1991), 24–27.
27. Ibid.
28. Norman H. Wright, *Beating the Blues* (Ventura, CA: Regal Books, 1988), 30.
29. Ibid., 67.
30. George Colt, *The Enigma of Suicide,* 48.
31. Ibid, 283.

32. Jerry Johnston, *Why Suicide?* (Nashville: Oliver Nelson Publishers, 1987), 9.
33. Anthony, *Suicide: Knowing When Your Teen Is at Risk,* 147.

Chapter 17

1. Mike Warnke, *Schemes of Satan* (Tulsa: Victory House, 1991), 54.
2. Bob Larson, *Satanism* (Nashville: Thomas Nelson Publisher, 1989), 31.
3. Ken Magid, and Carol A. McKelvey, *High Risk* (New York: Bantam Books, 1987), 5.
4. Larson, *Satanism,* 140.
5. Ibid., 141.
6. Warnke, *Schemes of Satan,* 188.
7. Marcia Goodavage, "Stalking the Night Stalker," *USA Today,* February 1991.
8. Larson, *Satanism,* 140.
9. Sandi Gallant, "Occult Investigator," Gannett News Service, November 1990.
10. Larson, *Satanism,* 103.
11. Ibid., 104.
12. Ibid., 104.
13. Larry Kahaner, *Cults That Kil.(* New York: Warner Books, 1988), 133.
14. Larson, *Satanism,* 142.
15. Ibid., 101.
16. Ibid., 145.
17. Anton Szandor LaVey, *The Satanic Bible* (New York: Avon Books, 1969), 25.
18. Jerry Johnston, *The Rise of Evil* (Dallas: Word Publishing, 1989), 159.
19. Warnke, *Schemes of Satan,* 46.
20. LaVey, *The Satanic Bible,* 33.
21. Ibid., 33.
22. Ibid., 30.
23. Larson, *Satanism,* 192.
24. John Weldon, and James Bjornstad, *Playing with Fire* (Chicago: Moody Press, 1984), 24.
25. Larson, *Satanism,* 49–50.
26. Johnston, *The Rise of Evil,* 106.

27. Warnke, *Schemes of Satan,* 107.
28. Ibid., 107.
29. Ibid., 108.
30. Kim Painter, "D and D and Death," *USA Today,* 1990.
31. Marilyn Elias, "Multiple Shootings Related to Dungeons and Dragons," *USA Today,* 1988.
32. Warnke, *Schemes of Satan,* 211.
33. Ibid., 209.
34. Ibid., 210.
35. Larson, *Satanism,* 201.

Chapter 18

1. Bob Larson, *Satanism* (Nashville: Thomas Nelson Publishers, 1989), 113.
2. Ibid., 113.
3. Jerry Johnston, *The Rise of Evil* (Dallas: Word Publishers, 1989), 169.
4. Ibid., 169.
5. Ibid., 169.
6. Larry Kahaner, *Cults That Kill* (New York: Warner Books, 1988), 47.
7. Larson, *Satanism,* 114.
8. Ibid., 108.
9. Ibid., 108–110.
10. Ibid., 101.
11. Ibid., 108.
12. Mike Warnke, *Schemes of Satan* (Tulsa: Victory House, 1991), 195.
13. Ibid., 112.
14. Ibid., 112.
15. Kahaner, *Cults That Kill,* 140.
16. Ibid., 164.
17. Ibid., 163–164.
18. Ibid., 201.
19. Warnke, *Schemes of Satan,* 196.
20. Ibid., 196.
21. Ibid., 200.
22. Ibid., 200.
23. Kahaner, *Cults That Kill,* 36.

24. Warnke, *Schemes of Satan,* 113.
25. Larson, *Satanism,* 102.
26. Warnke, *Schemes of Satan,* 89.
27. Ibid., 89.
28. Ibid., 91.
29. Ibid., 92.
30. Larson, *Satanism,* 89.
31. Stephen Arterburn, and Jack Felton, *Toxic Faith* (Nashville: Oliver Nelson Publishers, 1991), 31.

Chapter 19

1. George Barna, *Absolute Confusion* (Regal Books, Ventura, CA. 1993), 139.
2. Fran Sciacca, *Generation at Risk* (Moody Press, Chicago. 1990–1991), 142–202.
3. Ibid., 142.

Acknowledgments

We gratefully acknowledge permission to quote from the following musical compositions.

Excerpts from "For What It's Worth." Used with permission of Cotillion Music Inc. Stephen Stills. © 1966 Ten East music and Springalo Toones. Warner Tamerlane Publishing Corp.

Excerpts from "Yesterday." Used by permission of Apple—Capitol Records. Produced by Paul McCartney, George Martin and John Lennon. Written by Paul McCartney and John Lennon. Published by Northern Songs Limited, 1965.

Excerpts from "Dust in the Wind." Distributed and produced by CBS Records © 1977. Producer Kerry Livegren — Kansas — used by permission.

Excerpts from "Heart of the Matter." Used by permission. Giffen Records. Distributed by MCA © 1989. Produced by Don Henley and Danny Kortchmar.

Excerpts from "Stairway to Heaven," *Led Zepplin IV* – produced by Jimmy Page – Atlantic Recording Corporation – Warner Communications Company © 1971. Wirtten by Jimmy Page and Rober Plant. Printed in U.S.A.

Excerpts from "Smells Like Teen Spirit", produced and engineered by Butch Vig and Nirvana, © 1991. David Geffen Company Los Angeles, CA. Written by Kurt CoBain and distributed by David Geffen Company U.S.A.

Excerpts from "Like a Rolling Store". *Bob Dylan's Greates Hits* written and produced by Bob Dylan – Columbia Records CBS Inc.,. New York, N.Y. 1976 CBS – Columbia Corporation.

Excerpts from "Eleanor Rigby" – The Beatles 1966. Apple Records Capital Corp. Written by John Lennon and Paul McCartney. Produced by George Martin. Published by Northern Songs Limited.

Excerpts from "We Built This City." Recorded and distributed by BMG Music, New York, NY. Written by Bernie Taupin and Martin Page. Produced by Dennis Lanbert and Peter Wolf, 1985.

Rapha

The heart of Rapha is combination of the finest medical care and Christ-centered therapy. Our multidisciplinary approach addresses not only one's mental and physical needs but the spiritual needs as well. Hurting people often base their self-worth on their performance or on others' opinions. This gives birth to intense fears of rejection and failure and to an overwhelming sense of shame and hopelessness. Depression, substance abuse, eating disorders, or other emotional problems often result. Those who come to Rapha learn a whole new way of dealing with these painful emotions, strained relationships, and unhealthy patterns of behavior.

Rapha is one of the nation's largest managers of psychiatric care and substance abuse treatment from a distinctively Christian perspective. In hospitals located nationwide, Rapha offers a continuum of care for adults and adolescents including acute inpatient, sub-acute, and partial hospitalization; day, evening, and weekend programs; intensive outpatient therapy; an outpatient network; conferences; support group training; books and materials.

For more information about Rapha's counseling resources for you or someone you love, call 1-800-383-HOPE.

To order Say You Want a Revolution or other materials, call 1-800-460-4673 or write:

Rapha Resources
12700 North Featherwood
Suite 250
Houston, TX 77054.